MASCULINITIES IN BRITISH ADVENTURE FICTION, 1880–1915

For my brother Anthony, for many adventures

Masculinities in British Adventure Fiction, 1880–1915

JOSEPH A. KESTNER
University of Tulsa, USA

ASHGATE

Published by
Ashgate Publishing Limited
Wey Court East
Union Road
Farnham
Surrey, GU9 7PT
England

Ashgate Publishing Company
Suite 420
101 Cherry Street
Burlington
VT 05401-4405
USA

www.ashgate.com

British Library Cataloguing in Publication Data
Kestner, Joseph A.
  Masculinities in British adventure fiction, 1880–1915.
  1. Adventure stories, English–History and criticism.
  2. Masculinity in literature. 3. English fiction–19th century–History and criticism.
  4. English fiction–20th century–History and criticism.
  I. Title
  823'.087'09353'09034–dc22

Library of Congress Cataloging-in-Publication Data
Kestner, Joseph A.
  Masculinities in British adventure fiction, 1880–1915 / Joseph A. Kestner.
    p. cm.
  Includes bibliographical references and index.
  ISBN 978-0-7546-6901-2 (hardback : alk. paper) — ISBN 978-0-7546-9594-3
  (ebook) 1. Adventure stories, English—History and criticism. 2. English fiction
  —19th century—History and criticism. 3. English fiction—20th century—History
  and criticism. 4. Masculinity in literature. 5. Imperialism in literature. I. Title.
  PR830.A38K47 2010
  823'.087093521—dc22

2009031160

ISBN 9780754669012 (hbk)
ISBN 9780754695943 (ebk)

Mixed Sources
Product group from well-managed
forests and other controlled sources
www.fsc.org Cert no. SA-COC-1565
© 1996 Forest Stewardship Council
FSC

Printed and bound in Great Britain by
MPG Books Group, UK

Contents

Acknowledgements

This book could not have been written without the cooperation of individuals, libraries and institutions. The author wishes to express his gratitude for the assistance rendered by these individuals and institutions.

The author is grateful to the library of the University of New York at Albany for access to its outstanding periodicals collection. The author is particularly grateful to Ann Blakely of the McFarlin Library at the University of Tulsa for exceptional professional diligence in locating articles and reviews from Victorian periodicals.

The author is grateful to the University of Tulsa for the academic leave which enabled the completion of this book.

For their advice and support, the author wishes to thank Lynn Alexander, Thomas Benediktson, Lars Engle, Thomas Horne, Holly Laird, Russell Renfrow, Robert Spoo, Gordon Taylor, Steadman Upham, Jeff Van Hanken, Sandra Vice, Joseph Wiesenfarth and Carl Woodring. The author is grateful to Patrick Scott Belk for his precision, advice and assistance during the preparation of the final manuscript.

The author wishes to thank Ann Donahue, Senior Editor at Ashgate, for her stellar professionalism, expertise and support. He also thanks Whitney Feininger, Assistant Editor at Ashgate, for her scrupulous attention to the manuscript in preparing it for production.

The author is also grateful for permission to reproduce an image on the jacket from the film of *The Secret Sharer* (1973) and thanks the following: Encyclopaedia Britannica Educational Corporation, the producing company; Larry Yust, producer/director; Isidore Mankofsky, director of photography; and David Soul, actor.

For her unending loyalty, undying love to Topaz.

Love to Ari for his golden-eyed vigilance.

Anna H. Norberg has been a strong and loving source of support during the writing of this book.

Introduction:
Masculinities and Adventure Fiction

In the first chapter of his novel *Lord Jim* (1900), Joseph Conrad constructs the narrative to alert the reader about a formative experience of its protagonist: 'He could see the big ships departing, the broad-beamed ferries constantly on the move, the little boats floating far below his feet, with the hazy splendour of the sea in the distance, and the hope of a stirring life in the world of adventure' (47).

The mechanism for this 'hope of adventure' is then delineated:

> On the lower deck in the babel of two hundred voices he would forget himself, and beforehand live in his mind the sea-life of light literature. He saw himself saving people from sinking ships, cutting away masts in a hurricane, swimming through a surf with a line; or as a lonely castaway, barefooted and half naked, walking on uncovered reefs in search of shellfish to stave off starvation. He confronted savages on tropical shores, quelled mutinies on the high seas, and in a small boat upon the ocean kept up the hearts of despairing men – always an example of devotion to duty, and as unflinching as a hero in a book. (47)

Conrad underscores the crucial importance of adventure literature imprinting codes of masculinity: rescue, heroism, survival, courage, duty, isolation, voyaging. In the case of Lord Jim, the young man is unable to live up to this modelling – the imprinting is inadequate, fantasy superseding actualisation. Joseph Conrad does acknowledge the crucial role of adventure literature in the formation of masculine codes. In Conrad, this masculine formation process is a crucial focus of his texts.

However, Conrad indicates that the interrogation of masculine codes is as important as the processes of imprinting. In the last two decades of the nineteenth century, Elaine Showalter notes, 'adventure fiction is thus important training' (80). Joseph Bristow (1991) contends that 'towards the end of the Victorian period, the type of adventures absorbed outside school would be modified and so make their way into the classroom' (27).

In *Allan Quatermain* (1887), H. Rider Haggard's protagonist-narrator states explicitly:

> That is what Englishmen are, adventurers to the backbone; and all our magnificent muster-roll of colonies, each of which will in time become a great nation, testify to the extraordinary value of the spirit of adventure which at first sight looks like a mild form of lunacy ... . The names of those grand-hearted old adventurers

> who have made England what she is, will be remembered and taught with love
> and pride to little children … Yet have we done something. (101)

Being an adventurer is part of being English in the final decades of Victoria's reign. Still, Haggard's phrasing of a declaration which looks like a question ('Yet have we done something') also implies that adventure can be the focus of inquiry, examination, challenge, doubt and dispute.

The intention of this book is to study in adventure fiction these processes of imprinting and interrogation in four dimensions: first, those of initiation; second, those of encountering the Other; third, those involving explicit imperialising contexts; and fourth, those concerning sexual relations.

1880–1915

This study begins with texts from the 1880s and ends in 1915, the clear end of the 'long nineteenth century' and the end of 'British naval domination of the world that extended from 1815 to 1914' (John Peck 7). Lee Horsley notes the same encompassing dates: 'From the time of the scramble for Africa in the closing decades of the nineteenth century until the outbreak of the First World War, the imperialist enterprise provided a context for heroic action' (20).

According to David Bunn, the representation of individual masculinities is especially challenging from the 1880s and following because the state apparatus assumed an increased role in the 1880s: 'After 1880, … individual achievements paled before the prospect of imperialist state organization. The private voyeurism of the romance writers now seemed threatened, as did the continuance of the romance genre' (8). The writers studied in this book, therefore, represented individual masculinities in imposing state contexts. Hence, one reason for beginning this study in the 1880s is that adventure fiction assumes a new valence of intensity to confront the larger and larger role of the state.

Robert Kiely comments that 'in the decade of the 1880s there were signs of a small but vigorous movement in Great Britain' (21) against the novels represented by George Eliot and Anthony Trollope. In his 1882 'A Gossip on Romance', Robert Louis Stevenson argued, as Kiely puts it, for 'the importance of event' (25) and the role of chance in adventure narrative, 'the random nature of the human adventure' (26). For Stevenson, as he observes in his essay, 'romance' is 'the poetry of circumstance' (56). The 1880s, according to Bristow (1991) marked a significant change: 'There was, then, in the 1880s a concerted movement among conservatives to mould the idea of the finest novel to a wholly depoliticized and universalized set of masculine terms' (118).

Martin Green (1979) contends that by the 1880s the temperament of England was hostile to the content of adventure narratives. 'This disapproval of the military, aristocratic, and adventurous hero was a very powerful impulse within English seriousness … . English literature had organised itself into a system, of which the central seriousness was hostile to the material of adventure and therewith of empire and frontier' (64). In Victorian culture, the reigning realistic novel shunned adventurousness in favour of marriage, home and domesticity. Green stresses: 'Serious fiction writers in England were warned away from the adventure tale, and toward the domestic novel, even though ... the adventure material bore much more directly upon the serious history of England' (58). The ironies are many, as Green concludes: 'The modernist adventure tale probably was more influential than the serious novel' (49).

However, there are other compelling reasons for beginning a study of adventure fiction and masculinity in the 1880s. The Zulu War had begun in 1879. In 1880 the First Boer War commenced. The Revolt of the Mahdi in the Sudan began in 1881, followed in 1882 with the British occupation of Egypt. The death of General Charles Gordon in 1885 at Khartoum transfixed the nation, with its attendant celebration of masculine heroism and questioning of the effectiveness of British troops for the failure to rescue him.

Another factor about the 1880s, as E.C. Mack has noted, was the dominance of games ideology in schools: 'By 1880 or thereabouts [the mania for games] had come to dominate all the schools, including the once studious Shrewsbury ... . At Harrow the government of the Houses was passing from boys high in studies to those high in athletics; at Rugby where the athlete did not officially rule, he began to do so unofficially as the monitorial system began to decay' (123–4). This emphasis on physical strength finds its representation in texts such as Haggard's *King Solomon's Mines* or Rudyard Kipling's *The Man Who Would Be King*. Lawrence Millman emphasises: 'Maleness is validated by an involvement with guns, and male loyalty is all, sanctified by the powerful spirit of the English public school, which presses into later life' (18).

Alan Sandison argues that 'British expansion after the 1880s was clearly negative in purpose and achievement', as confidence gave way to fear concerning the Empire:

> Individual enterprise ... seemed to flag, and the self-confidence which had carried Victorians so far and revealed a world so full of promise also began to wane; fears of subversion and disloyalty took its place encouraged by the various rebellions in India, Ireland and South Africa. Nationalists refused to be assimilated to British purposes; the old faith in influence and moral suasion declined. (19)

One could cite, for instance, the British defeat by the Boers at Majuba Hill on 27 February 1881, which led to the loss of the Transvaal. Additional sources of anxiety included the rise of Germany as an imperial power and the growth of terrorism in late-Victorian Britain. In the light of these problems, to compensate the adventure novel becomes more intense, as John Peck has argued: 'After 1880 the adventure story acquired fresh energy, reached out in new directions and began to appeal to a much broader audience than just boys' (151).

Craig Smith provides a sharp distillation of events and contexts that 'saturated readers and texts between the "Scramble" [for Africa] and World War I':

> Consider these arrivals on the national scene: the New Woman of the 1880s and 1890s, demanding access to higher education, recognition and liberation from her customary subordination; radical and working-class politics of the 1880s, plus the 1893 founding of the Labour Party, which quickly secured the allegiance of the Trades Union Congress; the wider importance of class interests in elections evident in the Liberals' 1906 triumph; the victory of manufacturing capital over the old elites. Consider also the newly organized pressure for male franchise extension … and the Suffragette Movement's call for universal suffrage … And factor in the growth of eugenics as a science, aiming to prove why Brtitain did and should rule the world and arousing fears about the purity of the national blood. (178–9)

Combined with anxiety about the imperial attitudes of Germany, the economic challenges posed by the United States, and concern about the physical deterioration of the English male, these conditions contributed to the intensified agendas of the adventure genre from the 1880s to 1915.

While novels like Haggard's *King Solomon's Mines* and *Allan Quatermain* might be seen as reinforcing imperial agendas, others such as Kipling's *The Light That Failed* or Stevenson's *The Ebb-Tide* perceive the imperial project as very conflicted. And, as Andrea White argues, even Haggard 'introduced an adversarial element, a contentious note' (82) in his novels, for example by 'questioning commercialism' (93) or adulating Zulus. By the time Conrad writes his tales, there is clearly a subversion of the adventure genre, accompanied by a profound interrogation of masculinity, which is regarded as conflicted and problematical. Millman remarks that 'Conrad's world … is an indisputably male world, and its constant evocation of the "heart of darkness" is an immense complication of Haggard's cliché of "the dark continent"' (iii). George, Lord Curzon believed that a legacy of British involvement in the Empire might be 'a sense of manliness' (cited in Sandison 7), but this agenda increasingly encountered challenges from nationalist movements and revolts. Sandison records an 'upsurge of strong imperialist feeling that occurred in the last thirty years of the nineteenth century' (3), but this shift did not necessarily entail optimism, as the texts of Kipling or Stevenson or Conrad indicate.

The 1890s brought what Showalter has described as a 'crisis of masculinity', citing observers who note 'a crisis of masculinity in the 1890s of the male on all levels – economic, political, social, psychological, as producer, as power, as role, as lover'. She writes: 'The crisis of masculinity marked an awakening consciousness of what it meant to be a man' (9).

Andrew Roberts (2000) supplies a definition of 'masculinity' that is sufficiently broad in its scope: 'Masculinity, then, might be regarded as a psychic structure, as a fantasy, as a code of behaviour, or as a set of social practices and constraints'

(5). It is legitimate to claim that under the rubric of masculinity, each of the four subsets examined in this book (initiation, othering, imperialising, loving) might apply, recognising that as a construct, there can be no essentialist 'masculinity' but rather 'masculinities', as Arthur Brittan argues: 'This assumption – that we can know and describe men in terms of some discoverable dimension is problematic – because it suggests that masculinity is timeless and universal … My position is that we cannot talk of masculinity, only masculinities' (1–2).

However, each of these subsets might be subject to 'crisis' as Showalter indicates. For example, the increased surveillance of homosexuals following the passage of the Labouchere Amendment in 1885 altered assessments of codes of behaviour by authorising state-controlled constraints, such enforcement becoming severe after the Wilde trials of 1895. Millman details the result of the Wilde trials: 'Such was the late Victorian cultural mood that the virtues of this sort of [adventuring] maleness had to be asserted in the face of increasing cultural onslaughts: it's not accidental that manliness should be so thoroughly extolled at exactly the period when Oscar Wilde had become such a prominent figure … The popular male hero of this period seems like an aggressive response to all that Wilde himself represented' (28–9). As another example, the inability to find recruits for the Army in the late nineteenth century due to physical defects undermined psychic confidence that the Empire could be supported.. Roberts supplements Herbert Sussman's more narrow definition of masculinity as 'those multifarious social constructions of the male current within the society' (13).

Adventure Fiction

One response to these crises, both abroad and at home, was the rise of an intensified adventure fiction, often described as the romance genre by critics such as Andrew Lang and Robert Louis Stevenson. In his essay 'Realism and Romance' published in the *Contemporary Review* in 1887, Lang argued that both realism (the novel of domestic life, the novel of manners) and romance might peacefully co-exist, albeit his preference was for the latter: 'Fiction is a shield with two sides, the silver and the golden: the study of manners and of character, on one hand; on the other, the description of adventure, the delight of romantic narrative' (684). He continues: 'What is good, what is permanent, may be found in fiction of every *genre*' (685).

Lang objects to 'the exclusion of exciting events and engaging narrative' in novels of realism, arguing that 'though full of talent, [they] are limited in scope' (688). Bristow (1991) observes that 'the critical debate about realism and romance, conducted in many periodicals during the 1880s, took place when Britain's own imperial treasures loomed more largely than ever before in the nation's mind' (95–6).

Lang argues that civilised people still long for adventure: 'Not for nothing did Nature leave us all savages under our white skins; she has wrought thus that we might have many delights, among others "the joy of adventurous living"' (689).

In his defence, he cites Stevenson's *Treasure Island* and *Kidnapped* and Rider Haggard's *King Solomon's Mines* and *She* as texts meriting public attention, albeit they are adventure tales rather than domestic texts, although Lang is willing to elevate Stevenson above Haggard. Lang contends: 'Whatever the merits and demerits of modern English romance, one thing is certain. It is now undeniable that the love of adventure, and of mystery, and of a good fight lingers in the minds of men and women' (692). Stevenson in his 1884 essay 'A Humble Remonstrance' even admits that adventure 'appeals to certain almost sensual and quite illogical tendencies in man' (70).

Lang claims that 'it will always be possible to combine the interest of narrative and of adventure with the interest of character' (692). In arguing the two types (adventure, character) can be welded, Lang foresees the achievement of Conrad in novels like *Chance*. Victory, however, was on the side of the adventure novelists. Susanne Howe comments that 'the reading public slipped away in droves [from the realist novel], as many Victorian memoirs record, and escaped to *Treasure Island* [and] *The Prisoner of Zenda*' (8). Joseph Bristow (1996) asserts that 'it was in the 1880s that the adventure story for the first time reached a large and enthusiastic adult readership' (xiv). Millman argues that the adventure novel 'would illuminate the interests of an entirely different segment of the reading public: men' (7–8). Millman adds: 'The product [of adventure fiction] was the "male novel", written by men, for men …, and about the activities of men' (22).

This popularity intersected with the rise of what Arthur Conan Doyle (1890) marked in Stevenson, 'the modern masculine novel' (652). This focus on the masculine novel increased to such an extent that Anthea Trodd states about the Edwardians:

> Literature was increasingly seen in a masculine context. This was a period when the voice of the masculine ruling class was particularly dominant in the culture … . In the Edwardian period Englishness was closely associated with masculinity, and 'manliness' was seen as a dominant characteristic of English literature … [There was] an equation of literature with masculinity. (6–9)

George Salmon writing the essay 'What Boys Read' for the *Fortnightly Review* in 1886 remarked that the home country itself could no longer supply fields of action: 'Englishmen sought to gratify mentally a passion for romance, which it was yearly becoming more difficult to gratify physically' (248). Hence the importance of adventure fiction in providing an imagined masculine ideal. Salmon also contended that the adventure genre was significant: 'It is impossible to overrate the importance of the influence of such a supply on the national character and culture' (248). As did Lang and Stevenson, Salmon emphasised that 'fiction for young or old should endeavour to give force and colour to facts' (49).

Stevenson in 'A Humble Remonstrance' injected gender into his evaluation of adventure: 'Life is monstrous, infinite, illogical, abrupt and poignant; a work of art, in comparison is neat, finite, self-contained, rational, flowing and emasculate'

(70). This interesting final term recognises the masculinising project of adventure narratives. It is not that Stevenson excludes sex and women from his texts, which he does. It is that in its focus on masculine experience, often homosocial, Stevenson is emphasising that his stories are 'masculate', about maleness. This is the primary if narrow agenda of many adventure texts, to model masculinity and interrogate it, albeit this may entail the exclusion of women or the relegation of sexual relations to a secondary role. Millman contends: 'The male novel is in fact a conservative backlash to an overwhelming association of the Victorian novel with women, often made by people who neither liked novels or women' (13–14). In fact, however, as the fourth chapter of this study suggests, women often play a central role in the adventure narrative.

Martin Green (1979) defines the adventure genre as follows: 'Adventure seems to mean a series of events, partly but not wholly accidental, in settings remote from the domestic and probably from the civilized (at least in the psychological sense of remote), which constitute a challenge to the central character. In meeting this challenge, he/she performs a series of exploits which make him/her a hero, eminent in virtues such as courage, fortitude, cunning, strength, leadership, and persistence' (23). John Batchelor (1982) argues that an adventure text is 'both a sophisticated study of private experience and a story of action and adventure' (100). For Green and Batchelor, the emphasis is on the personal aspect of the adventure.

Linda Dryden, however, sees national agendas in addition to personal ones. She asserts about adventure fiction that its focus is 'on heroes anxious for thrilling adventures in tropical locations where they prove their manliness, assert English racial superiority, and plunder the land of its riches'. There was a desire 'to explore the geography and peoples of those parts of the world that the expanding British Empire was bringing to the attention of those at home' (4). According to Dryden, however, 'Conrad's fiction challenges notions of confident Empire and the assumptions of white superiority' (8).

Graham Dawson (1994) notes the association of *adventure* with fortune, chance, hazard, enterprise and assertion of will at various points since the Middle Ages (53). He writes: 'A paradoxical tension between risk and control remains at the heart of adventure … Adventure in the modern sense is balanced between anxiety and desire' (53). Dawson adds that adventure often involves quest: 'The adventure quest therefore provides a powerful metaphor for the human capacity to endeavour, risk and win through; for the prevailing of human purpose in the world' (55).

The great theoretician of the adventure novel, however, remains Jacques Rivière, with his essay 'The Adventure Novel' published in *The Ideal Reader*. According to Rivière: 'Adventure is what occurs … what is added, what happens in addition to the bargain, what one did not expect, what one could have done without. An adventure novel is the tale of events that are not contained the one within the other … The sentiments described overflow those of the preceding chapter' (115). Adventure demands an orientation to everything future in the text:

'The adventure novel is a novel that advances through constantly new events. Instead of using the initial data with wise economy, instead of making it last, the author spends all his wealth each time. In order to go further on, he has only what he does not yet have; he borrows everything from the future' (116).

Hence, Rivière asserts: 'Adventure is the form of the work rather than its material' (116): its structure demands a new event with each chapter. 'It reflects our state of newness before the world' (117) and exists in 'two great species' (116): 'In addition to the adventure novel in the usual sense, there is also place for a psychological adventure novel [which] becomes deep and essential' (117). This psychology is emphasised by 'the emotion of awaiting something, of not yet knowing everything, of being led as close as possible to the edge of what does not yet exist ... something that is *going to happen*, something both absolutely unknown and absolutely inevitable' (119). 'It is a surrender to uneasiness ... to experience, in the very depths of our marrow, this obscure, indefatigable question which moves and torments all living beings' (120).

But, as Rivière argues, it is not only emotion which is aroused by adventure fiction: 'The intellect will be mixed with the emotion that the novel of adventure will give us. It will aerate it, illuminate it [with] the joy that the intellect experiences in foreshadowing, in calculating, in putting events together, in guessing them, in explaining them to itself' (120–21). As an exemplary text of adventure, Rivière cites Stevenson's *The Ebb-Tide*, discussed in Chapter 2 of this book. Hence, for Rivière, adventure fiction is marked by its form dictating its content, its insistence on the forthcoming and the unexpected, its exhaustion of each episode before the next and its sharp psychology.

John Cawleti (1976) states there are two kinds of heroes involved in adventure fiction, one a superhero, consigned to boys' literature; and the other an 'ordinary hero', a character who is 'one of us', generally the province of adventure fiction for 'sophisticated adults' (40). The focus of this study is on the latter kind of protagonist. Indeed, the protagonist might be 'ordinary' in Cawleti's terms, but the challenges arising test this kind of heroism in the course of the narrative.

Owen Knowles and Gene Moore (2000), in assessing Conrad's place in this tradition, note two kinds of adventure texts. One is 'naïve' colonial literature 'in which the mission of the British Empire itself furnished patriotic adventure, heroic possibilities, and recurring tests upon manhood'. Knowles/Moore argue, however, that Conrad's early fiction 'belongs to a period when the imperial mission fell increasingly under suspicion ... forging a passage from the "naïve" tradition of British Empire fiction to a new kind of skeptical and interrogative colonial novel' (7). This study examines masculinities in both kinds of adventure texts in these terms, both the 'naïve' (e.g., Haggard, Buchan, Hope), and the 'skeptical' (e.g., Conrad, Kipling, Schreiner). Stevenson, it will be argued, is predominantly in the latter category.

In his 1911 essay 'The Adventurer' Georg Simmel argues that 'adventure' 'bears a twofold meaning: it revolves about its own center ... and at the same time is a segment of a course of life' (187). 'An adventure is certainly a part of our existence, directly contiguous with other parts which precede and follow it; at the same time, however, in its deeper meaning it occurs outside the usual continuity of this life' (188). Hence, the adventure is paradoxical – both exceptional and continuous.

Yet, adventure is clearly demarcated according to Simmel: 'We ascribe to an adventure a beginning and an end much sharper than those to be discovered in the other forms of our experiences … The adventure … is independent of the "before" and "after"… We speak of adventure precisely when continuity with life is thus disregarded on principle … something alien, untouchable, out of the ordinary' (188–9). Still, it is also continuous: 'The adventure is defined by its capacity, in spite of its being isolated and accidental, to have necessity and meaning. Something becomes an adventure only by virtue of two conditions: that it itself is a specific organisation of some significant meaning with a beginning and an end; and that, despite its accidental nature, its extraterritoriality with respect to the continuity of life, it nevertheless connects with the character and identity of the bearer of that life' (190).

Furthermore, chance and continuity do intersect, as Simmel contends:

> The adventurer similarly lets the accident somehow be encompassed by the meaning which controls the consistent continuity of life, even though the accident lies outside that continuity. He achieves a central feeling of life which runs through the eccentricity of the adventure and produces a new, significant necessity of his life … The great forms in which we shape the substance of life are the syntheses, antagonisms, or compromises between chance and necessity. Adventure is such a form … By adventure we always mean a third something … . The adventure … is that incomparable experience which can be interpreted only as a particular encompassing of the accidentally external by the internally necessary. (191–2)

The adventure texts examined in this study create this 'third' of Simmel's by combining the necessity of adventuring with its constitutive contingency. He notices the typical fatalism of the adventurer. 'The obscurities of fate are certainly no more transparent to him than to others; but he proceeds as if they were … This is only a subjective aspect of the fatalist conviction that we certainly cannot escape a fate which we do not know: the adventurer nevertheless believes that, as far as he himself is concerned, he is certain of this unknown and unknowable element in his life' (194). For Simmel, 'adventure is a *form of experiencing*. The *content* of the experience does not make the adventure' (197). Simmel stresses 'the perception of contrast characteristic of adventure, viz., that an action is completely torn out of the inclusive context of life and that simultaneously the whole strength and intensity of life stream into it' (198). The 'forms of experiencing' in the texts considered here advance or critique masculinising agendas.

The adventure genre is then paradoxical in embracing both the random and the requisite. Writing about maritime fiction but applicable to much adventure narrative is John Peck's position: 'The need for risk-taking is set against the need for regulation and control; the need for aggression and individual freedom is set against the need to respect individual liberties; the masculine culture of the ship, business and war is set against the feminine-influenced values that dominate domestic life' (6).

Hence, as Peck notes, there is 'a pattern of transgression' (6) in this evolution of male identity. To take risks, to travel, to voyage out is to leave the masculinity of the shore or metropolis. Hence, transgression, which in some of these texts means capitalist exploitation and even murder, is nevertheless inherent in the processes of masculine formation or experience. Paul Zweig observes about the adventurer: 'The invisible boundaries, the decorum, the obsession with right behavior, do not extend very deeply into his psyche' (59). To be masculine is to be in revolt.

Martin Green (1990), noting that 'the adventure tale [is] historically speaking the most important of all our literary forms' (1), argues that 'adventure has ... been the liturgy – the series of cultic texts – of masculinism ... [the] intensification of male pride' (2). He argues that Daniel Defoe's *Robinson Crusoe* of 1719 contains elements – shipwreck, the island, solitude – that constitute basic elements of the adventure story, leading to a tradition of the Robinsonade, that is, those texts deriving from Defoe's model. These books stress specific elements: the island, storm, work, survival, whiteness, power and moral justification (21–3). Green argues that 'adventure is reading for men, not for readers' (5), contending that between 1880 and 1910, adventure fiction, by Stevenson and Kipling, attempted to amalgamate both 'literary ambitions' and 'adventure subject matter' (5).

According to Paul Zweig, this adventure subject matter will entail 'abrupt intensity', 'risk', 'the energy of survival ... . This is the view developed in adventure stories. They offer us heroes obsessed by risk and confrontation ... . Adventure stories transpose our dalliance with risk into a sustained vision' (3–4). In the testing of masculinity, 'the adventurer's most serious obstacle is himself. The world extends before him like a fabulous text. Only his ability to "read" it is in doubt' (24).

In addition, there is a strong psychological component to the content of adventure narrative, which Zweig observes: 'Adventure and action literature ... may well be attempts to objectify the vertigo of inward disorder which is for most intimate knowledge of the unknown ... The psychic unknown and the outward unknown seemed related ... [These] suggest a connection between the two sets of adventure' (29–30). Indeed, as Norman Etherington (1984) has argued: 'The imperial situation made a grand metaphorical stage for encounters and battles between different sections of the self' (54). In much adventure fiction, the external journey is of course an internal one, as texts by Conrad and Childers, for example, demonstrate.

Adventure fiction enables the investigation of masculinities because its premise is wandering, encountering all sorts and conditions of men, especially men of other classes, nationalities and races. This adventuring is a four-stage process: 1. departing; 2. encountering; 3. transgressing; 4. potential re-integrating. Leaving the home or native country, driven sometimes by economic necessity (which can mask psychological necessity), the protagonist encounters dangerous and hazardous challenges. In the course of surmounting these challenges, the protagonist must often transgress Christian morality, engage in suspect activity like surveillance or spying, even 'go native' or murder. These may constitute rites of passage; all involve testing. Bristow notices that in adventure texts 'Africa ... is being used ... to articulate a universal truth about masculinity: an instinctual violence to which imperialism has given terrifying rein' (163).

At the conclusion, the protagonist will have a re-formed and transformed sense of masculine identity. The paradox is that a man must transgress conventional behaviours to achieve integration into the masculine order approved by the culture, eloquently expressed in texts such as *Prester John*, *The Four Feathers* or *The Riddle of the Sands*. All the protagonists must transgress in the process of achieving a masculine identity. Adventure fiction enables this negotiating of masculinity, since it is at a distance from the shore or native country or metropolis. To fit in one must go out. On the other hand, some men undergo transformative experiences but are not integrated, such as the protagonists of *The Ebb-Tide*, *Green Mansions* or *A Smile of Fortune*, who are exiled rather than integrated at the end. Sometimes, transgression leads to the death of the protagonist, as in *Trooper Peter Halket of Mashonaland*, *The Light That Failed* or *The Man Who Would Be King*.

This distancing has additional advantages, as Millman comments about Haggard: 'The arcane nature of Haggard's kingdom in the far reaches of Africa ... has protected him from censorship' (50). Thus, even as some reviewers denounced the violence in Haggard's texts, he generally got a pass because the violence was 'over there' rather than 'here' in England. In addition, Millman continues, distance enabled veracity: 'Action in Haggard and Stevenson occurs where the veracity of fantasy cannot be questioned, in the strange outer limits of time and space' (22).

Paul Zweig argues that adventure fiction endorses transformative masculinising processes. 'The initiated adult undoes his original birth from woman, replacing it by a wholly masculine birth. But adventure, too, is an initiation. Through it, the adventurer becomes a child of his own deeds, his own bravery. He becomes not only his own father – that represents the "Oedipal" side of the initiation – but also his own mother' (70–71). And this process is never terminated: 'If adventure is a form of initiation into the emperion of the masculine, then it is curiously imperfect, because it must be reaccomplished incessantly ... The project of self-birth is keen and exciting, but unlike the original birth it cannot be done once and for all' (71). Hence, even if certain texts give an impression of stabilised masculine identity at their conclusions, the texts are nevertheless open-ended because this masculine identity will be challenged and contested. This self-birth is a repudiation of women in terms outlined by Millman: 'The origins of the male novel [are] in the desire to establish a male fiction impervious, if not hostile, to the demands of women' (61–2). Partly this is due to the adventurer's very nature: 'In a sense the adventurer's career violates all standards of responsible "male" behavior. It does not uphold morality; it lacks the productive logic of work [by] yielding intuitively to the rhythms of chance' (71).

Masculinities

As Andrea White emphasises about adventure texts, 'so powerful were these books that they often preempted actual experience itself' (59). J.S. Bratton comments about the nineteenth century:

> Many educators consciously turned to fiction to solve problems of the transmission of the [dominant masculine] ideology. Fiction had the advantage of a much more nearly universal availability: anyone educated to the level of basic literacy was accessible through a story. It was also private, enabling the direct messages inculcating imperial ambition, and national, familial and racial pride, to be received without a blush; and apparently optional, so that no one need feel repelled by being forced to undergo indoctrination ... Perhaps the most compelling virtue of fiction as a vehicle for ideology was (and is) that it appeals to and employs the readers' imagination ... The elaborated idea of the school itself, or of the battle, or the expedition, when set in the ideal and shapely world of art, may be far more potent than the messy and unsatisfactory reality. (76)

The function of imprinting masculinities through adventure texts has been analysed by Graham Dawson. Dawson (1994) writes:

> Masculinities are lived out in the flesh, but fashioned in the imagination ... If masculinity has had a role in imagining the nation, then so too has the nation played its part in constituting preferred forms of masculinity. These forms of manliness that have proved efficacious for nationalist endeavour have been approvingly recognized and furthered with all the power at the disposal of the state, while other subversive or non-functional forms (notably the effeminate man or the homosexual) have met with disapprobation and repression in explicitly national terms. A dominant conception of masculine identity – the true 'Englishman' – was both required and underpinned by the dominant version of British national identity in such a way that each reinforced the other. (1–2)

Hence, there is a reciprocity between the masculinity imagined, and imaged, in literary texts and the lived experience of males.

Dawson labels the function of these texts as 'the narrative imagining of masculinities':

> As *imagined* forms, masculinities are at once 'made up' by creative cultural activity and yet materialize in the social world as structured forms with real effects upon both women and men ... . The narrative resource of a culture

… therefore functions as a currency of recognizable social identities… . The narrative imagining of lived masculinities is powerfully shaped by such a repertoire of forms. It organizes the available possibilities for a masculine self … The cultural forms of masculinity enable a sense of one's self as 'a man' to be imagined and recognized by others. (22–3)

In this book, for example, texts involving male initiation into manhood by Conrad, Childers, Stevenson or Kipling demonstrate imagined males undergoing this process. They constitute a cultural product which reveals to young men or old a discourse about a process which involves most men. For men, these texts then present challenges and evaluate responses to initiation. Dawson adds, however:

Since the imagining and recognition of identities is a process shot through with wish-fulfilling fantasies, these cultural forms often figure ideal and desirable masculinities, in which both self and others may make investments … Since the demands and recognitions of social life are not uniform but many-faceted and contradictory, the achievement of an absolutely unified and coherent gendered social identity, for masculinity as for femininity, is an impossibility. Lived masculinities will necessarily be composed out of various forms from the range of possibilities within the repertoire. (23)

The validity of this variety of forms is demonstrated by the diversity of narratives, locales and occupations apparent in the texts studied herein: from autodiegetic first-person accounts to homodiegetic observer records to heterodiegetic 'third-person' accounts of an undramatised narrator; from Asia to Africa; from sailors, soldiers and explorers to imperialists, capitalists, mercantilists, drifters and lovers. Dawson concludes: 'the modern adventure hero [is] a plurality of forms rather than a singular, abstract figure' (57).

If as Middleton argues '[m]asculinity is socially constructed' (2), adventure fiction participates in this process. Adventure fiction posits that this process can be spectacularised. Kimmel and Messner theorise: 'Men are not born … to follow a predetermined biological imperative … . To be a man is to participate in social life as a man, as a gendered being. Men are not born; they are made' (8–10). In texts as diverse as Hudson's *Green Mansions*, Conrad's *Typhoon*, Kipling's *The Light That Failed* and Schreiner's *Trooper Peter Halket of Mashonaland*, males are represented as being 'made' as opposed to being 'already' masculine.

This four-stage process of adventuring (departing, encountering, transgressing, potential re-integrating) is displayed for males in adventure fiction, where the purpose is to present the spectacle of masculinity and maleness. Bette London has noted 'the historical specificity of the construction of masculinity … that masculinity, as much as femininity, is created by cultural negotiations and contestations … . It brings to light the constitution and distribution of the male body in the making of cultural identity … . Male spectacle is an integral part of masculinity' (261). Steve Neale argues that masculinity *is* a spectacle, stressing 'how heterosexual masculinity is inscribed and the mechanisms, pressures, and contradictions that inscription may involve' (9):

> Identification is never simply a matter of men identifying with male figures on the screen … . [It] draws on and involves many desires, many forms of desire. And desire itself is mobile, fluid, constantly transgressing identities, positions, and roles. Identifications are multiple, fluid, at points even contradictory … . A series of identifications are involved, then, each shifting and mobile. Equally, though, there is constant work to channel and regulate identification in relation to sexual division, in relation to the orders of gender, sexuality, and social identity and authority marking patriarchal society. (9–11)

Lee Horsley reinforces this idea of masculinity as spectacle: 'The territory of the adventure is above all a space of possibility and performance' (24).

If masculinity is a spectacle, then the gaze of the male is the device for negotiating masculinity. In her landmark essay 'Visual Pleasure and Narrative Cinema', Laura Mulvey argues that the gaze serves two ends: first, scopophilic, that is, 'pleasure in looking at another person as an erotic object' (815). In adventure texts, there is often the possibility of the homosexual desire existing in the homosocial space. Second, the gaze serves narcissistic ego-formation purposes for men. Males viewing the representation of males contemplate the phallus as the symbolic presence, the visible mark of male empowerment. This gaze legitimates the phallic order. The represented male is 'the more perfect, more complete, more powerful ideal ego' (810).

Steve Neale notes that 'the narcissistic male image' is 'the image of authority and omnipotence' (13). The gaze enables white men to be in the subject active position, possessing power, control, authority. Women and racial Others are in the object position, objects of the gaze and hence passive and receptive rather than creative in terms of identity. In these texts, white males are frequently peering at, gazing at or undertaking surveillance over ethnic or racial Others. This is the 'determining male gaze' noted by Mulvey (808).

The spectacle of masculinity and the imprinting of masculinity depend on discourses representing the male. Michael Hatt argues that 'the stability of masculinity depends upon the visibility of the male body; to be learnt or consolidated, masculinity requires a visible exchange between men … Authority demands recognition; in order to function, it needs to be looked at' (63, 65).

According to Michael Roper, 'making men visible as gendered subjects has major implications for all the historian's established themes' (2). And the locales of this representation are often homosocial, such as the ship or the regiment, as Hatt comments: 'A division between heterosocial and homosocial [spaces] is both more useful and more accurate [in describing the nineteenth century]. The crucial difference is that some of these spaces only men … may enter. Moreover, it is in the homosocial realm that young men are inculcated with the ideals of their gender roles … The transmission of masculinity is dependent on the visual economy of these spaces' (62). Hence, many of the texts examined here are predominantly homosocial, such as Kipling's *Captains Courageous*, Haggard's *Allan Quatermain* and Conrad's *The Secret Sharer* or *The Shadow-Line*.

Adventure fiction, in both establishing masculine paradigms and questioning them, concentrates on the issue of the penis/phallus equation discussed by Kaja Silverman in *Male Subjectivity at the Margins*. Silverman argues that the dominant fiction of masculinity in culture is represented by the penis/phallus equation, that is, that being biologically male (penis) automatically entails authority (phallus). Silverman's point is that in actual experience, most men discover this is not so, that this dominant concept is a fiction. Whether by virtue of race, size, ethnicity, class, experience, religion, or a combination of these, males, while possessing the penis, do not in fact have the phallus. Adventure fiction negotiates this difficult situation. Silverman contends: 'Because of the pivotal status of the phallus, more than sexual difference is sustained through the alignment of that signifier with the male sexual organ … . Hegemony is keyed to certain privileged terms … [the] dominant fiction of the phallus/penis equation … . believing in the commensurability of penis and phallus, actual and symbolic father' (15–16, 42).

Males in adventure fiction possess the penis. The question is, do they possess the phallus, which Jacques Lacan argued was impossible for men or women? White males prevail in adventure texts, but in a distant geographical space. Males in these texts sometimes end by believing in the penis/phallus equation, as in *Prester John*, *Captains Courageous*, or *The Riddle of the Sands*. Some protagonists begin already believing in the penis/phallus equation, as in *King Solomon's Mines* or *Allan Quatermain*. Ambiguity persists, however, because many protagonists of adventure fiction are rarely shown back in the metropolis, if at all for only a few concluding pages. They might return home, but this is often unrepresented in the text. When the return is depicted, the men may be ruined physically, as in *The Man Who Would Be King*, or psychologically, as in *Treasure Island*. Back in the metropolis, other protagonists move warily, as in *The Four Feathers* or *Heart of Darkness*. All these males evolve a new conception of their masculinity, but it may not accord with that of the dominant fiction.

In adventure fiction, one often confronts not so much conviction in the penis/phallus equation as a contestation of the equation in writers like Conrad, Hudson, Mason or sometimes Kipling. On the other hand, in a writer such as Haggard or Childers, there is at the conclusion a tentative validation of this equation. Being biologically male in no way guarantees the consolidation of a masculine identity. Adventure fiction investigates the processes of a formation of such an identity without making it either easily available or conclusive. In a text such as Conrad's 'The Planter of Malata', for instance, the process leads to self-destruction; in the same writer's *A Smile of Fortune*, to psychological paralysis. James Adams focuses on the conflicted nature of male identity: 'Norms of masculinity [are] sites of profound internal stress and instability … . The understanding of "manhood" depends importantly on the analysis of transgression, as a dynamic which defines and energizes the authority of the norm' (208).

Graham   Dawson   (1991)   argues   that   these   constructions   have   real consequences:

> This 'imagining' of masculinities is not simply a matter of defining those roles, traits or behaviours considered normal or appropriate for 'men' in any particular cultural context. Rather, it indicates the process by which such norms are subjectively entered into and lived in, or 'inhabited', so as to enable a (relatively) coherent sense of one's self as 'a man' to be secured and recognized by others. An *imagined identity* … has real effects in the world of everyday relationships. (118)

Dawson stresses that the representation of process is the crucial factor, whether or not anything conclusive about masculinities is achieved in the text:

> A necessary distinction must be made here, however, between the representation of masculinities in images and narratives, and the complexities of any such identity as it is lived out amidst the contradictory demands and recognitions generated by any actual social relations. Representations furnish a repertoire of cultural forms that can be drawn upon in the imagining of lived identities. These may be aspired to, rather than ever actually being achieved, or achievable … . The forms furnished by representations often figure ideal and desirable masculinities, which men strive after in their efforts to make themselves into the man they want to be. (118–19)

No one can contend that the models presented in adventure fiction can pass without question in the domestic or metropolitan spheres. Factors of distance by their very nature prevent any inflexible adoption. Yet, it is clear that adventure writers want to address issues about masculinity, in many instances selecting homosocial foreign spaces (countries, islands, ships, outposts) that reveal contradictions in male paradigms. Hence, the dedications made by writers like Haggard to grown men reveal that masculinities are still in process. Carrigan contends: 'There is a distance, and a tension, between collective ideal and actual lives' (92). Distance and tension distinguish such texts as Kipling's *The Man Who Would Be King*, Haggard's *She*, Buchan's *Prester John* or Stevenson's *The Ebb-Tide*.

If adventure fiction interrogates models of masculinity, it does so at a distance. Hugh Ridley argues that while the genre could be seen as supporting imperialism, there was another equally compelling side to the form. 'The adventure story contained … a silent resistance to European society. It took refuge in a world of escape and adventure … . The adventure story contains a double structure: a sublimation of the uncomfortable pressures of the European class-system into a positively heroic encounter with the world outside' (25). There is 'an implicit critique of European civilization … the basic attraction of primitiveness, the sense of dissatisfaction with an excessive and decadent civilization' (112).

In adventure fiction, aggressivity not tolerated at home is permitted abroad. Thus, a protagonist like the Scottish David Crawfurd in Buchan's *Prester John*, economically at a loss, could go to South Africa, save English imperial interests and return home wealthy. As Ridley argues, landscapes in adventure fiction 'symbolized the exotic writers' escape' (63) from England, again an element evident in Buchan's text. Men in colonial fiction evolve a self that in some respects rejects European masculine models for a more authentic, real or manly model than that available at home.

While the 1880s mark a resurgence of interest in the adventure novel, this resurgence results from the interest in masculinity earlier in the century, especially in the work of Thomas Carlyle, whose 1840 lectures *On Heroes, Hero-Worship, and the Heroic in History* were published the following year. Carlyle's heroes, such as Odin, Mahomet or Cromwell, were marked by their galvanising energy, vitality, fearlessness, self-reliance, earnestness and intensity. In Martin Green's words (1979), Carlyle in his lectures supplies 'value-images' (209).

George Salmon writing in 1886 argued that 'boys' literature' constituted 'a vast system of hero-worship' (250), noting: 'It is the God-fearing courage of a Gordon which [a young man's] reading should engender, not the ignoble daring of a Ned Kelly' (258). According to Lee Horsley, Carlyle's ideas support the cult of action: 'The association of high moral standards with the activities of the energetic, event-making man is central to the tradition of hero-worship which runs through the nineteenth century … . Hero-worship and the excitement of Empire were sustained by the late nineteenth-century proliferation of tales of adventure' (21–2).

These are traits associated with masculinity from the 1880s in Victorian England, although the protagonists of adventure fiction at this time are not supermen but 'ordinary' men tested in foreign circumstances. Wendy Katz notes: 'Bourgeois society could be many things, but it could not be courageous or gallant. Sheer material success was not the stuff of heroism' (60). Yet the legacy of Carlyle exists in the adventure hero, as he is or becomes distinct from his culture even as he embodies it. Katz continues:

> The imperial hero, whether a soldier, an adventurer, or simply an embodiment of 'manliness', has no ideological dispute with his society – although he may believe that his society is losing its integrity, getting soft, or somehow straying from its true course. He is a hero who embodies its moral and social norms and turns restive only when his society exhibits signs of weakness … He [is] a traditional man of action who expresses the politically conservative aspirations of his society. (61)

There are several legacies from Carlyle to adventure fiction. According to Susanne Howe: 'The cult of the hero was not all that empire owed to Carlyle; it owed him the Gospel of Work as well' (73). In a text such as Buchan's *Prester John*, the protagonist David Crawfurd establishes commercial enterprises in South Africa with relentless energy. Katz regards the 'twin burdens of exile and hard work' (66) as components of Empire.

In addition, Carlyle inscribes violence into his heroic paradigm when he declares: 'Divine *right*, take it on the great scale, is found to mean divine *might* withal!' (429). One result is that violence in adventure fiction, as Hugh Ridley argues, becomes 'a kind of initiation into an in-group, the racial elite' (141). Again in Buchan's text, the titular hero is, in Howe's words, a 'Noble Savage, who has borrowed enough from the white man to further his own schemes for his people … He is a tragic and impressive figure on the grand scale' (120), but nevertheless, Howe adds, 'it was left to the British to finish off' the Zulus (121).

The adventure texts studied in this book date from the 1880s and later. However, these texts are influenced by predecessors. In particular, Robert Ballantyne's one-volume *The Coral Island* of 1858, itself strongly influenced by *Robinson Crusoe*, remains a signature text of mid-century Victorian adventure narrative. It does so because it established motifs such as islands, voyaging and encounters with racial Others that will be major elements in subsequent adventure texts.

Ballantyne: *The Coral Island* (1858)

Published as a single volume in 1858, Robert Ballantyne's *The Coral Island* is one of the most important novels of adventure to appear in nineteenth-century England. Its influence is marked and acknowledged in later novels from Stevenson's *Treasure Island* to William Golding's *Lord of the Flies*. As many critics have attested, with its motifs of shipwreck and exploration, it is one of the most famous of all the Robinsonade tales descended from Daniel Defoe's 1719 masterpiece. Richard Phillips stresses the importance of Ballantyne's novel: '*The Coral Island* mapped the British Victorian world … What *Robinson Crusoe* seemed only to suggest to Victorian Britons, *The Coral Island* spelled out. It was more arrogantly ethnocentric, more fervently religious, more exuberantly adventurous, more optimistic and more racist than its predecessor' (36). Frank Kermode contends that *The Coral Island* 'could be used as a document in the history of ideas' (203).

The narrative recounts the experiences of three young men, Jack Martin, who is eighteen; Ralph Rover, the narrator, who is fifteen; and Peterkin Gay, who is thirteen, almost fourteen. The young men are shipwrecked on an island in the South Pacific. There they explore the island, examine coral formations, encounter a shark, discover fruits and vegetables, examine the fauna and flora, and observe penguins in the first eighteen chapters of the novel.

With Chapter 19, however, the narrative turns from idyllic to violent. Ralph is captured by pirates. The youths observe a horrific massacre of one tribe by another. Cannibalism is witnessed. At the end, the youths are saved only by the intervention of an English missionary, who converts the vicious native chief Tararo to Christianity and saves the young men, who return to England. With its voyaging, mapping, and invading, the novel anticipates many of the elements later adapted by Stevenson, Hudson, Conrad, Stacpoole and Buchan. Although there are no sexual encounters by the three youths, Ralph recognises the love of comrades as part of their young heroic code.

Ralph Rover states in his Preface that 'I was a boy when I went through the wonderful adventures herein set down' (xxx). His retrospective account begins with his frank admission of being an adventurer: 'Roving has always been, and still is, my ruling passion, the joy of my heart, the very sunshine of my existence. In childhood, in boyhood, and in man's estate, I have been a rover ... an enthusiastic rover throughout the length and breadth of the wide, wide world' (1).

Since we never witness Ralph's adult adventures, we can assume he has remained an inveterate traveler and perhaps a coloniser and imperialist. He tells us that his ancestors for three generations were involved with the sea. The influence of the novel's narrator's name extended to the twentieth century when Sir Robert Baden-Powell named his handbook for young men *Rovering to Success* in 1922.

Like the later protagonist of Conrad's *Lord Jim*, Ralph is entranced by stories of exotic places, in this instance the stories told him by seamen in the coasting trade:

> I freely confess that my heart glowed ardently within me as they recounted their wild adventures in foreign lands – the dreadful storms they had weathered, the appalling dangers they had escaped ... But of all the places of which they told me, none captivated and charmed my imagination so much as the Coral Islands of the Southern Seas ... where summer reigned nearly all the year round; where the trees were laden with a constant harvest of luxuriant fruit; where the climate was almost perpetually delightful; yet where, strange to say, men were wild bloodthirsty savages, excepting in those favoured isles to which the Gospel of our Saviour had been conveyed. These exciting accounts had so great an effect upon my mind that, when I reached the age of fifteen, I resolved to make a voyage to the South Seas. (3–4)

Ballantyne anticipates the young Charles Marlow who will determine in Conrad's *Heart of Darkness* to 'go there' to Africa. Ballantyne also establishes the trope of the seeming paradise which nevertheless seethes with violence.

Ralph, however, is an enigma from the beginning. For example, we never learn his true surname: 'My Christian name was Ralph, and my comrades added to this the name of Rover, in consequence of the passion which I always evinced for travelling. Rover was not my real name, but as I never received any other, I came at last to answer to it as naturally as to my proper name; and as it is not a bad one, I see no good reason why I should not introduce myself to the reader as Ralph Rover' (3). Why this disguise?

This camouflage is especially strange because Ralph introduces his other two companions, whom he meets on a ship to the South Pacific, with their real names. 'Jack Martin was a tall, strapping, broad-shouldered youth of eighteen, with a handsome, good-humoured firm face ... lion-like in his actions ... My other

companion was Peterkin Gay. He was little, quick, funny, decidedly mischievous'
(7). Jack undoubtedly stands for the values represented by the Union Jack. Among
the three young men, Green (1990) labels Jack as representing 'the military' and
Ralph 'the ministerial' (120).

After the shipwreck, the first to sound the imperial note is Peterkin: 'I have
made up my mind that it's capital – first-rate – the best thing that ever happened
to us, and the most splendid prospect that ever lay before three jolly young tars.
We've got an island all to ourselves. We'll take possession in the name of the
king; we'll go and enter the service of its black inhabitants. Of course we'll rise,
naturally, to the top of affairs. White men always do in savage countries. You shall
be king, Jack; Ralph, prime minister' (18). Jack has a pocket-handkerchief with
'sixteen portraits of Lord Nelson printed on it, and a Union Jack in the middle'
(19). For these youths, Nelson is the indubitable hero of the sea. Dryden notes that
'Ballantyne's young adventurers in *The Coral Island* are intellectually sharp in
contrast to the sluggish intelligence of his Polynesians' (105).

The young men are quick to take possession: 'My heart glowed within me
and my spirits rose at the beautiful prospect which I beheld on every side' (21).
Ralph hints at the rites of passage these friends encounter: 'We afterwards found
… that these lovely islands were very unlike Paradise in many things' (28), but
this realisation emboldens rather than disturbs their ideas about white superiority.
Ralph rapturously records: 'We found this to be the highest point of the island,
and from it we saw our kingdom lying, as it were, like a map around us' (47). The
island becomes 'our island' (47), 'our homestead' (50). Phillips comments: 'While
both *Robinson Crusoe* and *The Coral Island* describe the colonial acts of white
British males, the latter is more explicitly and arrogantly colonialist … Seeing was
explicitly equivalent with possessing the island' (40).

To view the island from this vantage point is to possess it by the male gaze.
As Hannabuss (1983/84) comments: 'Islands like these are metaphors of religious
and imperialist attitudes' (77). The island provides the perfect locale for young
men's rites of passage, as Robert Anderson observes: 'The island has come to
symbolize an escape and to provide a place to test the possibilities of other styles
of life within known limits' (54).

A part of this imperialising attitude is the influence of Thomas Carlyle's ideas
about the hero, especially that the hero should be a person of action and not mere
cogitation. Jack remarks: 'But come; … we are wasting our time in *talking* instead
of *doing*' (17). Ralph states about Jack: '[He] would have induced people much
older than himself to choose him for their leader' (24). Jack also espouses Carlyle's
doctrine of work: 'Let us finish our work before eating' (25). Peterkin claims: 'I
would *have* nothing. I didn't say I wanted to *have*; I said I wanted to *do*' (112).
Jack exhibits the will of Carlyle's heroes, as Ralph declares: 'Jack did it. He was
of that disposition which *will* not be conquered' (129). Ralph stresses: 'Jack was
very tall, strong, and manly for his age, and might easily have been mistaken for
twenty' (168). Brian Street asserts that the three young men 'soon dominate their
environment due to their Victorian skills' (115). These three young men exhibit a

quality noticeable in later adventure texts, a devotion to duty, as Millman records: 'Thus the activity of adventuring itself becomes simply a necessity, a form of duty genuinely Victorian despite its often esoteric jungle garb. You just grit your teeth and carry on' (33).

Ballantyne stresses initiation rituals such as communal bathing and swimming (34, 58, 91–2, 113). The youths are united by their intense comradeship: 'I am now persuaded that this [harmony] was owing to our having been all tuned to the same key, namely, that of *love*! Yes, we loved one another with much fervency while we lived on that island; and, for the matter of that, we love each other still' (125). This intense male homosocial bonding is regarded as the most crucial experience for a young male. This bonding enables their exploration. After building a boat, they can range: 'The prospect of being so soon in a position to extend our observations to the other islands and enjoy a sail over the beautiful sea afforded us much delight' (135).

With Chapter 19, the narrative introduces gruesome realities. Canoes arrive, and the youths witness a ferocious battle among the natives:

> The battle that immediately ensued was frightful to behold. Most of the men wielded clubs of enormous size and curious shapes, with which they dashed out each other's brains. As they were almost entirely naked, and had to bound, stoop, leap, and run in their terrible hand-to-hand encounters, they looked more like demons than human beings. I felt my heart grow sick at the sight of this bloody battle. (173)

In this novel, as Street comments, 'Ballantyne revels in detailed descriptions of native atrocities which "prove" his missionary to be right' (71). Only white Christianity can rescue savagery from itself.

This encounter with the racial 'Other' is inflected by racist language. Ralph observes the 'frizzed' hair of the chief, with his body 'as black as coal ... He seemed the most terrible monster I ever beheld' (173–4). They witness cannibalism: 'The monsters cut slices of flesh from [a slain man's] body, and, after roasting them slightly over the fire, devoured them' (175). Green (1990) notes that Ballantyne gives 'horrific images of pagan and cannibal rites in the Fiji Islands (a place that missionary accounts were then turning into *the* site of horror)' (115). Street argues: 'That such bloodthirsty scenes are an everyday event in "savage" society is a central theme of the novel' (131).

For the three white English young men, the invasion by 'savages' forces a brutal awareness: 'We had lived for many months in a clime for the most part so beautiful that we had often wondered whether Adam and Eve had found Eden more sweet; and we had seen the quiet solitudes of our paradise suddenly broken in upon by ferocious savages, and the white sands stained with blood and strewed with lifeless forms' (187–8). Ralph describes 'the awful realities which we had witnessed so lately' (188). Indeed, Ralph discovers that he himself might be becoming savage: 'I began to find that such constant exposure to scenes of blood was having a slight effect upon myself, and I shuddered when I came to think that I too was becoming callous' (243). Martine Dutheil argues that 'Ballantyne's novel can be said to epitomize this turn from the confidence and optimism of the early Victorian proponents of British imperialism to self-consciousness and anxiety about colonial domination … . The repetition of cannibal scenes ends up subverting the author's celebration of white values and morals by prompting a recognition of the narrator's own savagery' (106).

This witnessing of native savagery leads to a rethinking of one of Carlyle's major dicta. Jack tells Ralph: 'Now, I understand from you, Ralph, that the island is inhabited by thorough-going, out-and-out cannibals, whose principal law is, "Might is right, and the weakest goes to the wall"?'(283). Ralph assents. If the Carlylean model of a hero applies especially to Jack, another legacy of Carlyle, which is that might = right, forces Jack to confront and accept violence.

If the natives fighting on the shore are one form of alternative masculinity, the pirates the youths encounter are another: renegade white men, 'white *savages*' (193). When Ralph is captured by the pirates, the pirate Captain tells him he is like another of the pirate crew, seeing the potential dark side of Ralph: 'You're a brick, and I have no doubt will turn out a rare cove. Bloody Bill there was just such a fellow as you are, and he's now the biggest cut-throat of us all' (202). The Captain pretends to Ralph that he is 'a lawful trader' (205). Ballantyne connects commerce with piracy. The Captain is revealed as a murderous villain when he slays hundreds of natives by cannon from his ship.

Religion, commerce and civilisation merge as Ballantyne advances his Christianising agenda. Bill tells Ralph: 'We find that wherever the savages take up with Christianity they always give over their bloody ways' (221). Jack exclaims: 'God bless the missionaries!' (231). Later, Ralph reinforces Ballantyne's religious advocacy: 'I could not help again in my heart praying to God to prosper those missionary societies that send such inestimable blessings to these islands of dark and bloody idolatry' (296). Here, Christianity and racial superiority reinforce economic exploitation.

Bloody Bill remains thoroughly racist. When Ralph observes there are no serpents on the islands, Bill remarks: 'No more there are any … if ye except the niggers themselves' (229). Joseph Bristow comments on his function in the text: 'Bloody Bill is there, in part, to demonstrate that the lowest type of white man is infinitely more dignified than the Fijian' (105). Parker observes: '[Ballantyne's] racism was part of a view of mankind which saw a natural hierarchy of gentlemen leaders and humble followers, which embraced the concept of class as well as race' (46).

It is a Christian missionary who saves the youths from death after they have been captured by natives. Stuart Hannabuss (1989) stresses 'the aggressive work of the missionaries, who combined belief in God with a belief in British nationhood' (60). Ralph remembers: 'I was again led to contrast the rude huts and sheds and their almost naked, savage-looking inhabitants with the natives of the Christian village' (305). Images of painted bodies, human bones and hideous executions anticipate Marlow's account of Kurtz's station in Conrad's *Heart of Darkness*.

The missionary manages to convert the chief Tararo, save the Christian Samoan woman Avatea, and rescue everyone from savagery. Parker emphasizes: 'The father figure who helps to convert Jack is a native missionary; and Jack's maturation, from a "presumptuous boy" to a Christian gentleman, is paralleled by the islanders' conversion to Christianity' (46). The three young men depart for England. Religion in *The Coral Island* is a means of dominating indigenous tribes, and indeed John Peck calls the novel 'a classic text of imperialism' which 'confirms the national destiny' (150). For Phillips, 'the Christian island the boys leave behind them will be more accommodating to European imperialism' (40). In the novel, one trader notes this connection between religion and economics: 'The captain cares as much for the Gospel as you do (an' that's precious little), but he knows, and everybody knows, that the only place among the southern islands where a ship can put in and get what she wants in comfort is where the Gospel has been sent to' (213).

The imprinting power of *The Coral Island* was confirmed by Arthur Conan Doyle in an 1894 essay 'My First Book' for *McClure's Magazine* when he noted:

> I do not think life has any joys to offer so complete, so soul-filling, as that which comes upon the imaginative lad whose spare time is limited, but who is able to snuggle down into a corner with his book, knowing that the next hour is all his own … You lie out upon the topsail yard, and get jerked by the flap of the sail into the Pacific … It was all more real than the reality. Since those days I have in very truth both shot bears and harpooned whales, but the performance was flat compared to the first time that I did it with Mr Ballantyne … at my elbow. (92)

Phillips summarises: 'Few adventure stories have been gaudier, more muscular, more arrogant than *The Coral Island*, in which Ballantyne simplified and exaggerated the certainties of Victorian Britain, along with the middle-class, Christian, white, male colonial values of *Robinson Crusoe*' (36). In addition, Dutheil contends that 'Ballantyne's novel, written in the realist mode and addressed to public school boys who would eventually grow into the administrative cadres of the British Empire, is didactic in intent … . Ballantyne's narrative in fact addresses its lesson to the British boys whose access to manliness is symbolically achieved through their role as colonial instructors' (109–10).

When the young men leave the Coral Island, they carve their names 'on a chip of ironwood' (281) to leave a mark of possession. Hannabuss (1989) claims of Ballantyne that 'his large output of books makes him a considerable influence on boys, young men and men of the time. He mediated many powerful ideals about heroism and Christian courage through [his] stories' (54). The enigmatic narrator Ralph, who assumes the surname of 'Rover', demonstrates that the adventure hero has earned the right to name himself, discarding any remnant of previous existence, to become a man. The novel itself, as Green (1990) remarks, renders Ballantyne one of the 'powerful lawgivers of manliness' (122) of his time.

As he does in *The Coral Island*, Horatio Nelson might represent the great man to many adventurers, but imagined protagonists could still be paradigmatic. Bratton details the effect of Nelson: 'The officer quality of leadership is not so much feudal or charismatic, connected with the mystique of blood, but rather an exaltation of the gentry qualities of efficiency and intelligence and moral worth' (83). The connection between sea stories and Empire is stressed by Bratton: 'The adventure at sea also allows for another dimension in the imaginative patterning of these books which is useful in the transference of their values to the support of the Empire: such adventures necessarily take place far from England, while the inspiration and the ultimate reward lies at home' (85). Transformative experiences at sea define masculine character back home, as in 'Youth', *The Riddle of the Sands*, or *Captains Courageous.*

This book is organised in four chapters which seek to study adventure fiction from four different perspectives. In Chapter 1, Voyaging, the focus is on departure from shores, especially as it involves not only removal from the metropolis or home country but also as it concerns processes of initiation in homosocial spaces as part of that removal from the home country. This chapter focuses on works by Stevenson, Kipling, Childers and Conrad. Chapter 2, Mapping, concentrates on writers' increasing sophistication in dealing with the construction of masculinities by experiencing 'Other' cultures, with analysis of texts by such writers as Haggard, Kipling and Schreiner. Chapter 3, Invading, engages narratives particularly focused on imperializing texts by Conrad, Buchan, Mason and Hudson. Chapter 4, Loving, examines texts involving adventure and sexual encounters which transform the characters' understanding of masculinities. Here, works by Haggard, Stevenson, Hope, Stacpoole and Conrad will be studied.

'The modern masculine novel.' So Arthur Conan Doyle, writing in the *National Review* in 1890, labels the movement begun with Stevenson's *Treasure Island*. He describes this kind of novel:

> [It] deal[s] almost exclusively with the rougher, more stirring side of life, with the objective rather than the subjective ... a reaction against the abuse of love in fiction. This one phase of life in its orthodox aspect, and ending in the conventional marriage, has been so hackneyed and worn to a shadow that it is not to be wondered at that there is a tendency sometimes to swing to the other extreme and to give it less than its fair share in the affairs of men. In British fiction, nine books out of ten have held up love and marriage as the be-all and end-all of life. Yet we know, in actual practice, that this is not so. (552)

Some of the texts considered here do stress male homosocial spaces such as the ship or the regiment (*Typhoon*, *Trooper Peter Halket of Mashonaland*, *The Shadow-Line*, *Captains Courageous*, *Treasure Island*), but just as frequently heterosexual relationships inflect adventure agendas (*The Light That Failed*, *She*, *The Prisoner of Zenda*, *Green Mansions*, *The Blue Lagoon*). If, as Allan Quatermain declared, Englishmen are adventurers, then this book concentrates on one aspect of this adventuring, the adventure of masculinity itself. In that sense, they do constitute examples of Doyle's 'modern masculine novel'.

Martin Green (1990) concludes: 'Thus many adventures … have recommended themselves to their readers as real. They have been read in sequence with, side by side with, narratives of real-life exploration, of feats of courage and strength and force, of sailing around the world alone, of flying across the Atlantic when that was dangerous, and so on. This is not naïve reading any more than those are naïve actions. It is not necessarily self-deceptive. It is certainly not unimportant' (11).

Chapter 1
Voyaging

The texts examined in this study concentrate on the masculinities of their protagonists and the formation of masculine identity through adventure fiction. J.A. Mangan argues:

> Central to the evolution of the male image was the Victorian ideal of 'manliness' … as embracing qualities of physical courage, chivalric ideals, virtuous fortitude with additional connotations of military and patriotic virtue. In the second half of the nineteenth century … the concept underwent a metamorphosis. To the early Victorian it represented a concern with a successful transition from Christian immaturity to maturity, demonstrated by earnestness, selflessness and integrity; to the late Victorian it stood for neo-Spartan virility as exemplified by stoicism, hardness and endurance … 'Manliness' symbolised an attempt at a metaphysical comprehension of the universe. It represented an effort to achieve a *Weltanschauung* with an internal coherence and external validity which determined ideals, forged identity and defined reality. (1–3)

Hence, the texts examined in this book record a process of masculinisation which differed from that prevalent earlier in the nineteenth century. 'A neo-Spartan idea of masculinity was diffused throughout the English speaking world with the unreflecting and ethnocentric confidence of an imperial race' (3).

Norman Vance contends that '"manliness" can be summarized as physical manliness, ideas of chivalry and gentlemanliness, and moral manliness, all of which tend to incorporate something of the patriotic and military qualities which "manliness" may also connote' (10). This process of masculinising is key for culture because as Arthur Brittan notes, 'The fact that masculinity may appear in different guises at different times does not entitle us to draw the conclusion that we are dealing with an ephemeral quality which is sometime present and sometime not' (2). Masculinity describes the codes of male behaviour in culture that construct male subjectivity.

For males a key phase of this process of constructing male subjectivity is initiation into codes of masculine behaviour. Often these initiations occur apart from the influence of women or family or even the father, who may have his role usurped by an alternative male figure who may or may not accord with the father's prerogatives. This other individual may be a sea captain, an older man or a renegade male. Part of the attraction of the adventure genre is that it provides males a way out of and beyond the domestic and legal constraints of shore life or the home country.

Hence, voyaging is often a mechanism of both escape and initiation in many adventure texts. Lionel Tiger has observed:

> That initiations are frequently bizarre, cruel, and of profound significance to both members and aspirants suggests the importance of the initiation process and the exclusivist and selective principle it functions to defend. The fact that membership is often voluntary perhaps underlines the important role of these societies in the social lives of their members. The usually unisexual composition of the groups emphasizes the special part they may play in members' and communities' socio-sexual equilibrium. (126–7)

The texts considered in this chapter focus on initiation into masculine paradigms in homosocial spaces. In Robert Louis Stevenson's *Treasure Island*, Jim Hawkins signs on the *Hispaniola* at the urging of the local squire after Jim's father dies. In the course of his voyage, he encounters a number of surrogate fathers, several of whom are criminal and all of whom are inadequate. In contrast to the Hanoverian setting of *Treasure Island*, Rudyard Kipling locates his *Captains Courageous* on an American fishing vessel in the late nineteenth century. There, a spoiled son of an American Captain of Industry abandons his arrogant ways in the classless environment of the ship. Two loners are the focus of Erskine Childers' *The Riddle of the Sands*. Together, especially in the case of one of the men, the men cement a tenuous friendship and save England from the threat of a German invasion. Joseph Conrad's tales 'Youth', *Typhoon*, and *The Secret Sharer* concern voyages which entail initiations and transformations for some of the men on the ships.

John Peck stresses the significance of initiation as one major subject of sea stories: 'The story of initiation … focuses on the testing of a young man in an unfamiliar situation … A young midshipman, put to the test, proves that he has the qualities that will make him a true sailor … . Being at sea can be seen as the real situation and the voyage the true condition of humanity. Voyaging consequently acquires a positive meaning' (13–14, 15). In all cases, these texts by Stevenson, Kipling, Childers and Conrad show adventure writers using the genre to analyse rites of passage for their protagonists. In some instances, such as in *Treasure Island*, the protagonist remains wretched. In others, such as *Typhoon*, an initiation may be imperfect. In others, such as *Captains Courageous*, there is passage but also progress. In assessing these voyages of initiation, one should bear in mind Conrad's declaration in *Notes on Life and Letters*: 'The mere love of adventure is no saving grace. It is no grace at all. It lays a man under no obligation of faithfulness to an idea and even to his own self' (189).

Stevenson: *Treasure Island* (1883)

Robert Louis Stevenson's *Treasure Island* was serialised from October 1881 to January 1882 in the magazine *Young Folks*. Substantially revised, it appeared in book form in 1883. The novel is the quintessential adventure narrative, including voyaging out; residence in a strange territory, here an island; murderous plotters; lost treasure; daring escapades. It is also the *rite de passage* of its young hero, Jim Hawkins, who works at his father's inn, the Admiral Benbow. After his father's death, Jim becomes a cabin boy on the *Hispaniola* when he sails with the wealthy landowner Squire Trelawney and the physician Dr Livesey to find the treasure on Treasure Island.

The novel, narrated for the most part by an adult Jim, recounts Jim's search for a father and his having to choose among a range of potential father surrogates, including Livesey, Trelawney, Captain Smollett and even the dreaded, psychopathic one-legged pirate Long John Silver. The novel records a contestation of masculinities. As Fraser notes, the novel is 'the founding text in the revival of quest romance' (26).

This *rite de passage* occurs on board the homosocial space of the *Hispaniola*. As many critics have noted, Jim's mother disappears soon after the opening of the narrative. It is a man's world, and it is there that Jim must find an identity. The narrative embraces a strong imperialistic ethos, where both the pirates and the more respectable men (Livesey, Trelawney) believe they have the right to seize the territory, exploit the land and grab the treasure. All the men are proto-imperialists. Joseph Bristow (1991) claims that the squire and the doctor have 'dubious morality guiding their actions. Both men are as wealth-grabbing as the despicable seamen in their plotting for the gold' (113).

Peck labels the novel 'an exceptionally nasty book' (153). Still, it is typical of the kind of adventure fiction appearing in the 1880s, as Peck observes: 'It seems to embody more than one aspect of a change of mood in Britain that can be dated from the early 1880s. A taste for action and adventure is rediscovered' (158).

As Martin Green has noted in *The Robinson Crusoe Story*, the adventure novel is concerned with national power, *potestas*, and this power is completely marked as masculine. Most of *Treasure Island* is not about treasure-hunting but about power; only two of the thirty-four chapters involve the hunt. As Green observes, adventure is a way of eschewing inherited masculinism and moralism. Kiely notes its 'exhilarating sense of *casting off*' (68).

In *Treasure Island*, Hawkins is forced to achieve an identity, but this process is riddled with ambiguity, including the fact that Jim commits murder and remains haunted by the experience as a nightmare, both literally and ontologically. Manhood is achieved, but only by extreme transgression. The treasure represents Jim's independence, identity and selfhood, yet he is haunted by it.

The opening chapters of the novel are filled with men with damaged bodies. The men are mutilated and inadequate. These include Billy Bones with a scar on his cheek; Black Dog, 'the emissary of Flint's crew' (Hardesty 3), who is missing two fingers; Pew, who is blind; Long John Silver, one-legged; and Jim's sickly father. These mutilations are marked from the beginning of the text and signal the crisis of masculinity Stevenson wishes to present, even though he locates the narrative in the eighteenth century. Jim notices the 'sabre cut across one cheek' (1) of Billy

Bones. At first, Jim fantasises about his status: 'He had none of the appearance of a man who sailed before the mast; [he] seemed like a mate or skipper accustomed to be obeyed or to strike' (2).

Later, Jim realises: 'I was, in a way, a sharer in his alarms' (3), anticipating by decades Conrad's *The Secret Sharer.* Being advised to watch for a man with one leg, Jim soon has ferocious dreams of this individual, all strongly implying castration fears: 'Now the leg would be cut off at the knee, now at the hip; now he was a monstrous kind of a creature who had never had but the one leg, and that in the middle of his body. To see him leap and run and pursue me over the hedge and ditch was the worst of nightmares' (3).

One January morning, Black Dog appears. Almost immediately, he tells Jim he has a son almost like Jim, setting up another father/son pair. Jim's father dies, and the next instant blind Pew arrives, delivers the Black Spot to Bones, who has a stroke and dies. Jim and his mother open Bones' chest and find coins from many nations. Jim has taken a packet belonging to Bones and brings it to Dr Livesey and Squire John Trelawney. As greedy as the pirates, Trelawney and Livesey decide to outfit a ship and sail from Bristol to Treasure Island. The captain is Alexander Smollett.

 Jim's fantasies about the forthcoming venture and adventure are based on imperialist assumptions:

> I brooded by the hour together over the map, all the details of which I well remembered. Sitting by the fire in the house-keeper's room, I approached that island in my fancy, from every possible direction; I explored every acre of its surface; I climbed a thousand times to that tall hill they call the Spy-glass, and from the top enjoyed the most wonderful and changing prospects. Sometimes the isle was thick with savages, with whom we fought; sometimes full of dangerous animals that hunted us; but in all my fancies nothing occurred to me so strange and tragic as our actual adventures. (36)

The strangeness begins when Trelawney engages Long John Silver as ship's cook. Trelawney believes him a 'man of substance' (38) although Silver's wife 'is a woman of colour' (39). Jim, however, immediately recognises a pirate when he sees Silver: 'I thought I knew what a buccaneer was like' (42). Later, Livesey also declares Silver is 'honest' (50). Jim already exceeds these two fathers in perception, albeit not in status.

Jim is soon proved correct on the *Hispaniola*. Getting into the apple barrel, Jim is on the verge of sleep when a man rests on it. It is Silver. Then the terror begins:

> The barrel shook as he leaned his shoulders against it, and I was just about to jump up when the man began to speak. It was Silver's voice, and, before I had heard a dozen words, I would not have shown myself for all the world, but lay there, trembling and listening, in the extreme of fear and curiosity; for

from these dozen words I understood that the lives of all the honest men aboard depended upon me alone. (56)

The apple barrel represents the locale of the knowledge of good and evil. It is also the womb, from which Jim emerges in a re-birth – to knowledge of good and evil, to maturity and to self-reliance. For Jim, the voyage is now completely one of self-discovery. Whatever innocence Jim has left is destroyed when Jim overhears Silver plotting a mutiny. To Jim, Silver becomes 'an abominable old rogue … I think, if I had been able, that I would have killed him through the barrel' (58). Silver describes his group as 'gentlemen of fortune' (58).

Jim must now masquerade before Silver. 'He did not know, to be sure, that I had overheard his council from the apple barrel, and yet I had, by this time, taken such a horror of his cruelty, duplicity, and power, that I could scarce conceal a shudder when he laid his hand upon my arm' (64). The Squire can scarcely believe Jim when he tells of the plot: 'And to think that they're all Englishmen!'' (67) he declares. Hence, Stevenson enlarges the issue of masculinity beyond Jim's maturation to question the probity of England itself. Wandering the island, Jim at first feels 'the joy of exploration' (73), but soon he witnesses Silver kill Tom with his crutch and then his knife. Jim labels Silver a 'murderer' (76).

It is part of this *Bildungsroman* that Jim must wonder: 'Could anyone be more entirely lost than I?' (77). Echoing the Robinson Crusoe narrative, alone Jim meets the marooned Ben Gunn, who was with Captain Flint when the treasure was buried. He has been abandoned on the island for three years. While Robert Fraser's position that 'male bonding is at work [in the novel] in a particularly efficient way' (25) has validity, Stevenson complicates the situation because it is also the case that Jim Hawkins, from the time of the death of his father, is agonisingly isolated.

Chapters 1 to 15 have been narrated by Jim. Chapters 16, 17 and 18 are narrated by Livesey. He recounts how he, Trelawney, and their party had managed to occupy the fort in Captain Flint's stockade. Like an imperialist land grab, the men 'flew British colours on the log-house in Treasure Island' (98). Jim resumes the narration in Chapter 19 to recount several exploits. The men in the stockade repulse an attack by the pirates. As Hardesty et al. argue, having Livesey narrate these chapters allows a demarcation between the youthful Jim of the first part of his narration and the adult Jim of the remainder (5).

The *Hispaniola* constitutes the all-male homosocial space of initiation, as Fraser observes 'a floating male society' (21). Yet, as Fraser continues, the Island becomes another ship, 'with its three mountain tops – "Foremast Hill", "Spyglass Hill", and "Missenmast Hill" – standing for the masts on deck. The stockade at the south end of the island is placed in exactly the same position as the captain's quarters on the schooner, immediately behind the missen hill or mast – that is, figuratively behind the wheelhouse... The buccaneers, in the meantime, situate themselves further to the north, in an area of the terrain equivalent, in nautical terms, to the foc's'le' (21).

Jim, however, must test himself in extreme circumstances. He now faces the ultimate challenges in his *rite de passage*: 'The scheme had an air of adventure that inspired me, and the thought of the water-breaker beside the fore companion doubled my growing courage' (129). Jim rows out to the *Hispaniola* and sets it adrift. Later, when the ship is adrift, Jim manages to board it by the bowsprit. Jim takes command of the ship: 'I was greatly elated with my new command. I ... was quieted by the great conquest I had made' (135).

Pursued by the vicious coxswain Israel Hands, Jim finds himself in the position of kill or be killed: 'I felt a blow and then a sharp pang, and there I was pinned by the shoulder to the mast. In the horrid pain and surprise of the moment – I scarce can say it was by my own volition, and I am sure it was without a conscious aim – both my pistols went off, and both escaped out of my hands. They did not fall alone; with a choked cry, the coxswain loosed his grasp upon the shrouds and plunged head first into the water' (142).

This is Jim's supreme transgression in the text, but Stevenson appears to argue that maturation and manhood may well involve these extremes. Jim is terrified at first. He has a 'horror' of falling from the cross-trees, but then 'I was once more in possession of myself ... . I was my own master again' (143). Stevenson stresses this emergence of a new identity. Jim records: 'The habit of tragical adventures had worn off almost all my terror for the dead ... . For the rest, the *Hispaniola* must trust to luck, like myself' (144–5).

Returning to the stockade, Jim finds it occupied by Silver and his men. Silver tells Jim he is 'the picter of my own self when I was young and handsome' (150); Silver addresses Jim as 'my son' (151). Jim must finally confront this renegade father. Stevenson suggests there is a parallel between Silver and Jim in their use of violence and maybe even potential identity. When Jim recounts how he foiled the pirates' plans, some of the crew wish to kill Jim, but Silver saves him.

When the pirates go to find the treasure, they discover it gone. Ben Gunn had removed it to his cave. Trelawney and his party find the treasure. At a West Indies port, Gunn assists Silver to escape. The *Hispaniola* then returns to England, where everyone receives 'an ample share of the treasure' (191). Stevenson devotes no time to the spending of money since, as Fraser notes, 'the spending of money is a landlubbing tale' (21).

The universe of *Treasure Island* contains much violence. Christopher Harvie contends this represents great cultural anxiety at the end of the nineteenth century: 'There is a sense in which *Treasure Island* could be seen as a sort of social parable: an embattled microcosm of civil society – squire, doctor, captain and retainers – being menaced by the lower orders under brutal and materialistic leadership. That establishment is saved by chance and Jim Hawkins' (120). Harvie observes the many instances of civil violence around the time of the novel's publication, such as the 6 May 1882 'murder of the Irish Chief Secretary, Lord Frederick Cavendish and his senior administrator, Thomas Burke in Phoenix Park, Dublin' (121). There is some belief that the Treasure Island in fact represents Ireland. There is also speculation about whether the pirates represent the lower classes, anxious for the vote, reform and power. The novel may also represent fears of socialism and of international terrorism.

Stevenson complicates Jim's assumptions about manliness by presenting a class-ridden society in *Treasure Island*. Though low-born, even Jim is conscious of class from the very beginning, when he comments about Dr Livesey: 'I remember observing the contrast the neat, bright doctor, with his powder as white as snow, and his bright, black eyes and pleasant manners, made with the coltish country folk' (5). Although Supervisor Dance saves Jim and his mother from the pirates, when Dance asks Jim for the packet of evidence, Jim prefers to give it to Livesey. Dance responds: 'Perfectly right … perfectly right – a gentleman and a magistrate' (29). Jim records that the Squire treats Dance in a 'condescending' manner (30).

Seeing the pirates cowering before Livesey, Hawkins analogises them to 'charity school-children' (165), which reflects again his snobbism. The eighteenth-century hierarchy is marked in the death of Tom Redruth, Squire Trelawney's gamekeeper. Trelawney asks the dying Tom to forgive him 'for taking him to the tropics' (Jackson 30). Tom asks: 'Would that be respectful like, from me to you, squire?' (94).

Stevenson's ironic comment on Jim's class consciousness is to have Silver declare Jim a gentleman 'for a gentleman you are, although born poor' (165). Even at the conclusion of the novel, Captain Smollett recognises Jim's class consciousness: 'You're a good boy in your line, Jim; but I don't think you and me'll go to sea again. You're too much of the born favourite for me' (185). Before the voyage began, Jim had aligned himself with the Squire against Captain Smollett, when the latter had raised suspicions about the crew: 'I assure you I was quite of the squire's way of thinking, and hated the captain deeply' Jim records (51), an attitude Smollett perceives as unchanged at the conclusion of the narrative.

The final two paragraphs of the novel epitomise the brutality of Jim Hawkins' passage to manhood. He first states: 'Of Silver we have heard no more. That formidable seafaring man with one leg has at last gone clean out of my life.' Then Jim allows: 'The bar silver and the arms still lie, for all that I know, where Flint buried them; and certainly they shall lie there for me' (191). But does 'lie' mean 'rest' or 'await'? Jim's final thoughts are immortal: 'The worst dreams that ever I have are when I hear the surf booming about its coasts, or start upright in bed with the sharp voice of Captain Flint still ringing in my ears: "Pieces of eight! Pieces of eight!"' (191).

The fact that treasure exists in nightmare more than in actuality is key to the novel, where the stress is on process rather than product, as Millman emphasises:

> Nor do the fantasies in *Treasure Island* and *King Solomon's Mines* underscore a bourgeois profit motive. Though near the ends of both novels a treasure is placed as a reward for an adventure well-performed, it is more for the sake of spurious purpose, to provide the adventurer with some ostensible motivation beyond his real motivation, which is simply the spirit of adventure itself. Excitement is

conferred on the way to acquisition, rather than in the act of acquiring. This is
the fantasy of action, not wealth. (20)

The purpose is the pursuit of masculine identity, the genuine if nightmarish
treasure.

The result of Jim's maturation is the nightmare of adult manhood. Stevenson
reflects not the eighteenth century but the nineteenth-century crisis of masculinity
in *Treasure Island*. Peck goes so far to state that Stevenson in the novel 'touch[es]
upon a deeper sense of malaise in not being able to manufacture and motivate
a manly hero' (158). Masculinity in this novel is policed at every turn, as the
spy-glasses and telescopes attest. No male escapes this surveillance, even in
his dreams. Jim awakens to an existential world of nightmares, paralleling the
nightmares he had experienced at the beginning of the text about brutal surrogate
fathers. The still-roving Silver represents the return of the repressed, terrifying
even for a newly-initiated young man like Jim Hawkins.

Kipling: *Captains Courageous* (1897)

Rudyard Kipling's *Captains Courageous* is a very strong adventure initiation tale.
It is a superb maritime novel in a century that saw many great ones, including
Herman Melville's *Moby Dick* (1851), Robert Ballantyne's *The Coral Island*
(1858), R.L. Stevenson's *Treasure Island* (1883), and Joseph Conrad's *The Nigger
of the 'Narcissus'* (1897). The novel is quintessential as a Kipling text, Norman
Vance (1979) notes: 'For Kipling the masculine world he entered so early and
so eagerly involved community, solidarity, hierarchy, and exclusiveness, with the
concomitant rituals of initiation, recognition, dressing up, and esoteric forms of
communication' (83).

A *Bildungsroman* more complex than is supposed, *Captains Courageous*
records the transition of fifteen-year-old Harvey Cheyne, arrogant and spoiled
American son of a Captain of Industry, into a young man. Cheyne falls off an
ocean liner and is saved by the crew of a cod-fishing schooner, the *We're Here*, out
of Gloucester, Massachusetts.

On the schooner at the Newfoundland banks, Cheyne learns a different way of
life as he fishes from May to September. Eventually he is reunited with Cheyne Sr,
his father, a railway and shipping magnate, and sent to Stanford. After graduation,
he assumes control of the family business. He will remain a capitalist, but a more
enlightened one than his father. At the end, 'the new Harvey had come to stay'
(125).

The narrative is a story of Harvey Cheyne's re-birth, a re-birth into manhood.
Kipling underscores this re-birth when he records Harvey's fall from the liner: 'He
was fainting from seasickness and a roll of the ship tilted him over the rail on to
the smooth lip of the turtle-back. Then a low, grey mother-wave swung out of the

fog, tucked Harvey under one arm, so to speak, and pulled him off and away to leeward' (6).

As Norman Vance (1985) has commented: 'Kipling's most "manly" narrative ... celebrates the character-building discomfort and harshness of life with the Grand Banks fishing fleet. This transforms a spoilt brat of an American millionaire's son into a resourceful and self-reliant young man. The book was much admired by Theodore Roosevelt' (197). This transformation results from several processes.

For one, Harvey Jr must choose between two fathers, the skipper of the fishing schooner Disko Troop and his own captain of industry natural father, who has neglected him. Each father is a 'captain courageous' in his own sphere. This transition is also a cultural one, for by the end of the novel the experience of training on the schooner is shown to be inadequate or incomplete in the modern world, which prefers land-based education, even formal education at university.

Yet, this experience on the *We're Here* emphasises an issue important to Kipling, work, as Vance (1979) argues: '*Work* is a key-word for Kipling, who continually celebrates the skills and achievements of those who possess manual or technological expertise' (86). But this emphasis on work also marks initiations and exclusivity: 'All Kipling's heroes are experts in some field or other, and the possession of a craft or special skill repeats, of course, the familiar pattern of initiates and excluded majority' (87). Vance claims that Kipling, when planning to write *Captains Courageous*, demanded actual demonstrations of preparing the cod for the hold of a fishing vessel.

What has been neglected in appraisals of this novel, however, is its deployment of ancient Greek ephebic ideas as the *modus operandi* of this transition. However, Kipling marks this paradigm from the beginning of the novel, especially in the name of the captain of the *We're Here*, Disko Troop. While named for his birth place, an island off the coast of Greenland, in the novel one of the crew, Long Jack, salutes the skipper as 'Discobolus' (23), evoking the famous sculpture signifying the age of heroic Greek athleticism. Furthermore, his last name, Troop, indicates the all-male band of the Greek warrior formation, the phalanx. Thus, the values celebrated on the schooner are collective, unlike the extreme self-reliance of Cheyne Sr, an orphan who started out with nothing and became a self-made millionaire.

Vance (1985) notes that the stress in *Captains Courageous* is on manliness, but not the Christian manliness of Thomas Hughes (197). Instead, as Disko Troop's name indicates, Kipling substitutes a Greek process of initiation leading to ancient *andreia* or manliness. In the fifth paragraph of his novel, Kipling refers to 'education' (3) and that Harvey has not yet begun his. The 'educative' process recorded in the novel, however, is very ancient, that of the ephebe from young man to hoplite-warrior status in the Greek state. Disko Troop's son Dan tells Harvey: 'You'll know more 'fore you're through' (9). 'You've a heap to learn' (19).

Many elements of the novel incorporate such initiatory markers: the removal to a liminal/boundary/frontier location (particularly signified by the waters of the Banks); the all-male unit (the crew); the sequestration of the initiates (Harvey aboard ship); the change in clothing after Harvey is rescued, when he puts on a set of Dan Troop's fisherman's clothes (33); the rough physical treatment, as when Disko slugs Harvey (14); the range of masculinities represented aboard ship by the crew; the ritual testing of life aboard ship (swinging dories, cleaning, hooking, salting, etc.); the competitive struggle of the *We're Here* with other boats in the fleet in the famous Chapter 8 about the 'town' of massed fishermen; and the code, as in 'keepin' things sep'rate' (82).

Other elements of this ancient initiation include: the description of Harvey's behaviour as 'boylike' as he learns: 'Boylike, Harvey imitated all the men by turns' (70); the token shared between men, as with the knife of the deceased Frenchman that Dan gives Harvey (106); the common mess; the loyalty, for the men have shipped together at least six years (17); the phalanx-like support of every man for every other: '[Harvey] felt for the first time in his life that he was one of a working gang of men' (29). Harvey is a member of the phalanx at the novel's conclusion: 'Same as they treat me down at Wouverman's wharf. I'm one of the crowd now' (139). Harvey now feels like 'the most ancient of mariners' (155).

When Harvey had fallen from the liner at the beginning, when he was rescued he asked 'Where am I?' (7). At the conclusion, his masculinity transformed, he has achieved a sense of his manhood. As Daniel Karlin (1989) observes, Harvey's fall from the liner was 'a fortunate fall' (14). Harvey has learned communal loyalty, discipline and compassion during his time on the *We're Here.*

The irony, however, is that this sea-based discipline must be reinforced by land-based education and progress. Even Dan Troop recognises that his strong, admirable father is not progressive: 'Them new haddockers an' herrin boats … Dad can find fish, but he ain't no ways progressive – he don't go with the march o' the times. They're chock full o' labour-savin' jigs an' sech all' (65).

Reunited with his father, Harvey listens to the man's chronicle of how he made it on his own, the self-made Captain of Industry. But Harvey Sr sees his time is passing; "I can handle men, of course, … but – I can't compete with the man who has been *taught*! I've picked up as I went along, and I guess it sticks out all over me … . Now *you*'ve [*sic*] got your chance. You've got to soak up all the learning that's around' (143). He insists that his son Harvey attend Stanford.

At the conclusion, as Karlin (1989) asserts, Cheyne Sr begins this embrace of the future 'by taking [Dan] out of the fishing industry altogether and transplanting him from the east to the west coast of America. Cheyne [Sr] places Dan in the shipping line he owns, and gives the line to Harvey as his graduation present' (21). Harvey Cheyne Jr combines experience with learning. As Linda Dryden observes: 'Even the spoilt and work-shy Harvey Cheyne … becomes an accomplished seaman' (82). An anonymous reviewer of *Stalky & Co.* in the *Atheneaum* in 1899 compared it to *Captains Courageous* in terms of masculine imprinting: 'In both cases the type of boy to be turned out is that of the military or commercial organizer' (Green, ed., *Critical Heritage* 227).

On the final page of the novel, young Harvey and Dan meet several years later. Harvey announces he is coming into the business in a year, fulfilling the prophecy of the Negro cook that they would be Master and Man. When Dan declares he owes much to the *We're Here*, Harvey adds 'Me too' (156). In truth, however, both Harvey and Dan have embraced a more advanced form of capitalism that renders their fathers nostalgic figures of the past.

John Peck stresses that the novel focuses on 'a male fraternity' and 'a world of masculine fellowship' (161). It is a novel which emphasises Carlyle's doctrine of work in its unremitting scenes of toil. Peck argues: 'This involves reviving a masculine culture, where men live by their physical strength and their skill at their trades. There is, however, something not only wistful but also doomed about hoping to recover all this' (160). He observes: 'In *Captains Courageous* there is a sense of strain as [Kipling] tries to revive a sense of masculine values in a period that has little time for such an idea' (159). However, this masculine solidarity does prevail at the conclusion, albeit in a new context.

There is a nostalgia and even doom about both Disko Troop and Cheyne Sr, but the male fraternity is sustained. Economic power, however, has been reconstituted. For Mark Kinkead-Weekes, Dan's 'brotherly' (156) smile at the end indicates he is indeed 'a brother, not an employee' (215), in reality as much a master and a man (not a servant) as Harvey. The future belongs to being on land and educated. Masculine values have shifted from sea to shore. Kipling's point is to analyse this transition, not to celebrate a dead sea ritual but to record a reformulation of masculine values.

Kipling had derived the title *Captains Courageous* from the ballad 'Mary Ambree', which he may have read in Percy's *Reliques*. He had used the title in an article about 'businessmen as the new adventurers' (Ormond 157), which he had published in *The Times* in November 1892. In it, Kipling declares that the adventure tradition lives on in captains of industry: 'The adventurers and captains courageous of old have only changed their dress a little and altered their employment to suit the world in which they move. [They are] selling horses, breaking trails, drinking sangaree, running railways beyond the timber-line, swimming rivers, blowing up tree stumps, and making cities where no cities were' (cited in Karlin 16).

In *Captains Courageous*, Kipling argues to move Greek *andreia* into the twentieth century by melding it with formal education and training. As Karlin (1989) writes about both Dan and Harvey at the conclusion of their *rites de passage*: 'They are not here but there' (21).

Conrad: 'Youth' (1898)

Joseph Conrad finished the tale 'Youth' by 3 June 1898. The text was published in September 1898 in *Blackwood's Magazine*. The narrative reflects Conrad's experiences on the barque *Palestine*, a ship carrying coal, during 1881–82. 'Youth' is one of the very greatest tales about evaluating masculine paradigms. Conrad explained to his publisher: 'Out of the material of a boys' story I've made "Youth" by the force of the idea expressed' (cited in Knowles/Moore 407). Conrad explicitly links the narrative with the tradition of adventure literature. The story, conceived by many as a quest narrative marked by a *rite de passage*, involves the voyage out, the testing, the contact with new shores and the evolution of a concept of manhood. Daniel Schwarz (1980) argues that Conrad 'created Marlow to explore himself ... Conrad creates a double who clarified and ordered the very problems that haunted him. Marlow is a surrogate figure coping with versions of Conrad's own psychic turmoil and moral confusion' (52).

The tale is famous as being the first involving Charles Marlow as narrator. His narrative, however, is contained by a frame entailing an unnamed narrator, who recounts Marlow's narrative. The external narrator characterises such a voyage not as an 'amusement' but as 'life itself' (71), signalling this contestation of masculinities. His listeners involve four men, an all-male grouping which will reappear in *Heart of Darkness*. This all-male group of auditors marks gender boundaries. Women are not privileged to hear the tale, which focuses on masculine issues, which are Conrad's priority here. Their exclusion shows Conrad at this phase of his career stressing male experience. The group of all-male auditors intensifies the masculine inflection of the tale.

Marlow ships as a second mate on the *Judea* taking a shipment of coals from England to Bangkok. The ship's name, evoking the Wandering Jew, underscores the youthful male experience of being an exile and outcast before a sense of male identity is achieved. The motto of the ship 'Do or Die' (72), evoking Tennyson's 'Charge of the Light Brigade', reinforces the concept of initiation.

Of great significance, Marlow, narrating at age forty-two, is discussing a voyage which occurred when he was twenty. 'The narrative is thus composed of two voices, immediate and retrospective, innocent and experienced' (Simmons 82). Hugh Epstein notes that 'Young Marlow's restless spirit colours and agitates the prose of the older man's account' (3).

It is Marlow's first voyage to the East, and the middle-aged narrator recognises its significance for himself as young protagonist: 'You fellows know there are those voyages that seem ordered for the illustration of life that might stand for a symbol of existence' (71). He continues: 'There was a touch of romance in it, something that appealed to my youth' (73). The challenge of masculine imprinting is marked, as well, by the name of the chief mate, Mahon 'pronounced Mann' (72). Despite this name, Mahon 'had never got on' (72), hence a masculine paradigm to be rejected.

During the voyage to Bangkok, the ship experiences three setbacks which almost become disasters: 1. It takes sixteen days to get from London to the Tyne because of inclement weather, 'the famous October gale' (73); 2. The ship is rammed by a steamer; 3. A storm in the channel causes the hull to leak, necessitating repairs in Falmouth. These 'tests' at first, however, do not dismay the youthful Marlow.

Marlow recounts: 'This is the deuce of an adventure – something you read about; and it is my first voyage as second mate – and I am only twenty ... I had moments of exultation... . O youth! The strength of it, the faith of it, the imagination of it! ... To me she was the endeavour, the test, the trial of life' (77). Clearly, one inspiration for the youthful Marlow is the genre of adventure. 'Remember I was twenty and it was my first second mate's billet, and the East was waiting for me' (79). 'For me there was also my youth to make me patient. There was all the East before me, and all life ... I lived the life of youth in ignorance and hope' (81).

South of Java Head, the cargo of coal catches fire from 'spontaneous combustion' (82). Yet even in this peril, the youthful Marlow is staggered by the beauty of the sea: 'The sea was polished, was blue, was pellucid, was sparkling like a precious stone ... one colossal sapphire, a single gem fashioned into a planet' (83). Marlow is finally assailed by an explosion on the ship, one which transforms him physically: 'I did not know that I had no hair, no eyebrows, no eyelashes, that my young moustache was burnt off' (85). His psychic life is presaged by this bodily catastrophe.

The Liverpool crew is forced to pump water into the hull in an attempt to extinguish the blaze. It occasions from Marlow a nationalist encomium: 'That crew of Liverpool hard cases had in them the right stuff. It's my experience they always have. It is the sea that gives it – the vastness, the loneliness surrounding their dark stolid souls' (87). When Marlow asks the crew to make extraordinary efforts, they respond.

Marlow begins to embrace his English manhood by reflecting on the crew's behaviour:

> They had no professional reputation – no examples, no praise. It wasn't a sense of duty ... . No; it was something in them, something inborn and subtle and everlasting. I don't say positively that the crew of a French or German merchantman wouldn't have done it, but I doubt whether it would have been done in the same way. There was a completeness in it, something solid like a principle, and masterful like an instinct ... that gift of good or evil that makes racial difference, that shapes the fate of nations. (89)

As Simmons notes, the tale 'is a narrative of Englishness' (83).

When the *Judea* finally sinks near Indonesia, Marlow takes his first command, of one of the lifeboats: 'I thought I would part company as soon as I could. I wanted to have my first command all to myself ... I would beat the other boats [to Java]. Youth! All youth! The silly, charming, beautiful youth' (93). Having 'made a mast out of a spare oar and hoisted a boat-awning for a sail' (94), Marlow sails his boat past that of Mahon, 'a malicious old man' (94). That kind of 'Mann' he abandons. The result is an achievement of edgy consciousness: 'I did not know how good a man I was till then ... I remember my youth and the feeling that will never come back any more – the feeling that I could last for ever, outlast the sea, the earth, and all men; the deceitful feeling that lures us on to joys, to perils, to love, to vain effort – to death' (95).

According to Epstein, Marlow's 'landfall consists of two episodes' (5). One is a false arrival as Marlow rows into the harbour, still attending to Western tasks: 'Then before I could open my lips, the East spoke to me, but it was in a Western voice' (96). The true arrival occurs after Marlow sleeps through the night and receives a symbolic rebirth/regeneration on awakening: 'I pulled back, made fast again to the jetty, and then went to sleep at last. I had faced the silence of the East. I had heard some of its language. But when I opened my eyes again the silence was as complete as though it had never been broken' (97). The East stares at the old Western men, the captain Beard and the chief mate Mahon: 'The East looked at them without a sound' (98). The West is noise (commercial), the East is silence (mystical).

Marlow has a celebrated vision of the East 'with strange odours of blossoms, of aromatic wood ... the first sight of the East on my face. That I can never forget' (95). 'This was the East of the ancient navigators ... full of danger and promise' (98). While for others 'Nemesis lies in wait, pursues, overtakes so many of the conquering race', for Marlow 'all the East is contained in that vision of my youth' (98). He ends with a query: 'Wasn't that the best time, that time when we were young at sea?' (99). As Alan Simmons comments, 'Despite its title, "Youth" is about age' (82).

At the conclusion of the voyage, the young Marlow sees the old skipper, whose name was John Beard, the hairy father who must be rejected: 'He looked as though he would never wake.' Mahon appears 'as though he had been shot' (98). The young Marlow bypasses these old men, almost the living dead, embracing his newly-found masculinity.

This new masculinity, however, has a strong imperialist bias. After the gale which delays the voyage out, Marlow has time to do some reading: 'Meantime I read for the first time [Thomas Carlyle's] *Sartor Resartus* and [Frederick] Burnaby's *Ride to Khiva*. I didn't understand much of the first then, but I remember I preferred the soldier [Burnaby] to the philosopher [Carlyle] at the time; a preference which life has only confirmed. One was a man; and the other was either more – or less' (74). Marlow makes a snide reference to the rumours of Carlyle's sexual impotence.

Marlow's preference for Burnaby's book, first published in 1877, aligns him with a daring soldier who was a pro-imperialist conservative whose book denounces Russia's threatened moves against British interests in India. At the battle of El Teb, 9 February 1884, according to Todd Willy, Burnaby 'managed to kill thirteen Sudanese Moslems with a double-barreled shotgun' (43), an act for which he was both lauded and condemned. Burnaby was to die at the battle of Abu Klea, 17 January 1885, part of the Gordon Relief Expedition. (This was the battle in which the Mahdists broke the square.)

Willy argues that the conservative attitude of Burnaby paralleled the similar attitude at *Blackwood's Magazine* where the story first appeared. Marlow's stress on the English nature of the crew's achievements, noted above, reflects notions of English superiority which were key to the year, 1898, and even month, in which the story was published. In the spring of 1898, British and Egyptian forces had defeated the Mahdists 'at Atbara in the Sudan' (Willy 40). The battle of Omdurman, 2 September 1898, yielded a great victory for England under Horatio Kitchener, the climax of the Reconquest of the Sudan after the devastating loss at Khartoum, with General Charles Gordon's death, in 1885.

Marlow's conservative, pro-imperialist stance had been hinted at when he mused in the narrative while thinking of the East: 'I thought of men of old who, centuries ago, went that road in ships that sailed no better, to the land of palms, and spices, and yellow sands, and of brown nations ruled by kings more cruel than Nero the Roman and more splendid than Solomon the Jew' (81). This passage, published the same month as Kitchener overcame the 'brown' Mahdists, suggests that Marlow's ecstatic first view of the East also entailed a desire for conquest, if not military then certainly economic. The golden age he remembers celebrates British imperialism.

Schwarz (1980) believes that 'Youth' 'is about Marlow's efforts to create a significant yesterday so that his life will not seem a meaningless concatenation of durational events ... . The act of telling is a desperate attempt to suppress the knowledge of experience in a song of innocence ... . Marlow's psychic need to create a sustaining myth asserts itself' (54, 55, 56). There are several perspectives in 'Youth', most notably those of the young Marlow and the mature Marlow. This situation means that the narrated tale of his youth serves Marlow as a camouflage to conceal the reality, or even the futility, of his life by generating a glorious myth of origin. Masculinity becomes a process of negating the past as much as fabricating the future.

Because this is a story of initiation, inevitably it is not the end of defining manhood. The final paragraph indicates that the convictions of youthful self-realisation will pass. The external frame narrator notes of the group listening to the tale of an adventure twenty years old that 'our faces [were] marked by toil, by deceptions, by success, by love; our weary eyes looking still, looking always, looking anxiously for something out of life, that while it is expected is already gone – has passed unseen, in a sign, in a flash – together with the youth, with the strength, with the romance of illusions' (99). The word 'illusions' inspires fear and existential skepticism. This narrator may well be commenting on the far less confident attitude to Empire twenty years after the youthful Marlow's experiences.

This rite of passage occurs in the all-male context of the ship. Earlier the Captain had advised Marlow that no sailor should marry. Yet, for the young Marlow, these tests inspired a maturing self-confidence, a small but first command and a rejection of outworn male paradigms (skipper, first mate) in favour of his own energetic one. The *Judea* (symbolising religious codes) sinks, but Marlow does not. He lives for another excursion, ten years later, during which all his masculine idealism is destroyed to the Congo, which he narrates in *Heart of Darkness*, also to appear in *Blackwood's Magazine*.

Conrad: *Typhoon* (1902)

Completed in January 1901, Conrad's novella *Typhoon* was published in the *Pall Mall Magazine* from January to March 1902. It is a tale of initiation involving the young first mate Jukes and his interactions with the skipper of the steamship *Nan-Shan*, Captain MacWhirr, as the ship transports two hundred coolies 'from an unnamed Eastern port for Fu-Chau on the south China coast' (Knowles 377). This initiation, however, is complex, since MacWhirr is an ambiguous masculine model for Jukes, who is racist and unappealing.

Conrad's novella records a maturation process where the leading model of masculinity, invested with captaincy, is ordinary and unimaginative. As Paul Bruss remarks, Jukes is exposed to 'three physical and psychic "typhoons": MacWhirr's verbal absurdity, the tremendous storm, and finally the tumbling of the coolies' (46). There are at least two other views of MacWhirr presented in the text, that of MacWhirr's wife and that of the chief engineer, Solomon Rout.

In the initial paragraphs of the story, Conrad sets up the juxtaposition of Jukes with his Captain. MacWhirr is described as 'simply ordinary, irresponsive, and unruffled … medium height, a bit round-shouldered [with a] powerful, hairy fist' (3). The Captain carries an unrolled umbrella, which Jukes assiduously furls. Jukes perceives even this simple deficiency in his Captain.

Their next confrontation occurs over the flying of the Siamese flag on the ship. For racist reasons among others, Jukes, 'looking at it bitterly', objects that it seems 'queer' over a ship manned by British sailors (8). MacWhirr counters that 'that elephant there … stands for something in the nature of the Union Jack in the flag … "Does it!" yelled Jukes' (9). The incidents of the umbrella and the flag establish the ambiguity of MacWhirr as a masculine paradigm for Jukes. The flag incident shows MacWhirr's 'literal-mindedness' (Simmons 68). Jukes writes a friend about MacWhirr: 'Sometimes you would think he hadn't sense enough to see anything wrong … I believe he hasn't brains enough to enjoy kicking up a row … We get a laugh out of this at times; but it is dull, too, to be with a man like this' (13).

Racial inflections about the Far East are introduced early in the story. Jukes shows the clerk of the Bun Hin Company the location where the coolies being transported will be lodged during the passage. Conrad contrasts Jukes and the clerk: '[Jukes] was gruff, as became his racial superiority, but not unfriendly. The Chinaman, gazing sad and speechless into the darkness of the hatchway, seemed to stand at the head of a yawning grave' (10). 'The image of "a yawning grave" powerfully suggests the inhuman conditions under which the coolies are going to live' (Goonetilleke 47). When Jukes speaks to the Chinaman, 'having no talent for foreign languages [he] mangled the very pidgin-English cruelly' (10). As Goonetilleke observes: 'The Chinese were transported to the West Indies, Peru and Malaya by the British to provide labour for their profit-bringing ventures … . The "coolie trade" was called the "pig trade" by dealers' (47, 48).

When the threat of the typhoon looms, Jukes expresses his concern for the 'passengers' (23), as he calls the coolies. At first, this might appear sympathetic.

When MacWhirr asks 'What passengers?' Jukes replies 'The Chinamen', at which MacWhirr expostulates: 'The Chinamen! … Never heard a lot of coolies spoken of as passengers before. Passengers, indeed! What's come to you?' (23). To MacWhirr the coolies are cargo, not passengers. Jukes appears concerned for the Chinese as human beings, but, as Goonetilleke observes: 'Jukes desperately refers to the Chinese to cover his concern for the ship and his fellow seamen' (48).

When the hurricane commences, there is an emphasis on MacWhirr's responsibility. MacWhirr decides that, with a steamship rather than a sailing ship, he will confront the storm directly rather than go around it. Even Jukes recognises the value of the Captain taking responsibility: 'Jukes was uncritically glad to have his captain at hand. It relieved him as though that man had, by simply coming on deck, taken most of the gale's weight upon his shoulders. Such is the prestige, the privilege, and the burden of command … Captain MacWhirr could expect no relief of that sort from any one on earth. Such is the loneliness of command' (29).

When Jukes attempts to move on deck, imperiled, he 'finally was himself caught in the firm clasp of a pair of stout arms. He returned the embrace closely round a thick solid body. He had found his captain' (31). Indisputably at this moment, MacWhirr does serve to aid the young Jukes, who needs this masculine 'embrace': 'Jukes came out of it rather horrified, as though he had escaped some unparalleled outrage directed at his feelings. It weakened his faith in himself' (31). At this crisis of masculinity on Jukes' part, MacWhirr suffices. Schwarz (1980) contends that Jukes is 'threatened with complete psychic collapse' (114).

Jukes tells the Captain that two of their boats are gone. Again, MacWhirr offers physical reinforcement: 'Jukes felt an arm thrown heavily over his shoulders; and to this overture he responded with great intelligence by catching hold of his captain round the waist … . They stood clasped thus in the blind night, bracing each other against the wind, cheek to cheek and lip to ear, in the manner of two hulks lashed stem to stern together' (33–4).

Eventually Jukes is released to fare by himself: 'Captain MacWhirr removed his arm from Jukes' shoulders, and thereby ceased to exist for his mate, so dark it was' (35). Believing he is going to die, Jukes is not 'scared'. Rather, as the omniscient narrator remarks, 'There are the moments of do-nothing heroics to which even good men surrender at times', and Jukes experiences a 'numbness of spirit' (37). Such is part of his transition to manhood. As Bruss notes about Jukes, the typhoon 'is a full image of his own inner turmoil … It becomes another psychic, as well as physical, threat' (48).

In a brilliant passage of fragmented communication, MacWhirr commands Jukes to go below and attempt to bring order to the chaos of the coolies, who are fighting below decks among themselves as their money chests have all broken loose and scattered their dollars. Establishing order in this situation is Jukes' supreme challenge, which the narrative makes quasi-epical: '[Jukes] staggered away like a defeated man from the field of battle. He had got, in some way or other, a cut above his left eyebrow – a cut to the bone … It did not bleed, but only gaped red;

and this gash over the eye, his dishevelled hair, the disorder of his clothes, gave him the aspect of a man worsted in a fight with fists' (54).

The white men corral the coolies, who are as terrified of them as of the storm: 'The coming of the white devils was a terror … Several, whom the excess of fear made unruly, were hit with hard fists between the eyes, and cowered … Faces streamed with blood; there were raw places on the shaven heads, scratches, bruises, torn wounds, gashes' (57). Jukes, still retaining his racial superiority, advises MacWhirr: 'Let them only recover a bit, and you'll see. They will fly at our throats, sir. Don't forget, sir, she isn't a British ship now. These brutes know it well, too. The damn'd Siamese flag' (60). Leavis in *The Great Tradition* analogised the natural storm to 'the human hurricane of fighting coolies' (186). As it turns out, however, Jukes' fear of violent revolt against the white men is never realised. Conrad suggests it to underscore Jukes' immature and racist imagination.

While the final fury of the tempest is still to come, Jukes achieves a mastery over himself and attains a tentative form of maturation, aided in a bitter irony by his racial superiority. However, this achievement is qualified in its being partial. This result is because it is not Jukes alone who succeeds in restoring calm among the coolies. The achievement as much belongs to the carpenter, who finds 'chain and rope' and rigs 'life-lines' (56). The narrator records: 'The carpenter, with two hands to help him, moved busily from place to place, setting taut and hitching the life-lines' (57). When reporting to MacWhirr about the incident, Jukes does not specifically mention the carpenter's role, pretending he alone acted: 'I rigged life-lines all ways across that 'tween-deck' (63).

MacWhirr seems to suspect Jukes is less than forthcoming. He informs him: 'You are always meeting trouble half way, Jukes' (64). Then MacWhirr gives him solid advice: 'Don't you be put out by anything … Keep facing it. They may say what they like, but the heaviest seas run with the wind. Facing it – always facing – that's the way to get through. You are a young sailor. Face it. That's enough for any man. Keep a cool head' (64). Jukes passes the initiation: 'For some reason Jukes experienced an access of confidence, a sensation that came from outside like a warm breath, and made him feel equal to every demand. The distant muttering of the darkness stole into his ear. He noted it unmoved, out of that sudden belief in himself, as a man safe in a shirt of mail would watch a point' (64). The climax of the storm occurs on Christmas Day (68), probably to mark Jukes' 'birth' into manhood. The ship arrives safely and the money is distributed fairly by MacWhirr to the coolies.

It is in the final chapter of the novella that Conrad especially introduces ambiguities about MacWhirr. When MacWhirr's letter to his wife arrives, she is relieved that he is not coming home. Depicted as a mean-spirited, pretentious woman, she is proved a hypocrite and a liar as she pretends to lament his absence. In contrast, when Solomon Rout's letter to his wife arrives, she is pleased, retailing to Rout's mother his well-being and his success.

Jukes, however, has the last word. Writing to his friend, a former shipmate, he first conveys his still racist attitude that the coolies would have destroyed them all if given the opportunity. Jukes clings to his racist opinions, noting: 'Surely any skipper of a man-of-war – English, French or Dutch – would see white men through as far as row on board goes. We could get rid of them and their money afterwards' (71). About the coolies, Jukes observes: 'They had had a doing that would have shaken the soul out of a white man. But then they say a Chinaman has no soul … This would have laid out a white man on his back for a month' (73).

MacWhirr's attitude, as Schwarz (1980) argues, is also imperialist: '[Conrad] knew that the captain embodies the complacency, condescension, and, yes, racism of British imperialism. He does not idealise MacWhirr's commitment to the Chinese which is based simply on his conception of the White Man's Burden. MacWhirr insists that the coolies be given an equal chance to live and a share of their money, but does not tolerate the sentimental rhetoric of Jukes that equates Chinamen with passengers' (116–17).

Jukes concludes about MacWhirr: 'There are feelings that this man simply hasn't got – and there's an end of it' (71). 'I think that he got out of it very well for such a stupid man' (74). The validity of this opinion is questionable, however. Jukes is smarting from the rebuke MacWhirr delivers to him when a frantic Jukes armed some hands to ward off a revolt by the coolies, which never occurred. The exasperated Captain had asked: 'What the devil are these monkey tricks, Mr Jukes?' (72). Simmons contends that Jukes 'mistakes his captain's stolidity for stupidity' (73). Perhaps taking this statement by Jukes as a cue, Schwarz (1980) contends that Jukes 'proves his competence as a seaman *without* undergoing profound change' (111). However, it is possible that Jukes in the future will combine his innate imaginative nature with his hard-won awareness of the value of pragmatism.

One must recognise that the typhoon was also an initiation for MacWhirr. Early in the narrative, it is recorded:

> [The Captain] had never been given a glimpse of immeasurable strength and of immoderate wrath, that wrath that passes exhausted but never appeased – the wrath and fury of the passionate sea … Captain MacWhirr had sailed over the surface of the oceans as some men go skimming over the years of existence to sink gently into a placid grave, ignorant of life to the last, without ever having been made to see all it may contain of perfidy, of violence, and of terror. There are on sea and land such men thus fortunate – or thus disdained by destiny or by the sea … [MacWhirr] had no experience of cataclysms, and belief does not necessarily imply comprehension. (14–15)

The narrative establishes that such extreme testing is essential for a man to be his best. That MacWhirr, unimaginative and literal-minded, has not experienced that challenge, tells against him. Even though the Captain survives the test, one may wonder at the conclusion whether he has learned from it.

Jonathan Raban comments about Conrad's intention and strategy in *Typhoon*:

> When Conrad puts Captain MacWhirr at the wheel of the steamship, *Nan-Shan*,
> … the ship is like a great physical extension of the captain's dim and mechanical
> personality. The name 'MacWhirr' suggests the stupid revolution of a flywheel
> in an engine, and when ship and man drive blindly through the typhoon (as
> no ship should, and as no sailing ship could), they are affronting the nature of
> the sea. MacWhirr represents the unimaginative, industrial world that Conrad
> detested, and it is an anomaly that he should be at sea at all. (17)

According to Paul Bruss, MacWhirr retains a 'stiffness of determination which
precludes the possibility of awakening and change … This limited captain, who
has not had the sense to circle the perilous storm, regards the typhoon more as a
painful disruption to his routine than as a metaphysical horror of which he has
become aware … . MacWhirr never awakens … He knows only the possibility of
persistence in his routine' (54). Eberhard Griem, on the other hand, contends that
MacWhirr does achieve a new maturity while Jukes does not: 'Captain MacWhirr
experiences a crucial, existential crisis that completes his maturity, and … Jukes
remains relatively untouched by the experience, so that his case is that of a failed
initiation' (21).

Francis Mulhern has written a strong rebuttal to F.R. Leavis' reading of
Typhoon in *The Great Tradition* where Leavis 'celebrates the triumph of the
rational white male officer class over the chaotic bodily confusion of the Chinese'
(Roberts 75). Mulhern perceives that *Typhoon* instead records an appalling crisis
of masculinity:

> The [storm] that occupies most of Conrad's story is a literal event … But from
> the outset it is metaphorized as a psychic and political ordeal. The ship's captain,
> MacWhirr, is an obsessional … The storm attacks every established social
> relationship of the vessel. Masculinity is abandoned for hysteria; linguistic order
> fails … The lowering of the British ensign brings on a storm that unfixes identity
> … and *Homo Britannicus* is abandoned to a chaos of effeminacy, homoeroticism,
> and gibberish. (255–6)

For Mulhern, *Typhoon* records a cultural catastrophe with its ruined men.

Furthermore, to Mulhern, both Jukes and MacWhirr are individual failures as
officers: 'Jukes who, in his uncertain sexual orientation (his regular correspondent
is male) and openness to linguistic transgression (metaphor, pidgin), is socially
perverse. Worse, the protagonist himself is fatally ambiguous: MacWhirr, as we
have learned from an early narrative recollection, is not British but Irish. The chief
officers of the *Nan-Shan*, ultimate guarantors of imperial order, bear the typhoon
within themselves' (255–6). Even if one does not accept Mulhern's statement
about Jukes' sexual orientation (which may be true), the perils of initiation in
Typhoon are profoundly disturbing.

Hence, Christof Wegelin writing about this novella stresses 'Conrad's sense of
the absurdity of man's existence' (48), the 'sense of alienation' (49). In *Typhoon*,

this absurdity and alienation are demonstrated by the fact that, as Bruss notes, the tale is about Jukes' 'maturing into an officer ... who can respect the office of captain even in the dull MacWhirr' (50). It is absurd because the mentor Captain provides an unfinished and incomplete masculine paradigm at the same time that only a tentative maturation emerges in his alienated first mate. In *Typhoon*, Conrad reveals that a young man must find his models, however inadequate and fallible, and face the existential typhoon. The storm is within and without.

According to Roberts, 'Conrad's white male heroes ... are always, in fact, white male anti-heroes' (25). This situation was already addressed by Conrad in 'An Outpost of Progress' and *Heart of Darkness* before *Typhoon*. Those two narratives are famous for their analyses of racist attitudes, but *Typhoon* is quite similar. Goonetilleke stresses this element about the tale: 'The coolies are dehumanised because they are victims of the imperial economy, which was run partly on the lines of slavery... [They are in a] dehumanised, helpless state' (50). All three of these texts are eloquent narratives about masculinity, but *Typhoon* remains an especially brutal record of initiation, reflected in the equivocation the reader feels about its two protagonists.

Childers: *The Riddle of the Sands* (1903)

Erskine Childers, who was to die an Irish patriot by firing squad in 1922, published *The Riddle of the Sands* in 1903. The book was 'immediately greeted with rapturous acclaim ... A cheap edition sold several hundred thousand copies, making it in all probability the year's bestseller' (Kennedy 7). Childers 'thought about it for several years before he began working on it and spent two more years writing it ... [It] was finally finished, shortly after Christmas 1902' (Piper 71). The book was published in May 1903. 'By the end of the year it had gone through three editions, plus a special cheap edition' (Piper 72). There were editions in 1904, 'and one each in 1907 and 1908' (Piper 104). According to Childers' biographer Andrew Boyle, 'its overwhelming public reception stunned him' (109).

The novel involves two Englishmen, Carruthers, a clerk in the Foreign Office, and Arthur H. Davies, a loner, and their experiences aboard Davies' yacht the *Dulcibella*, as they sail along the Frisian coast. (According to Piper [67], the *Dulcibella* took its name from that of Childers' favourite sister.) In the course of their adventures, they discover that an English defector and traitor, Dollmann, whose ship is the *Medusa*, is assisting the Germans, including a commander named von Brüning aboard his torpedo ship the *Blitz*, in planning an invasion of the east coast of England.

The novel has as its 'riddle' this discovery of potential invasion, which is foiled by the enterprise of Davies and especially of Carruthers in their joint rites of passage in the text. The novel is part of the sub-genre of literature known as 'invasion scare' literature begun in 1871 with George Chesney's *The Battle of Dorking*. The Naval Act of 1900, by which Germany determined to have a world-class fleet, made the fear of a naval invasion by Germany a threat that England took seriously. While an alliance between England and Germany had been thought possible to avoid hostilities, the hostility of the Kaiser to the King meant that by 1901–1902, any hope of such an alliance was abandoned. Instead, it was an era of Germanophobia, the arms race, fear of spies and anxiety about terrorism.

John Buchan in a 1926 essay on adventure fiction declared *The Riddle of the Sands* 'the best story of adventure published in the last quarter of a century' (276). Its greatness lies in its legacy, because it epitomises the adventure genre even as it anticipates the spy novel of the early Georgian period. David Stafford (1981, *passim*) enumerates many reasons for the rise of the spy novel, especially that form of anxiety known as 'Tory pessimism' about Britain's defences: complex alliance systems; the armaments race; the erosion of British status after the Boer War; the use of crisis, often secret, diplomacy; invasion scares; the presence in Britain of Fenians and other anarchists; nihilists; plans to build a Channel tunnel; the Aliens Act of 1905; revolutionaries; the establishment of intelligence agencies as permanent features of government; concern about white racial deterioration; fear of urbanism and the working classes; the hostility of Germany to the Boer War; and the passage of the first Official Secrets Act in 1889. Childers sets his *rite de passage* for males against a genuine background of diplomatic and national turmoil.

According to David Seed, *The Riddle of the Sands* is divided into four sections: 'In contrast with Carruthers' previous life in London, which is a mere continuity, the voyage of the *Dulcibella* and therefore the structure of the novel breaks into four main phases, each with a clear beginning and end: the first (Chapters 1–9) concludes with Carruthers' decision to follow Davies in his quest to ascertain the true identity of Dollmann; the second section (Chapters 10–13) is transitional and takes the protagonists from the Baltic coast to Frisia via the Kiel Canal; the third (Chapters 14–20) opens their engagement with German antagonists; the final section (Chapters 21–end) focuses on the mystery of Memmert Island, with the confrontation with Dollmann and the solution of the riddle' (33). Childers imposes such a structure because he emphasises the *stages* of the men's remasculinising.

The call to save England by investigating German espionage, however, requires the transformation of the two Englishmen, especially of Carruthers, who narrates the text. The rites of passage require a regeneration, remasculinising and maturation of a smug Foreign Office clerk into a man of action and a spy, a man who is transformed from an adventurer, that is, a person of action, 'idiosyncratic, rebellious, a law unto himself', to a hero 'a virtuous man demonstrating qualities of courage, loyalty, charisma, and selflessness' (Hunter, 1982, 90, 89).

At the beginning of the novel, Carruthers is alone during the late summer sitting in the Foreign Office and going to deserted clubs in the solitude of September in London, marked by 'cynicism' (17): 'I was at the extremity of depression' (18). Then, he receives a letter from Arthur H. Davies, whom he had known at Oxford, to come and sail the Baltic with him. When he meets Davies, Carruthers experiences 'an irresistible sense of peace and detachment' (24); 'I saw my silly egotism in contrast with a simple generous nature ... The crown of martyrdom disappeared ... For though the change was radical its full growth was slow. But in any case it was here and now that it took its birth' (31). Carruthers recognises the time for his transformation into a man has come.

The ritual of all-male nude bathing represents the shedding of his former selfish life (33, 49–50, 216). Carruthers, for example, records: 'I stumbled up the ladder, dived overboard, and buried bad dreams, stiffness, frowziness, and tormented nerves in the loveliest fiord of the lovely Baltic. A short and furious swim and I was back again ... As I plied the towel, I knew that I had left in those limpid depths yet another crust of discontent and self-conceit' (33). A second bathing experience has a different inflection:

> Not even the searching wind could mar the ecstasy of that plunge down into the smooth, seductive sand, where I buried greedy fingers and looked through a medium blue ... Up again to sun, wind, and the forest whispers from the shore; down just once more to see the uncouth anchor stabbing at the sand's soft bosom with one rusty fang, deaf and inert to the *Dulcibella*'s puny efforts to drag him from his prey. Back, holding by the cable as a rusty clue from heaven to earth, to that bourgeois maiden's bows. (49–50)

This swimming episode has clear elements of sexual attack and male supremacy inscribed in it.

The stress on bathing in *The Riddle of the Sands* reflects wide national issues, as Jose Harris notes:

> 'Images of the sea and of Britain's oceanic dominion were deeply woven into national self-consciousness ... The late Victorian cult of both upper- and lower-class "clubland" was an almost exclusively, and often aggressively masculine sphere ... The report of the 1904 Interdepartmental Committee on Physical Deterioration ... reported that throughout urban Britain there was widespread physical unfitness, caused by poverty, malnutrition, and bad personal habits' (6, 27, 206).

Hence, Childers' insistent bathing scenes mark elements of both personal and national rites of passage. According to David Seed (1990), in the novel Childers 'generalised the desire for physical exertion into a national solidarity against potential German foes' (37).

As time passes on Davies' yacht, Carruthers recognises the stages of his remasculinisation: It is 'a passage in my life, short, but pregnant with moulding force, through stress and strain, for me and others' (35); 'the patient fates were offering me a golden chance of repairing' (37). Reading books about Admiral Horatio Nelson on board, Carruthers adopts this model, 'an undertaking the most momentous I have ever approached' (56). He knows a luxury 'even the Homeric gods knew not of' (58). Carruthers hopes he is no longer a 'peevish dandy' (93) and has left behind the 'foppish absurdities of a hateful past' (116). Chapter 12 Carruthers labels 'My Initiation' (107).

This remasculinisation takes place based on the incorporation of applicable past models. For example, there is a stress on ideals of knighthood and medievalism that buttress this new masculinity. Throughout the novel (89, 96, 112, 125, 136, 155, 169, 174, 191), the word 'quest' more and more characterises the adventures of Davies and Carruthers. 'Romance … handed me the cup of sparkling wine and bade me drink and be merry' (88) Carruthers thinks; before his final adventure, 'Romance beckoned' (154).

Carruthers records: 'If it imparted into our adventure a strain of crazy chivalry more suited to knights-errant of the Middle Ages than to sober modern youths – well, thank heaven, I was not too sober, and still young enough to snatch at the fancy … Galahads are not so common but that ordinary folk must needs draw courage from their example and put something of a blind trust in their tenfold strength' (182).

Works by James Fenimore Cooper, Stevenson, and Arthur Conan Doyle provide templates of masculinity incorporated in this self-fashioning. These include references to James Fenimore Cooper's novel *The Pathfinder* (1840) as a chapter title. There are several references to Stevenson's *Treasure Island*, including maps and charts (24, 68, 126, 190) and 'that dream-island – nightmare island as I always remember it' (115). The two men claim they cannot equal Sherlock Holmes in their investigation (78), but the model of Holmes fuels the drive behind their pursuit of the Germans, entailing Holmesian elements of decipherment (206) and disguise (238). Childers himself described the emerging narrative to his friend Basil Williams: 'It's a yachting story, with a purpose, suggested by a cruise I once took in German waters. I discovered a scheme of invasion directed against England. I'm finding it terribly difficult as being in the nature of a detective story' (cited in Boyle 109).

There are numerous references to 'clues' and 'mystery', even one to Scotland Yard. Key masculine elements, such as pluck (75, 120, 282), detail traits of this remasculinising. Davies and Carruthers are adventurers turned scouts, living on a foreign frontier, evoking an organisation such as the 1904 Legion of Frontiersmen founded by Roger Pocock to defend British coasts, of which Childers was a member.

Carruthers revises his attitude about Davies, now seeing him as a masculine template. He has a 'devotion to the sea, wedded to a fire of pent-up patriotism' (96). Davies 'caught his innermost conviction from the very soul of the sea itself' (99). Davies is almost a Carlylean hero: 'You're so casual and quiet in the extraordinary things you do' (112), Carruthers observes. Carruthers knows that his previous 'work was neither interesting nor important' (17). Carruthers is transformed from Usborne's 'clubland hero' to a Carlylean hero.

Childers structures the novel by a system of emerging contrasts: German/ English; the seaman Davies/the landsman Carruthers; Davies explores the Frisian coast/Carruthers the hinterland; the plotting ex-Englishman now-traitorous

German Dollmann is Davies' personal opponent, while Carruthers' is the engineer Bohme. Finally grasping the meaning of the riddle, that Germany is planning an invasion of England, Carruthers receives 'life and meaning in the light of the great revelation', an awareness 'of vast national issues' (264).

This *Bildungsreise* enables British masculinity to assume superiority over the German when Carruthers (238ff.) impersonates a young German seaman, doubles back to the German coast, becomes a stowaway on a boat, steers the plotters' boat wrong, and retrieves the German conspirators' plans. German masculinity, from this perspective, is so counterfeit it can be impersonated if one knows German, as does Carruthers. There is a strong suggestion in the novel that masculinity is a question of role-playing like an actor, who changes costume to suit his agenda. Carruthers records: 'At 8.28 on the following morning, with a novel chilliness about the upper lip, and a vast excess of strength and spirits, I was sitting in a third-class carriage, bound for Germany, and dressed as a young seaman, in a pea-jacket, peaked cap, and comforter … The transition had not been difficult. I had shaved off my moustache' (238).

On the other hand, the traitorous Dollmann had been a British naval man. This betrayal reinforces the idea that the German masculine script can also be mastered. Beyond that, this change of clothes and language can also lead to aggressive acts against a man's former country. If Dollmann is a spy, Davies argues, then why shouldn't he and his friend Carruthers spy? 'I look at it like this. The man's an Englishman, and if he's in with Germany he's a traitor to us, and we as Englishmen have a right to expose him. If we can't do it without spying we have a right to spy, at our own risk – … It make me wild to think of that fellow masquerading as a German … Those Admiralty chaps want waking up' (86–7).

In addition to Dollmann being a traitor, however, Dollmann's daughter Clara falls in love with Davies, which could compromise Carruthers' friend. It is telling that, while this never happens, Childers concentrates in the last third of the novel on Carruthers. Not only does Clara sabotage the two men's male *camaraderie*. Though opposed to her father's traitorous activities, she might also weaken Davies' will against her traitor father. Hence, the emphasis of the text shifts to Carruthers.

Andrew Boyle observes about the two male protagonists: 'The two most finely finished characters were undoubtedly the English yachtsmen themselves, and the contrasting faults and attributes of Davies and Carruthers served to provide a low-key domestic drama, in the confined space of the *Dulcibella*, which in turn helped to hold and build up the general reader's attention from the start' (110). Boyle does not pursue his insight, but it is striking that Davies and Carruthers *are* a male couple in the manner of Sherlock Holmes and John Watson, suggesting a homoerotic context. Clara Dollmann splits up this male couple, as Mary Morstan does Holmes and Watson in *The Sign of Four*. Childers wanted to restrict his tale to a homosocial world, but he was compelled by publishing exigencies to include a heterosexual romance. He wrote to Basil Williams during its composition: 'I was weak enough to "spatchcock" a girl into it and now find her a horrible nuisance' (cited in Boyle 109).

Despite Clara's Germanic associations, Davies has 'no racial spleen' and acknowledges ambiguities about imperial aspiration, both British and German: 'We can't talk about conquest and grabbing. We've collared a fine share of the world, and they've every right to be jealous' (98). Both nations are imperialising, and competition is inevitable. Davies wonders: 'Germany's a thundering great nation … I wonder if we shall ever fight her?' (51). Davies advises Carruthers:

> Look at this map of Germany … Here's this huge empire, stretching half over central Europe – an empire growing like wildfire, I believe, in people, and wealth, and everything … . What I'm concerned with is their sea-power … They've got no colonies to speak of, and *must* have them, like us … The command of the sea is *the* thing nowadays, isn't it? (80)

Davies perceives the situation as desperate: 'We're a maritime nation – we've grown up by the sea and lived by it; if we lose command of it we starve. We're unique in that way, just as our huge empire, only linked by the sea, is unique … We want a man like this Kaiser, who doesn't wait to be kicked, but works like a nigger for his country, and sees ahead' (97). Davies goes so far as to indict British leadership for being ignorant of German depredations, lacking the aggressive and offensive vision of the Kaiser.

Eventually, Carruthers knows that the Germans are planning an offensive attack and that Britain itself cannot be passive but rather must be aggressive (if not actually offensive) in regarding its own circumstances. The plans of the German expedition against England are given in an Epilogue 'by the Editor' (275). Britain must do as does Carruthers: 'I pulled round and worked out my own salvation' (268).

During 1902–1903, British journals demanded that a North Sea naval base be established to oppose German ambitions, and in 1903 the British Admiralty announced plans for such a base at Rosyth (Kennedy, 1981, 7). Childers' inclusion of detailed invasion plans at the end of the novel includes Carruthers' decipherment of 'a confidential memorandum to the German government embodying a scheme for the invasion of England by Germany' (275). Such 'authentication' increased Edwardian anxiety about invasion. It is noted that the plan 'was checkmated but others may be conceived. In any case, we know the way in which they look at these things in Germany' (283). In a postscript added by Childers, he notes there are plans for a new North Sea naval base, 'an excellent if tardy decision' (283), and 'a new North Sea fleet has also been created' (284).

Carruthers at the conclusion becomes the Carlylean hero and completes the transformation of his masculinity. Carruthers is the paradigmatic clubland gentleman, marked by loyalty, sportsmanship, honour, duty, self-reliance, comradeship, fairness, honesty, love of adventure, pluck, competitiveness, persistence and patriotism (Usborne, 1953, 1–16). Yet added to these qualities, he now possesses experience based on the act of testing these qualities, not merely observing them or mindlessly living them.

According to Leonard Piper, *The Riddle of the Sands* is especially significant as a novel aimed at a male audience: 'The difficulty really was that, at that time, most novels in England were written for women … . Male readers, on the other hand, were almost totally neglected, at any rate by English novelists. The very word "novel" came almost to mean a book for women. *The Riddle of the Sands*, on the other hand, was a male-orientated book … leading the way through Buchan to Fleming … and the other masculine novels of every type that fill station bookstalls today' (72).

The Riddle of the Sands, then, not only describes initiation as remasculinisation. It also enacts it, since in fact its positions were acted upon in the interests of England's defence. Its imprinting of masculine behaviours became verified by a curious incident on 21 August 1910, when two 'English amateur yachtsman were arrested by the German authorities' (Piper 105). Both German and English newspapers fanned inimical hysteria. The men were found guilty and sentenced to four years' imprisonment. The Kaiser pardoned them in May 1913. At the trial, one of the men admitted that the two had been inspired by *The Riddle of the Sands*. As a result, needless to say, new editions followed in 1913 and 1914 as England entered the Great War. Childers was not surprised it was against Germany: he fought in the War as a reconnaissance officer in the Royal Naval Air Service.

Conrad: *The Secret Sharer* (1910)

Joseph Conrad's *The Secret Sharer*, a world-famous novella, was written in December 1909 and published in *Harper's Magazine* New York in August and September 1910. The story is narrated, retrospectively, by an unnamed young Captain experiencing his first command. Jakob Lothe notes that this narrator is 'omnipresent, but not omniscient' (59). The story is about his initiation/*rite de passage* on an unnamed ship in the Gulf of Siam. The Captain rescues and harbours a fugitive, Leggatt, from another ship in the area, the *Sephora*. Leggatt, the first mate, has killed an insubordinate sailor who refused to follow orders during a ferocious storm. The Captain conceals Leggatt on his ship for four or five days. Finally, shaving the coast, he manages to release Leggatt, who presumably swims to shore and embraces a new destiny.

The interpretations of this tale are legion. Much depends on the way in which Leggatt is perceived. These are some of the positions taken about the significance represented by Leggatt: 1. the superego/the ideal (Curley); 2. the id; 3. the *doppelgänger* or alter ego (Daleski, Steiner, Batchelor, Stallman); 4. the Captain's 'other' self; 5. an embodiment of evil (Wyatt); 6. a Satanic figure; 7. the Captain's hidden criminal self (O'Hara, Guerard); 8. the Captain's homosexual lover (Lansbury, Harkness, Snyder, Hodges, Ruppel [2008], Casarino, Phelan); 9. the saviour of the *Sephora* and the Captain's ship (Evans); 10. Cain (Williams, Leiter); 11. a component or agent of the Captain's *rite de passage*/initiation (Lorch, Hoffmann, Benson); 12. an image of fertility (White); 13. a figure of or about rebirth (Dassinger); 14. the irrational impulse; 15. a 'mirror' figure (Watts 1976); 16. the unconscious (the sea) (Devers, Rosenman, Ressler, Leiter); 17. Moses (Bidwell); 18. a figure representing castration anxiety – initially he appears headless (Johnson/Garber); 19. existential challenge (Brown); 20. Jonah (Leiter); 21. a sign of the Captain's Narcissism (Eggenschwiler); 22. death (Paccaud 1987#2); 23. Oedipus (Dobrinsky).

These varying interpretations of Leggatt suggest he may be anything from a moral son of a gentleman who takes decisive action to a vicious, violent, anarchic law-breaking murderer, deserter and outlaw. One may agree with Katherine Snyder this much about Leggatt:

> His crime represents, as he does himself, both the failure and the quintessence of properly regulated masculine desire and, thus, of properly regulated masculinity … Leggatt is both the narrator's main problem … and also the solution to his problem. In each of these positions, Leggatt is doubled: in his roles as the narrator's super-ego and his libido, as the emblem of the narrator's law-abiding conscience and his law-breaking desire. (153)

It is also significant that critics see the Captain himself as potentially several of these figures, including Cain, Jonah or Narcissus.

Much debate also centres on the young Captain as an unreliable narrator. To what extent does he misrepresent events? Why does he disparage Archbold? There is also debate about Leggatt as an unreliable narrator of events on the *Sephora*. All critics agree that the ship is a microcosm of existence, as well as a totally homosocial universe. A major symbol is the white hat the Captain places on Leggatt's head just prior to his escape. It stands for protection, reconciliation, conscience, re-integration of personality, surmounting of castration anxiety, the writer's blank page (Dobrinsky) or other ideas. With all these inflections, the text remains elusive.

Nearly all critics agree there is a rite of passage recorded here. Daniel Curley, for instance, asserts: 'The story is clearly an initiation-ritual story' (82). However, there is disagreement about whether or not the Captain matures or remains in ignorance of himself. Benson concludes that the story 'is not a story of full initiation into mature responsibilities; it is the beginning of the initiation' (87). If the Captain alters, does he do so in a morally satisfactory way, or is there merely change? Is he moral at the end or only full of his own ego? Or, does the Captain really change at all? The text is wondrously ambiguous.

What one can establish without a doubt is that the text is about masculinities, where the manhood of the Captain, Leggatt and Archbold, the skipper of the *Sephora*, represent various positions about masculinity, what Snyder designates as 'the competition within and among styles of manhood' (153). There is no doubt that the Captain experiences challenges to his self-conception and his masculinity during the narrative. As Perel argues: 'It will be Leggatt's presence on the ship that helps the captain shape his conceptions of masculinity' (123).

The unnamed ship is 'anchored outside the bar … at the head of the Gulf of Siam' (179). As Knowles/Moore note, the ship is 'becalmed' (336). This state, according to Lorch, signals a powerful psychological episode, separating youth from maturity, innocence from experience: 'In the sea stories this psychological pause is often symbolized by a calm or delay' (75). Such is the case also with the delays in 'Youth' and the ship in *The Shadow-Line*. These states of calm, particularly noted in the epigraph to *The Shadow-Line*, mark the psychological focus of the texts; 'calm grips the ship', Lorch notes (76), in *The Shadow-Line*. Lorch continues about the Captain in *The Secret Sharer*: 'His routine is violated, he passes through a period of suspension and uncertainty, and his ship passes through a spell of calm and light winds' (77).

Even the title can be read at least two ways. The word 'Secret' can be either a noun or an adjective (Dazey). If 'secret' is a noun, then the story is about concealed information that is shared: Leggatt is the 'sharer', revealing that he killed an insubordinate sailor. The Captain is also the 'sharer' since he receives the 'confidential information' (Dazey 201). In the magazine text, the title was *The Secret-Sharer*, that is hyphenated, stressing the sharer of a secret. If 'secret' is an adjective, the sharer 'becomes [a] hidden or concealed person' (202). When published in *'Twixt Land and Sea*, the story appeared without the hyphen, stressing the latter reading. Alternative titles for the story were 'The Secret Self', 'The Second Self', and 'The Other Self', all of which stress the adjectival construction.

The young skipper has a number of anxieties at the beginning of the text:

> I had been appointed to the command only a fortnight before. Neither did I know much of the hands forward. All these people had been together for eighteen months or so, and my position was that of the only stranger on board … What I felt most was my being a stranger to the ship; and if all the truth must be told, I was somewhat of a stranger to myself … I wondered how far I should turn out faithful to that ideal conception of one's own personality every man sets up for himself secretly. (180–81)

Lothe remarks 'how dependent the narrator's idealism is on his loneliness and social isolation' (71).

These remarks convey a sense of alienation both ontological and existential. Because he feels he needs to know his ship better, the Captain informs his officers that he will take the five hours' nighttime anchor-watch himself. Both the chief and second mates are incredulous at this violation of procedure. The Captain records: 'My strangeness, which had made me sleepless, had prompted that unconventional arrangement' (182). According to Peck, while traditional maritime fiction focused on external challenges, in this text 'there is a stronger sense of an internal challenge' (180).

The Captain goes on deck and notices that 'the riding-light in the fore-rigging burned with a clear, untroubled, as if symbolic, flame' (183). Because he dismissed the watch, a rope deck ladder is hanging over the side of the ship. He notices 'a faint flash of phosphorescent light, which seemed to issue suddenly from the naked body of a man' (183). The floating body appears like 'A headless corpse!' (184), indicating the castration complex. The Captain sees his own image in the water, like Narcissus. The Captain allows Leggatt, who has announced his name with a 'calm and resolute' voice, to come on board via the side-ladder. He gives Leggatt a sleeping-suit identical to the one he is wearing. He designates Leggatt 'my double' a second later (185). Leggatt tells the Captain he is the son of a parson in Norfolk (186). Hence, he is a gentleman and the son of a gentleman. On the most basic level, the attraction between the Captain and Leggatt is instant because the Captain is lonely, young and friendless.

Leggatt, who was chief mate, tells the narrator that he killed a recalcitrant crew member on the *Sephora*. The Captain immediately excuses him by saying it must have been a 'fit of temper' (186). There are extenuating circumstances: the violent gale, the insubordination, the need to save the ship. Leggatt's action saves the *Sephora*. According to Gettmann/Harkness: 'It is not a crime in the sense that Leggatt intended or premeditated a murder' (129). 'My double was no homicidal ruffian' the Captain concludes (187). Eggenschwiler argues that the Captain 'does not see Leggatt as a violent, irrational rebel. On the contrary, he has created Leggatt in his own best image' to serve a Narcissistic intention (33). In a Narcissistic reading Leggatt is 'the same' as the Captain. In addition, as Josiane Paccaud argues (1987#1) 'the fugitive … is the Other we harbour within' (95), who is and is not the self.

Curley contends: 'It must not be supposed that the choice Leggatt makes is the choice of violence; for his choice, like the captain's, is a choice of responsibility. Further, it is a choice made under trying circumstances when the natural source of responsibility, in the captain of the *Sephora*, has totally failed' (79). In fact, Leggatt tells the Captain that he refused to resort to violence on the *Sephora*. First, he refused to break out of his cabin where he was locked in every night: 'I wouldn't think of trying to smash the door. There would have been a rush to stop me at the noise, and I did not mean to get into a confounded scrimmage. Somebody else might have got killed' (190). Second, Leggatt worried about the violence if he were retaken after fleeing: 'Do you see me being hauled back, stark naked, off one of these little islands by the scruff of the neck and fighting like a wild beast? Somebody would have got killed for certain, and I did not want any of that. So I went on' (192).

These declarations, true or not, confirm for the Captain that Leggatt is not a killer. Curley argues that the circumstances render it not a murder: 'When the sailor came at him again, Leggatt was forced to adopt stronger measures and began to throttle him into submission. When the wave broke over the ship, Leggatt's reflex led him to hold fast to anything. Unfortunately, he happened to have hold of a man's throat. Here, then, is the murder in form that is not a murder in fact' (81).

As if pre-destined, the Captain conceals Leggatt in his *L*-shaped cabin, which he enters by going down, that is, into the psyche, which corroborates with his being unseen. The longer part of the room is 'recessed' as the Captain informs the reader (196, 204). Rosenman argues that this 'recessed' space is used 'to suggest the hidden world of the unconscious' (5). At one point, the Captain records about Leggatt: 'I saw him standing bolt-upright in the narrow recessed part' of his cabin (207), suggesting that Leggatt the double represents his unconscious desires and fears. The Captain tells Leggatt that he is 'almost as much of a stranger on board as himself' (193). As Schwarz (1982) notes: '[The Captain] identifies with Leggatt not as a criminal, but as an outcast' (5). In choosing to aid Leggatt rather than surrender him, the Captain 'privileges the "law of the sea" over that of the land' (Simmons 171).

Throughout the remainder of the text, the Captain labels Leggatt as his double or other self: 'double captain' (189), 'other self' (189, 200, 216), 'my double' (192, 195, 196, 197, 207, 215), 'my secret self' (195), 'the secret sharer of my life' (196), 'the unsuspected sharer' (198); 'my second self' (196, 198, 211, 217), 'my intelligent double' (201), 'my double down there' (201, 202), 'our secret partnership' (203), 'my secret double' (205), 'my very own self' (212), 'the double captain' (213), 'the secret sharer' (199, 217). Some of Leggatt's identities are clear in the text. He is 'Cain' the outcast (191, 209); like Moses in his early life, he has killed a man. As Hillis Miller has noted, the doubling motif even extends to Leggatt's name with its double set of double letters (233).

The Captain is mesmerized by Leggatt. When he puts him into his bed, the skipper thinks: 'He must have looked exactly as I used to look in that bed. I gazed upon my other self ... I was extremely tired, in a peculiarly intimate way ... . I felt more dual than ever' (194). This may well be homoerotic if not overtly homosexual. The Captain seems transfixed by Leggatt's body. He first sees Leggatt by 'a faint flash of phosphorescent light, which seemed to issue suddenly from the naked body of a man' (183). After he retrieves a sleeping-suit for Leggatt, 'coming back on deck, [I] saw the naked man from the sea sitting on the main-hatch' (185). Later the Captain records: 'I would smuggle him into my bed-place, and we would whisper together' (205). At their parting, 'Our hands met gropingly, lingered united in a steady, motionless clasp for a second' (213).

At the very least, according to R.W. Stallman, 'the Captain recognizes not alone this physical identity but also a psychic one' (99). Watts (1976) believes 'the sense of comradeship modulates towards homosexual love' (30). Behind these ideas is the myth of the three sexes from Plato's *Symposium*. There, the comedic playwright Aristophanes argues that at one time human beings were male-male, female-female and male-female, until Zeus in anger separated them. Aristophanes argues that each part continued to search for its counterpart. Hence, the male-male leads to searching for the homosexual counterpart. Paccaud (1987#1) regards the 'homosexual connotations' of the story as 'explicit' (94).

For Bruce Harkness (1965), the story 'is the earliest mature interpretation of homosexual relations in English literature' (56). He regards Leggatt's name, pronounced as Leg-it, to refer to the penis and sexual intercourse. (Leg-it can also refer to Leggatt's role as an escapee who has run away, as Joseph Dobrinsky asserts [42]). Harkness notes the numerous references (e.g., 189, 190, 194, 205,

212) to the 'bed' or the 'bed-place' in the story. Leggatt tells the Captain that when he came on board it was 'as if you had expected me' (193). The riding-light, phallic, was 'something to swim for' (192). Barbara Johnson and Marjorie Garber observe the phallic images of the ladder and the cigar, both hanging out (633). Cesare Casarino asserts that for much of the text, Conrad is depicting 'a male-male romance' (229) until the end, when the narrator betrays this romance: 'Now I forgot the secret stranger ready to depart … . But I hardly thought of my other self, now gone from the ship' (216). Casarino argues, 'the narrator attempts to exorcise all that Leggatt had allowed to crystallise in the enclosure of the cabin' (239). At the conclusion, therefore, the narrator represses his homosexual desire by marooning Leggatt on the shore.

For Casarino, the narrator instead embraces the ship, which has been presented as a woman, with the story becoming 'a tale of homophobic triangulation' (241), 'the narrator's full initiation into the bourgeois world of adult responsibilities, duties, and (hetero) sexuality' (242). The narrator records in the penultimate paragraph: 'And I was alone with her. Nothing! No one in the world should stand now between us, throwing a shadow on the way of silent knowledge and mute affection' (217). Leggatt, however, remains true to the Captain since, as Porter Williams Jr argues, he leaves the white hat in the sea to rescue the ship and the Captain (30), saving a ship a second time.

The Captain is tormented by the situation involving Leggatt. 'All the time the dual working of my mind distracted me almost to the point of insanity. I was constantly watching myself, my secret self … It was very much like being mad, only it was worse because one was aware of it' (195). 'Every day there was the horrible manoeuvring to go through' (205). The Captain even wonders if he has imagined Leggatt: 'An irresistible doubt of his bodily existence flitted through my mind. Can it be, I asked myself, that he is not visible to other eyes than mine? It was like being haunted … I think I had come creeping quietly as near insanity as any man who has not actually gone over the border' (207–8). The masculinity of the young Captain is tested *in extremis*.

When Archbold (presumably his name, since the skipper contends he is not certain), the Captain of the *Sephora*, comes to investigate, the young skipper deceives him. He pretends to be hard of hearing so Archbold will shout and Leggatt will hear everything. Trusting to Leggatt's craftiness in hiding, the young Captain gives Archbold a tour of his quarters to demonstrate that no one is concealed there.

Archbold's account asserts that as captain he gave the order to reef the foresail and saved the ship. Leggatt claims he was the agent of saving the ship. The young Captain believes Leggatt and scorns the veteran captain. He concludes that Leggatt, by killing one man, had saved twenty-four. He convinces Archbold that Leggatt's disappearance was suicide. Bonnie Scott concludes: 'Archbold becomes a figure for the law of the father. Leggatt and the Captain, in attacking his reasoning and reaching their own understanding, engage in a Freudian oedipal struggle to oust the father' (202).

Indeed, throughout *The Secret Sharer*, there is a powerful Oedipal scenario. There are two Oedipal fathers the young Captain encounters. The first is the chief mate, with his intimidating whiskers. The second is Archbold, Captain of the *Sephora*, who observes a strict interpretation of the Law of the Father, refusing to allow Leggatt to escape (locking him in his cabin for nearly seven weeks) and compelling him to submit to the law of the shore by being tried for murder. Dobrinsky contends that 'in this conflict between generations, the issue of virility is classically at stake … The fact that the old captain wears "a thin red whisker" seems equally emblematic of his inadequate masculinity' (36). Leggatt and the young Captain, however, defy these two men.

At the end, the Captain forces the chief mate to acquiesce to his manoeuvre to shave the shore. Leggatt refuses to 'explain such things [the killing on the *Sephora*] to an old fellow in a wig and twelve respectable tradesmen' in a trial (208–9). Paccaud (1987#1) observes that 'Both narrator and "hero" are involved in an open challenge to the law … [Leggatt refuses] to subject himself to men's Christian judgement and even less so to the hands of Providence' (94). For Dobrinsky: 'The younger protagonists will both assert their superior manhood in sharp contrast to the twinned older men … . The son-figures eventually carry the day, while the censorious father-figures are mocked at, and debased, in their defeat' (36–7).

It becomes necessary to maroon Leggatt on shore. The Captain risks his life, his crew and his reputation and veers to shore as close as he dares, considering it a 'matter of conscience to shave the land as close as possible' (214). The Captain gives Leggatt the white floppy hat to protect him from 'the sun' (213). But it protects Leggatt from being the *son* as well, a crucial homonym, one more device ensuring Leggatt's escape (leg-it) from his threatening fathers, Archbold and the jurymen. The white floppy hat he had given Leggatt appears on the water to mark his nearness to shore. It was noticed early in the tale that Leggatt was an excellent swimmer: 'I've had a prize for swimming my second year in the *Conway*' (190). Hence, the Captain did not need to veer so near the shore to save Leggatt. It is a matter of conscience because the Captain must prove to himself and the crew that he is a mature navigator deserving to be captain.

Furthermore, as Williams notes, 'it was a matter of conscience, ultimately, to offer Leggatt a compelling demonstration of absolute understanding and sympathy by indulging in an act of supreme daring … a demonstration of sympathetic understanding that momentarily involved the risk of sharing Leggatt's doom in order to justify deserting him' (627).

Because of this mark of the hat, the Captain avoids a crash on shore, navigates away from shore and heads out to sea. 'I was in time to catch an evanescent glimpse of my white hat left behind to mark the spot where the secret sharer of my cabin and of my thoughts, as though he were my second self, had lowered himself into the water to take his punishment: a free man, a proud swimmer striking out for a new destiny' (217). The value of Leggatt's resolve and daring has been transferred to the young Captain. Leggatt experiences the hell of existential choice: his freedom is his punishment.

One interpretation is that the Captain has achieved a transformed sense of manliness. He has done this by daring, by the transgressive act of imperiling himself and his ship. Conrad seems to suggest, like Stevenson in *Treasure Island*, that transgression is necessary for a young man to accomplish his *rite de passage*. As Hillis Miller observes: 'Both Leggatt and the narrator transgress against convention or law' (240). This process may or may not lead to success, fulfilment or even maturity. Goonetilleke regards this act of daring as disturbing: '[It is] a self-imposed expiation for violating social values and the seamen's code in harbouring Leggatt. Thus, the East becomes for the captain what it is going to be for Leggatt – a kind of purgatory' (38). Like Leggatt, the Captain might even remain a Cain, one physically in exile, the other mentally and morally.

According to John Peck, Leggatt as a *Conway* boy (a graduate of the merchant marine training ship *Conway* in Liverpool) with 'a thorough maritime education' ought to have exercised 'self-discipline' but 'in a crisis, however, Leggatt has yielded to instinct' (180). There can be no doubt that Conrad perceives this situation because he stresses the *Conway* connection between the two men. For Peck, the result is that 'in Conrad the fiction of the British naval or merchant officer as the embodiment of national virtues is falling apart' (180). Indeed this may be so for, after all, Leggatt did kill. Conrad however simultaneously endorses the Captain's transgression, evoking an ancient tradition.

This necessity of transgression recalls the Greek transition from ephebe to hoplite, which entailed killing others on the frontier. Miller remarks that 'these transgressions are absolutely necessary to make the narrator worthy of command … . Justice must be periodically interrupted by some decisive act that reaffirms the law by breaking the law … . The law can be preserved and reaffirmed only by acts that are apparently against the law' (250–51). These acts challenge and reaffirm the law, but they also potentially drive a young male to maturation by this process. Dobrinsky argues that in *The Secret Sharer* 'seamanship as well as lifemanship depend on brinksmanship' (38).

Wyatt argues, however, that these transgressions at the conclusion reveal the narrator's 'bad judgment' and that the narrator proves 'untrustworthy' and 'unstable' (23, 24): 'While the narrator professes to *reveal* what happened on his first command, he in truth *conceals*' (24). His greatest act of concealment is that he refuses to supply Archbold's version of the events on the *Sephora*: 'It is not worth while to record that version' (198) the Captain-narrator asserts. In a famous essay from 1965, J.D. O'Hara claimed the true 'moral center' (444) of the novella is Archbold, not the Captain/narrator or Leggatt. 'The narrator … is neither remarkably admirable nor remarkably bright … . The narrator of *The Secret Sharer* … learns just barely enough to save himself from Leggatt's fate … . Certainly he has not learned from his experience … The narrator is essentially the man he was before he met Leggatt' (444, 446, 450). For Wyatt and O'Hara, therefore, there has been an initiation process but no maturation.

Several critics have noted the process of repression in the Captain's marooning of Leggatt at the conclusion. For instance, in the text there are numerous references to people being locked up and psychologically locked down. On the *Sephora*, Leggatt had been 'kept under arrest in his cabin for nearly seven weeks' (189). He informs the Captain: 'They locked me in every night' (190). The Captain arranges for Leggatt to escape via the 'sail-locker' (212) where the men's hands meet 'gropingly' in a 'clasp' (213). Paccaud (1987#2) regards the tale as one of 'psychoanalytic repression' (68) necessary for the Captain to recover his self and survive. The Captain ruminates: 'Now I forgot the secret stranger ready to depart … I hardly thought of my other self, now gone from the ship' (216). The narrator represses, potentially, guilt, criminality, hostility to the father, homosexual desire, indecision, fear of death or some other components of his personality. Leggatt goes into the 'uncharted regions' (210) of the unconscious.

The Captain had told Leggatt: 'We are not living in a boy's adventure tale' to which Leggatt had replied: 'There's nothing of a boy's tale in this' (208). Hence, Conrad's brilliantly ambiguous text has transformed the adventure genre, turning it into an existential fable. Zivah Perel states that Conrad '[places] at issue the standards of masculinity established by this genre' (112):

> Conrad, as an early modernist, challenges the gender ideology of the nineteenth century, and his male protagonists repeatedly bring into question the notion of the hero lauded by the popular adventure fiction of the day... Conrad refigures the masculine hero and thereby conventional gender relations … [His tales] defy Victorian standards of masculinity [in a] literary assault on Victorian masculinity. (112–13)

The Captain, according to Gloria Dussinger, has embraced a new daring attitude at the end: 'That the narrator alters his world view from one of benign order to one of indifferent randomness is shown in his decision to steer toward the islands' (608). Dussinger regards the rope ladder as an umbilical cord and the sail locker as the womb, marking the Captain's re-birth (601). The Captain-narrator, after all, deploys the strategy (deceit, feigning) he uses with Archbold for 'psychological (not moral) reasons', as he admits (200). Paccaud (1987#1) observes about the Captain with Archbold: 'The screen of politeness … comes as another means of passive resistance, classically linked in psycho-analytic practice to fears of castration' (91).

Although a first command, at the conclusion there is command. 'The very dangerous course he has taken becomes incontrovertible evidence of his ability and his courage' (Phelan 134). The Captain has survived challenges and tests. 'Guilt is symbolized and repressed with the triumph of the son-figures over the debased father figures' (Paccaud 1987#1, 94). If Leggatt is the Captain's mirror image, the Captain seems to have overcome his Narcissism with Leggatt's disappearance. Schwarz (1982) comments: '[The Captain] *sacrifices* Leggatt for the unity of his own personality' (9). If Leggatt is a legate (*legatus*), he is the envoy or ambassador of manhood. Dobrinsky regards his name as deriving from the French *léguer* meaning 'to bequeathe' (35), which accords with this masculine imprinting.

Conrad complicates his novella by the question of whether or not either Leggatt or the Captain is a reliable narrator. The Captain may at the conclusion be embracing a stable manhood or manifesting a rashness and instability that is damaging to himself and his career. That said, however, *The Secret Sharer*, with all its contradictory inflections, remains one of the great texts analysing the rite of passage to manhood even as it also remains sublimely elusive.

The texts discussed in this chapter concentrate on one of the key subjects of sea fiction: initiation by voyaging. As Peck suggests, in such tales there is 'a particular emphasis on the masculine qualities of the hero, masculine qualities that will be tested to the limits' (12). In the texts examined here, the protagonists are severely challenged. All are survivors; some are victors. Jim Hawkins survives but is marked by nightmares. Harvey Cheyne profits in every sense from his experiences. Childers' protagonists secure the national borders, triumphing over international threats. In Conrad, Marlow, Jukes and the unnamed Captain survive, but they do so with varying degrees of ambiguity: Marlow recounts his narrative as a scarred older man; Jukes *may* change his character having learned from his initiation; the Captain is certainly a survivor, but ambiguously a victor, from his experience. The next challenge for these sailors is facing new alternatives when they arrive on a foreign shore, the subject of the next chapter.

Chapter 2
Mapping

This chapter engages a range of texts under the rubric 'Mapping' to analyse narratives concerning encounters with 'Other/ed' masculinities in Africa, Asia and the South Pacific. In these situations, white Europeans encounter a population often ideologically 'othered' as 'different' by virtue of the indigenous race, ethnicity or religion. Transporting one kind of masculinity, through encountering these other/othered masculinities the adventurers refine or redefine their senses of their masculine selves. Often these excursions represent encounters with geographical spaces which not only map the exterior geography but also map the internal responses of the protagonists. To adventure is to export masculinities.

In some instances, such as Haggard's *King Solomon's Mines*, the protagonists emerge with secure masculinities and wealth. In others, such as Haggard's *Allan Quatermain* or Kipling's *The Light That Failed*, some of the protagonists find death in a foreign terrain. The protagonist of Schreiner's *Trooper Peter Halket of Mashonaland* defies racism and virtually seeks death. The protagonists/exploiters of Stevenson's *The Ebb-Tide* and Kipling's *The Man Who Would Be King* find horrific ends. Actual maps or charts are central to many adventure texts. Of the texts considered in this study, one might note *Treasure Island*, *The Riddle of the Sands*, *Green Mansions* and *King Solomon's Mines* as examples. Gail Low notes that 'maps enable the white adventurers' (50).

Lindy Stiebel observes that 'a map is a source of power through knowledge … It is never a neutral activity, for the mapper brings a subjective gaze to bear upon the space … The political potential of mapping is obvious' (13). There is also particular emphasis on the 'empty' space. In *King Solomon's Mines*, Haggard's map 'is in effect empty of people … This myth of the "empty" landscape was pivotal to explorers seeking new lands to settle or exploit materially' (14). 'Naming, classifying, mapping and painting … were the cornerstones of a composite image of Africa and corresponding discourse of Africanism of Haggard's time' (16). Furthermore, as Stiebel continues, 'it is important … to note the masculinist tone of the explorers' accounts of what they saw in Africa' (18). Mapping therefore serves both imperializing and masculinizing goals.

Mapping, external and internal, was given an interesting inflection by Joseph Conrad in his essay 'Geography and Some Explorers' published in 1926. In the essay, Conrad distinguishes among various kinds of explorers, including those moved by an 'acquisitive spirit' and those moved by 'scientific' aims (143). Conrad labels the latter, in a strange phrase, an example of 'militant geography whose only object was the search for truth' (143).

However, the expression 'militant geography' accurately describes the motives of many men who were of the first kind, the 'acquisitive', moved by 'the idea of lucre in some form, the desire of trade or the desire of loot, disguised in more or less fine words' (143). Conrad was on to more than he would acknowledge when he coined this phrase.

Conrad describes himself as particularly moved by the daring and heroism of Sir John Franklin, lost in a search for the Northwest Passage in 1848, 'a stern romance of polar exploration' (144). Key to the adventure text is Conrad's admission that 'the great spirit of the realities of the story sent me off on the romantic explorations of my inner self' (144), the very description of the intention of much adventure fiction and particularly his own. A corollary was 'the discovery of the taste of poring over maps', leading to 'map-gazing, to which I became addicted so early' (144–5).

Conrad then reveals his special interest in 'Africa … Regions unknown!' (145). He cannot avoid military tropes describing his reaction to the white invaders of Africa: 'My imagination could depict to itself there worthy, adventurous and devoted men, nibbling at the edges, attacking from north and south and east and west, conquering a bit of truth here and a bit of truth there' (145). 'Conquering' and 'attacking' suggest the literally true military idea behind even scientific exploration. Conrad describes drawing an outline of Tanganyika which was sketchy, 'the heart of its Africa was white and big' (146). White it was, in several ways: unexplored and presumed unoccupied, a favourite fantasy of adventurers and imperialists that 'no one' lived in these unmapped locales, a fantasy which enabled conquest of the white spaces by whites. Low comments: 'The seeming absence of human life prior to the arrival of the European traveler is directly related to the colonial fantasy of virgin territory' (40).

In a famous anecdote, Conrad describes his desire by a map: 'One day, putting my finger on a spot in the very middle of the then white heart of Africa, I declared that some day I would go there' (147). This assertion parallels Marlow's famous declaration in *Heart of Darkness*: 'Now when I was a little chap I had a passion for maps. I would look for hours at South America, or Africa, or Australia and lost myself in all the glories of exploration. At that time there were many blank spaces on the earth and when I saw one that looked particularly inviting on a map (but they all look that) I would put my finger on it and say: When I grow up I will go there. The North Pole was one of these places I remember' (11).

Edward Said, writing about Conrad's *Heart of Darkness*, but in terms applicable to much adventure fiction, notes that 'during the 1890s the business of empire, once an adventurous and often individualist enterprise, had become the empire of business' (23). This situation was noted in the 1890s. For example, according to Alfred Lyall in 1894, the adventure novelists' 'field has widened with the expansion of British enterprise; they can draw their plots, descriptions, and characters from the colonies, from Africa, from the South Sea Islands, or from India … As for the Novel of Adventure, it is drawing copious sustenance from these outlying regions' (551).

Behind many of the novels considered in this chapter are a number of imperial wars fought for economic reasons, forming a palimpsest over which these texts are written or a context in which to engage them: the Zulu War 1878–79, the First South African War 1880–81, the Egyptian War 1882, the Sudanese War 1884–85, the Matabeleland War 1896, the Reconquest of the Sudan 1896–99, or the Second South African [Boer] War 1899–1902. These encounters with the racial or ethnic or even white (Boer) others represented consequences of mapping and results of economic endeavours.

The previous chapter examined challenges presented at sea. In instances of exploration, combat, imperialism or adventure, always contested was masculinity. How strong were British troops compared to those of the Zulus, for instance? Were black warriors the equal of white troops? John Peck notices this other form of challenge, beyond that at sea, presented to adventurers: 'The encounter might be on foreign shores, where the cultures encountered threaten insularity and the traveller's self-confidence' (13). Peck continues: 'The mysterious and unknown world beyond the seas [alters] to a world that is, increasingly, known, explored and mapped' (16). In the texts considered in this chapter, mapping of external and internal forces reveals masculinisation as a process of both daring and danger.

Haggard: *King Solomon's Mines* (1885)

H. Rider Haggard's *King Solomon's Mines*, published as a single volume in 1885, remains one of the greatest of all adventure novels. In his Introduction to the novel, Dennis Butts notes that it 'sold 31,000 copies during the first twelve months … [In] America at least thirteen different editions appeared before the year was out' (vii). As is well known, Haggard wrote the novel as a bet with his brother that he could outdo Stevenson's *Treasure Island* (1883). He nearly did. Its masculine imprinting function is apparent from the dedication: 'To all the big and little boys who read it' (2). Morton Cohen (1960) observes: 'It was a tale of adventure and heroic deeds, and its hero was a well-adjusted Englishman, competent, strong, sensible, in whom [readers] could believe. There was no heroine, nor should there have been. Penetrating Africa was strictly a man's job' (90).

According to D.S. Higgins, several elements of the publishing of the novel contributed to its popularity and its imprinting function:

> A revolution in book publishing was taking place … Haggard was … extremely fortunate that Cassell's chose to publish *King Solomon's Mines* as one of the first 6/-one-volume novels … Even more fortunately, 1885 was the year in which both typesetting processes, Linotype and Monotype, were developed, and Cassell's, one of the few publishers to own a printing works, took advantage of these new technological advances to produce four printings of the book, all of 2,000 copies, between 30 September 1885 and the end of the year … So in three

months 8,000 copies of the book were printed, whereas the total printing of each of Haggard's first two novels had been 500. (85)

David Patteson argues that *King Solomon's Mines* is one of a body of works defined as 'the imperialist romance' which 'chronicles the adventures of European explorers who travel into previously uncharted territory' (112). After the discovery of the Zimbabwe ruins in 1871 by Karl Mauch, whites regarded these as evidence of a previous white presence in Africa. Believing no blacks could construct such a place, 'the theory that they were the ruins of King Solomon's Golden Ophir' arose, not controverted until 1906 (Brantlinger 195). Hence, the new exploration 'constitutes restoration of the old (and correct) order' (112), that is, of a white race.

As Patteson and many other critics have recognised, the imperial romance is 'primarily a male-oriented genre' (116). Andrew Lang in an unsigned review in *The Saturday Review* (10 October 1885) commented: '[Haggard] was the very man to write a boy's book. He has written it, and we congratulate the boys. Since *Treasure Island* we have seen no such healthily exciting volume … . The slaying is Homeric … . [Haggard] has added a new book to a scanty list, the list of good, manly, and stirring fiction of pure adventure' (485–6). The reviewer in the *Academy* (7 November 1885, No. 705), also compared Haggard with Stevenson, but noted: 'Let it be said at once that *King Solomon's Mines* is not another *Treasure Island* … Mr Stevenson need fear no rival among living writers in the pourtrayal [sic] of character and in the finish of literary style' (304).

Again, the gender imprinting is unmistakable. *The Athenaeum* (31 October 1885) claimed the novel was 'one of the best books for boys – old and young – which we remember to have read … There is some fighting hardly to be beaten outside Homer and the great Dumas … We shall be surprised if it does not also prove to be the best [of the books of the season]' (568). The *Academy*, in its review (7 November 1885, No. 705), detailed this same imprinting function, observing about Haggard: '[He] has here combined his personal experience with his practice in fiction to write a traveller's story which will stir the pulses of juvenile readers, and will commend itself only in a less degree to the *blasé* critic' (304). This reviewer continued that the novel was 'a boys' book of the first class, which holds the attention from the first page to the last' (304). As Banks notes, 'the narrative of the novel, therefore, seeks out a narrowly constituted male audience' (10). Lawrence Millman concludes: 'Haggard's novels reflect the mind and interests of the late Victorian male' (ii). However, it is strongly in contrast to the protagonists of *The Coral Island* in having three mature men as protagonists.

Some reviewers regarded the novel as full of realistic and convincing detail. Others contended its events were literally extraordinary or a combination of both realism and romance. The reviewer (7 November 1885) in *Queen*, for example, commented that the text 'is done in a way that will satisfy most lovers of the marvelous … the spirit of the tale is well-sustained, and the local colouring indicates that the writer has had some South African experiences of his own' (512). The reviewer in *Public Opinion* (30 October 1885) emphasised the novel's 'wildest scenes of improbability, that might have emanated from the feverish imagination of Jules Verne', stressing it is 'impossible to describe the weird and exciting events which take place, and we can only say that nothing of the kind has ever been better conceived' (551).

Patteson lists twelve plot functions of the imperial romance, nearly all of which appear in *King Solomon's Mines*: 1. European adventurers 'plan a journey into unexplored regions' (112). In Haggard's novel, these are fifty-five year old hunter Allan Quatermain and his associates Sir Henry Curtis and Captain John Good of the Royal Navy; 2. preliminary adventures (here the elephant hunt); 3. a descent into caves (here the location of the mines of King Solomon); 4. evidence of a previous rule by an advanced civilisation, often white; 5. meeting with a native people (here the Kukuana); 6. verification of technical/racial superiority by whites (Good's use of the eclipse of the sun to stun the natives; Good's false teeth; the persistent references [119, 130, 131] to the whiteness of Good's skin); 7. Native religions divided along factional lines (Gagool's influence despised); 8. White alignment with a secular leader (Umbopa); 9. Women either treacherous and conniving (Gagool) or beautiful but helpless (Foulata); 10. No native woman lives if she falls in love with a white man (Foulata); 11. The more civilised faction of the tribe triumphs (Umbopa, who turns out to be Ignosi, the rightful heir to the throne of Kukuanaland, overcomes Twala and his associates); 12. Europeans get what they came for and depart (diamonds).

Allan Quatermain, albeit 'more accustomed to handle a rifle than a pen' (6) is the narrator. He aims to tell 'the story in a plain, straightforward manner' (6). In the first page of his narrative, he remarks that he has 'a big pile now' of money (7). He undertakes the adventure to get money for his son Harry, who is studying to be a doctor. Furthermore, Quatermain has no doubt that this is a male narrative: 'There is no woman in it – except Foulata … There is not a *petticoat* in the whole history' (9). Quatermain declares that he is a gentleman, although he admits that some 'niggers' (which he corrects to 'natives') have been gentlemen also and that many whites are not gentlemen (9). Yet, there is no doubt that women are ancillary to a male's evolution in this text.

Quatermain meets Sir Henry Curtis and John Good on a ship, the *Dunkeld*, to Natal, returning from a hunting expedition. Sir Henry is thirty, big-chested, 'with yellow hair, a big yellow beard, clear-cut features, and large grey eyes' reminding Quatermain of 'an ancient Dane … of Danish blood' (11). Good is thirty-one, a navy veteran: 'That is what people who serve the Queen have to expect: to be shut out into the cold world to find a living' (12). Good describes himself as 'turned out by my Lords of the Admiralty to starve on half pay' (19). The three men decide to go in search of Sir Henry's brother, George.

Quatermain shares with his friends a map of the location of King Solomon's diamond mines, which he obtained from a Portuguese explorer, José da Silvestra. This famous map, included to parallel the one in *Treasure Island*, is, as many critics have noted, different from Stevenson's, in that the map is actually an inverted nude female body, supine and passive. Hence, to explore Africa is to penetrate the female body, a confirmation of the sexualised and masculinised nature of the imperial project and this text. Quatermain admits again he is 'timid' (39), which is not true, as he willingly explores the female African body. Banks notes 'the relationship between mapmaking and discursive power' (11). To map is to control, whether Africa or woman.

Norman Etherington (1984) advises about the men's journey:

> The trek into Africa is a trek from the known into the unconscious unknown self … These three representatives of civilization undergo a series of punishing tests. The tests are progressively severe and are marked by changes of terrain … The greatest tests are moral and take place in the special secluded landscape of Kukuanaland … . Haggard's characters have moved progressively through a symbolic landscape from physical tests to moral tests. (41–2)

Hence, following a map leads to transformations of masculinity. Etherington emphasises: 'The real aim of the search is to rediscover or uncover lost aspects of oneself' (43).

The men encounter Umbopa at Durban, 'a very tall, handsome-looking man, somewhere about thirty years of age, and very light-coloured for a Zulu' (46). He admits he had been at the site of the Battle of Isandhlwana (1879), a disastrous British military defeat. He served both for and against Cetywayo. Standing naked, Umbopa 'was certainly a magnificent-looking man; I never saw a finer native' (49). He tells Sir Henry that they are 'men' (49). Quatermain had called himself 'a fatalist' (39), and Umbopa shares Quatermain's fatalism: 'What is Life? It is a feather, it is the seed of the grass, blown hither and thither … Man must die … . What is life? Tell me, O white men … . Life is nothing, Life is all. It is the hand with which we hold off Death' (67–8). He knows white men for what they are: 'The diamonds are surely there, and you shall have them since you white men are so fond of toys and money' (135).

Beyond famous is the description of the mountain range the men encounter, known as Sheba's Breasts, the quintessential sexualising of the African continent as the female body: 'Language seems to fail me. I am impotent even before its memory … These mountains … are shaped exactly like a woman's breasts … On the top of each was a vast round hillock covered with snow, exactly corresponding to the nipple on the female breast' (85). He declares: 'To describe the grandeur of the whole view is beyond my powers' (87). Anne McClintock (1995) calls this the white man's 'proprietary act of seeing' (243).

As extinct volcanoes, these mountains configure the feared sexuality of women and the great anxiety of men confronting the female body. As the men move forward, they are on the level of the lava wall 'connecting the two breasts' and out of the snow belt arises 'the nipple of the mountain' (93). As Rebecca Stott observes, 'The body is Africa signifying cultural and sexual otherness' (87). Joseph Bristow comments: 'As Europe is to Africa so is man to woman' (133).

This female land must be taken by men. An unsigned review in the *Independent* (vol. 37, 3 December 1885) resorted to understatement about the text: 'Its realism is admirably sustained, and some of the natural descriptions in it are of especial vividness' (13). This reviewer noted the text's similarities to *Treasure Island.*

The otherness of the Kukuanas compared to whites is manifest in various forms of both body and intention. Soon, the men confront the usurper to the throne of the Kukuanas, Twala, 'lips as thick as a negro's' with one eye (141) and the intimidating old woman, Gagool. She is the protector of the territory against white men and grasps their economic exploitative motives. She notes 'white man coming from afar … . I have seen the white man, and know his desires … . Ye come for bright stones; I know it' (148–9). When Sir Henry asks Ignosi to stop killing men without trial, Ignosi agrees because Curtis is an English 'gentleman', although Ignosi observes: 'The ways of black people are not as the ways of white men, Incubu [Curtis], nor do we hold life so high as ye. Yet will I promise it' (176).

Umbopa reveals himself as Ignosi, the rightful heir to the throne, by showing his naked abdomen with 'the mark of a great snake tattooed in blue around his middle' (154). Low astutely comments about this juxtaposition of clothed white man and naked black man: 'The visual and textual discourse that circulates around the black nude body can be read as the signifying negative to the semiotic of Otherness that accrues to cross-cultural dressing as empowerment... . The display of the black body … is caught up in the same movement of discrimination as the fetish of skin colour. The movement is linked to an atavistic trope of blackness, and marked against the white man's clothed and civilized body' (54). Both Umbopa in *King Solomon's Mines* and Laputa in Buchan's *Prester John* stand naked before white men to validate their authority. Buchan's use of the trope derives of course from Haggard.

Other differences between white and black emerge. When Twala offers the men some women, Quatermain, thinking that 'women bring trouble as surely as the night follows the day', tells the king: 'Thanks, O king, but we white men wed only with white women like ourselves' (178). He later opines: 'Women are women, all the world over, whatever their colour' (246).

For the final battle between Ignosi and Twala, Haggard launches into his most Homeric passages, as reviewers at the time recognised. Sir Henry tells Quatermain: 'We are in for it, so we must make the best of it … I had rather be killed fighting than any other way … But fortune favours the brave, and we may succeed. Anyway, the slaughter will be awful, and as we have a reputation to keep up, we shall have to be in the thick of it' (199). That is, the men must be Englishmen.

Sir Henry dresses 'like a native warrior', briefly 'going native' in a passage echoing the arming scenes in the *Iliad.* 'Round his throat he fastened the leopard-skin cloak of a commanding officer, on his brows he bound the plume of black ostrich feathers … The dress was, no doubt, a savage one, but I am bound to say I never saw a finer sight than Sir Henry Curtis presented in this guise … When Ignosi arrived presently, arrayed in similar costume, I thought to myself that I never before saw two such splendid men' (200). Etherington (1984) argues that such scenes show white men rediscovering or uncovering 'lost aspects' of the self (43), as Sir Henry is both black and, during the battle, a Viking.

Haggard deploys Homeric similes to describe the battle of Ignosi's troops against Twala's regiments: 'Then came a charge; the Greys ceased to give; they stood still as a rock, against which the furious waves of spearmen broke again and again, only to recoil' (222–3). Quatermain records: 'There came upon me a savage desire to kill and spare not' (224). There is a 'red mist of blood' (225). Higgins notes accurately: 'The relish with which Haggard described the defeat of the usurpers' armies may have owed something to his desire to expunge from his consciousness the horror of the Zulu victory over the British, using almost identical tactics, at Isandhlwana' (74) on 22 January 1879.

These Homeric strategies were not lost on reviewers. In the *Spectator* (vol. 58, 7 November 1885), the unsigned reviewer singled out 'the truly Homeric duel between King Twala and Sir Henry Curtis' (1473) for praise: 'It reeks, perhaps, a little too much of blood, but it is as effective a piece of writing as we have seen for a long time' (1473). This reviewer observed the 'stroke of genius' in the text, acknowledging that 'we were in the hands of a story-teller of no common powers; nor did the rest of the narrative, so skillfully and so high is the interest piled up, at all disappoint our expectations' (1473). To this reviewer, the text had a 'weird originality which takes away all idea from the reader that he has been reading the same things before' (1473).

The set piece of the battle is Haggard's description of the fighting Sir Henry: 'There he stood, the great Dane, for he was nothing else, his hands, his axe, and his armour, all red with blood, and none could live before his stroke … He shouted … like his Bersekir forefathers, and the blow went crashing through shield and spear' (226). Etherington stresses about this episode: 'The savage self and the ancient self are closely related and yet not identical. [Haggard reveals] alternative personalities hidden beneath the surface of Victorian propriety … . The Africa that is our deepest self … is also our past' (43, 46).

Throughout the novel, one part of its masculinising project is to echo ancient epic. At the conclusion of the battle, hearing Ignosi's chant, nothing will do for Quatermain but Homer: 'I once heard a scholar with a fine voice read aloud from the Greek poet Homer... Ignosi's chant, uttered as it was, [was] in a language as beautiful and sonorous as the old Greek' (237). The men's journey evokes the *Aeneid* (VI.268) 'Ibant obscuri': 'On we tramped silently as shades through the night' (74). There is an Homeric echo in this march of the crack Kukuana veteran troops, the Greys: 'At last the whole regiment of the "Greys" (so called from their white shields) … was marching behind us with a tread that shook the ground' (128). There is an unmistakable Homeric simile: 'At last the full bow of the crescent moon peeps above the plain and shoots its gleaming arrows far and wide, filling the earth with a faint refulgence, as the glow of a good man's deeds shines for awhile upon his little world after his sun has set, lighting the faint-hearted travellers who follow on towards a fuller dawn' (136). Evoking Achilles and Aeneas, Haggard incorporates these models into his masculine paradigm. (The Kukuanas, be it noted, are a fictitious ethnic group, according to Gail Fraser, 31.)

At least one reviewer (in the *Academy*), however, noted about the battle scenes that with all their heroism 'we have felt disgust at the lavish introduction of bloodshed to which no remembrance of the Zulu war can reconcile us. Under all the circumstances, we are glad that the book has come out without any illustrations' (304). This connection to reality would be reinforced in 1908, when Haggard wrote his essay 'The Zulus: The Finest Savage Race in the World', where he alludes to this 1879 war between the English and the Zulus. In 1908, Haggard still wonders if the Zulus will 'attempt to stamp out the white man ... . The question will have to be settled once and for all as to whether South Africa is to remain a white man's land or practically to pass back into the power of its original inhabitants' (764). Haggard then discusses the bloody history of the Zulu nation, noting that the British overcame the Zulus at Ulundi (4 July 1879) only by 'Martini bullets' (770). Because the Zulus are polygamous, Haggard ominously concludes: 'They do not die out' (770).

After the battle, Gagool takes the white men to the mines. Foulata accompanies John Good. The men finally enter Solomon's treasure chamber. 'There, alone, was enough ivory before us to make a man wealthy for life' (276). Also there are diamonds and gold. Quatermain tells his companions: 'We arc thc richest men in the whole world' (278). Gagool comments: 'There are the bright stones that ye love, white men' (278). Then the witch stabs Foulata as she tries to save the men from being locked in the chamber. Foulata's dying words solve the problem of miscegenation with Good: 'I am glad to die because I know that he [Good] cannot cumber his life with such as me, for the sun cannot mate with the darkness, nor the white with the black' (281). On the deaths of women in Haggard's novels, Millman observes:

> Because Haggard's novels rebel against the prospect of sexual feeling, they display it from a new perspective. When women do enter this male world, they become 'the enemy', so threatening are their attempts to compromise the essential maleness of adventuring ... They are the medium of an extraordinary psychic violence which includes the killing off of nearly every major female character by the end. These killings themselves are part of the adventure ritual. (iii)

Gagool stands against the mercenary white men, 'the idea of the three white men, whom, for some reason of her own, she had always hated' (282). Locking the men in the chamber, shc cxacts revenge for their greed and misogyny and racism. Millman concludes: 'Gagool represents not what Foulata might become, if not eliminated, but what she is beneath the illusion of her white flesh: an animal. Beauty seems just one more manifestation of feminine wiles. The almost simultaneous killing of both these women is Haggard's solution to his inability to combine vigor and purity in a single woman' (59). Eventually, the men find their way from the cave in a process McClintock (1995) designates as 'an extraordinary fantasy of male birthing, culminating in the regeneration of white manhood' (248).

Some of these diamonds are as big as 'pigeon-eggs' (279). McClintock continues:

> According to this phantasmic narrative of white patriarchal regeneration, the white men give birth to the new economic order of imperial mining capitalism … They have accomplished a new form of human reproduction, an autochthonous male birthing that annuls the mother. Finally, the pigeon eggs become the means for regenerating the declining gentry, for they allow Quartermain [*sic*], like Haggard himself, to return to Britain and buy a landed estate. (248)

Economic man in the person of a white male triumphs. Haggard records the lure of Africa after diamonds were discovered in Natal in 1867 and gold in 1884 (McClintock 249). Now that he has the wealth, Quatermain can disparage it: 'Truly wealth, which men spend all their lives in acquiring, is a valueless thing at the last' (287). Quatermain records that 'I had, by a lucky thought, taken the precaution to fill the pockets of my old shooting coat with gems, before we left our prison-house … So we had not done so badly' (302). Haggard elides the nature of this imperialist greed by making Quatermain's contradictory attitudes visible to everyone but himself.

Following the model of James Fenimore Cooper in *The Last of the Mohicans* (1826), Haggard has eliminated the threat of miscegenation. Quatermain spends time ruminating about Good and Foulata: 'Good never was quite the same after Foulata's death … I consider her removal was a fortunate occurrence, since, otherwise, complications would have been sure to ensue … No amount of beauty or refinement could have made an entanglement between Good and herself a desirable occurrence' (300). Acccording to Stott, 'to be absorbed is to become other, to go native, to regress. The frontiers of self, manhood, civilization and progress must be protected' (87). Millman notes about Haggard's women: 'Neither Stevenson nor Haggard, in their male novels, actually puts much energy into the description of women, except when they're in the act of dying and they suddenly acquire vitalities previously denied them' (13).

The parting with Ignosi draws a line between white and black. Now King of the Kukuanas, Ignosi delivers a blistering attack on white greed: 'Ye have the stones; now would ye go to Natal and across the moving black water and sell them, and be rich, as it is the desire of a white man's heart to be. Cursed for your sake be the stones and cursed he who seeks them … I have spoken, white men; ye can go' (305). Haggard presents his contradictory views of materialism by having a black deliver this speech. Then Ignosi expands his condemnation of the whites:

> 'No other white man shall cross the mountains, even if any may live to come so far. I will see no traders with their guns and rum. My people shall fight with the spear, and drink water, like their forefathers before them. I will have no praying-

men to put fear of death into men's hearts, to stir them up against the king, and make a path for the white men who follow to run on … None shall ever come for the shining stones.' (306)

Ignosi will resist all white invasion of his territory. Low notes that 'the strong black man … is necessary to a reproduction of the heroic male in contrast to his effeminised, civilised counterpart' the white man (62). Hence, the black male enables white heroism.

Quatermain's narrative is filled with racist attitudes and white superior postures. When a Zulu servant calls Sir Henry 'Incubu', Quatermain is insulted: 'It is very well for natives to have a name for one among themselves, but it is not decent that they should call one by their heathenish appellations to one's face.' The man sneers at him saying he is 'as great a man' (65) as Sir Henry. Here, a male black cedes nothing to white manhood. Quatermain thinks: 'I was angry with the man, for I am not accustomed to be talked to in that way by Kafirs … He was an impudent fellow, and … his swagger was outrageous' (65). At one point, Quatermain decides about Ignosi: 'The man knew too much', i.e., for a black (69). Of the Kukuana women, Quatermain observes that 'their lips are not unpleasantly thick as is the case in most African races' (129). At another point, Quatermain addresses a black 'with an imperial smile' (114).

After Sir Henry's brother George is found, Quatermain determines to sail for England. It is as if St George has arrived to bless their mission. Lawrence Millman terms a work such as *King Solomon's Mines* an example of the 'male novel … that which is written by men, for men or boys, and about the activities of men' (12). While, as Stott argues, such a text represents a 'confirmation of virility' (71), the novel is not without its cautions: Good is wrecked by his love for Foulata, Quatermain has been wounded in his leg by a lion, Good is an impoverished naval veteran.

Still, as Stephen Gray comments: 'Haggard ultimately condones what Quatermain actually does, which is to cause an entire black nation to be so divided that it all but exterminates itself, and can so be ruled' (28). While Ignosi intends to keep whites out of his land, he does tell the three adventurers that 'the path is always open' (306) to them. In fact, the three men do return, but to a different area of Africa, in Haggard's *Allan Quatermain* of 1887. While they do not meet Ignosi, they again find Africa. It is not without irony that, as Higgins observes, 'Earlier in 1885, people's attention had been caught by the Berlin Conference during which fourteen major countries divided the spoils of Africa' (84).

This mapping venture, as Cohen (1960) comments, had a huge impact: 'For many Englishmen, Africa became the Africa of *King Solomon's Mines* … Soon *King Solomon's Mines* was being read in the public schools, even aloud in class-rooms … . *King Solomon's Mines* helped bring the story of adventure up to date' (94, 96). Quatermain lived to become the narrator of the novel's successor, equally famous, *Allan Quatermain*, in which he dies imprinting masculine ideals.

According to Katz, Quatermain was 'Haggard's version of Everyman' (33). Etherington (1984) contends: 'As the embodiment of pragmatism and common sense, a crusty old hunter made a perfect foil for outrageously improbable events. He represented skeptical Everyman. Fantastic happenings were more believable because he narrated them' (75). As Everyman, Quatermain could imprint masculinity with conviction and flair. The reviewer in the *Academy* felt that 'Quatermain himself almost reaches the dignity of an original creation by force not so much of what he does as of his shrewd reflections and simple character' (304). Hence, it is not the actions of Quatermain which the reviewer stresses but his masculine nature.

In that connection, it is interesting to regard how Quatermain first presents himself: 'I am a timid man, and don't like violence, and am pretty sick of adventure' (7). By the end of the text, all of the above has been proved untrue. As Millman comments: 'By the time the novel is over, all of these negatives are reversed: Quatermain triumphs over the limitations of his age [and] revels in adventure and violence' (34). Far from undermining the function of Quatermain as masculine model, as might be suggested at its beginning, the novel confirms Quatermain in his modeling role. An additional confirmation of this modeling role is the fact that Quatermain is free of any sexual inclinations, as Millman stresses: 'Quatermain … became someone old enough to be free of those tests of the emotions which were much more perilous than the extreme tests contained in Africa' (37). Millman concludes that *King Solomon's Mines* 'is perhaps Haggard's most sexless novel' (19).

Haggard's protagonists are unlike those of Conrad or Kipling. In advancing his ideas about heroism, Katz stresses, Haggard differs from the emerging Joseph Conrad, who focuses on the 'indeterminate nature of heroism … Conrad seems to have felt that the heroic tradition was at an end' (60). Quatermain, on the other hand, exemplifies the hero by embodying the culture's 'moral and social norms … a traditional man of action who expresses the politically conservative aspirations of his society … . Haggard's heroes are a more exhilarating sort [than Kipling's]. They are relatively free adventurers, and … they are English gentlemen above all things' (61, 67).

Haggard made his intentions clear in a speech he made at the Grand Hotel on 20 May 1898 at a dinner of the Anglo-African Writers' Club. In the audience were a former Lieutenant-Governor of Natal, the Mayor of Durban and the Resident Commissioner of Rhodesia. In addition, Haggard read a telegram from Cecil Rhodes, who could not be present. Haggard proceeded to praise the special guest of the evening, Rudyard Kipling, as 'a true watchman of our Empire'. Then Haggard continued: 'I do not believe in the divine right of kings, but I do believe … in a divine right of a great civilising people – that is, in their divine mission' (Cohen ed., 35).

Haggard: *Allan Quatermain* (1887)

H. Rider Haggard is one of the supreme masters of adventure fiction in later nineteenth-century Britain. Having published *King Solomon's Mines* to great acclaim in 1885, Haggard continued the adventures of his protagonist hunter in *Allan Quatermain*. As with its predecessor, *Allan Quatermain* represents a contestation of masculinities black and white, played out against the African continent. This objective is evident in its dedication to Haggard's son Arthur John, in which Haggard declares that 'the highest rank whereto we can attain' is 'the state and dignity of English Gentlemen' (3).

At the novel's conclusion, Henry Curtis has a son by one of the queens of Zu-Vendis. He records: 'I hope I may be able to bring him up to become what an English gentleman should be ... the highest rank that a man can reach upon this earth' (282). Hence, the novel is flanked by this objective of imprinting the masculine paradigm. It is noteworthy that Curtis intends to accomplish this imprinting in Africa.

The novel begins with a diary entry by Quatermain about the death of his son Harry two years previously from smallpox. He is devastated: 'I would that it had been my soul and not my boy's' (7). He now desires, two years later, to escape back to Africa: 'I would go away from this place where I lived idly and at ease, back again to the wild land where I spent my life ... The thirst for the wilderness was on me; I could tolerate this place no more; I would go and die as I had lived, among the wild game and the savages ... No man who has for forty years lived the life I have, can with impunity go coop himself in this prim English country ... His heart rises up in rebellion against the strict limits of the civilised life' (9–10). To become an English gentleman, therefore, is to first have been an adventurer. Given that in *Allan Quatermain* the excursion is to East Africa, its focus differs from the concentration on the south of the continent in *King Solomon's Mines*.

Quatermain then speculates:

> Ah! This civilisation, what does it all come to? ... I say that as the savage is, so is the white man, only the latter is more inventive, and possesses the faculty of combination; save and except also that the savage, as I have known him, is to a large extent free from the greed of money, which eats like a cancer into the heart of the white man. It is a depressing conclusion, but in all essentials the savage and the child of civilisation are identical ... . Civilisation is only savagery silver-gilt. (10)

Quatermain expands this argument into a sweeping indictment of civilisation:

> Supposing for the sake of argument we divide ourselves into twenty parts, nineteen savage and one civilised, we must look to the nineteen savage portions of our nature, if we would really understand ourselves, and not to the twentieth, which, though so insignificant in reality, is spread all over the other nineteen,

making them appear quite different from what they really are, as the blacking does a boot, or the veneer a table. It is on the nineteen rough serviceable savage portions that we fall back in emergencies, not only the polished but unsubstantial twentieth … . Civilisation fails us utterly. (12)

Katz observes: 'The framing motive for adventure is simply escape from civilization' (43).

A week after the funeral of Quatermain's son, Sir Henry Curtis and Captain John Good, Quatermain's companions from *King Solomon's Mines*, appear. Quatermain, though sixty-three, is ready to go to Mt. Kenya in Africa and search for 'a great white race' (18) on the continent. Arriving in Africa, Quatermain finds his old black Zulu friend Umslopogaas, whose history includes his betrayal by a woman whom he slew with an axe. Quatermain assures him that 'we go to hunt and seek adventures … [We are] in search of adventure' (25). Both older men, one white, the other black, seek in adventure a restorative for the tragedies of their lives. In their search for lost cities, Quatermain muses: 'Gone! Quite gone! The way that everything must go … That is the inexorable law … a symbol of the universal destiny … The stern policeman Fate moves us and them on' (28). Both men seek affirmation of their masculinity, even if it is transient. Soon they must survive an attack by swimming Masai.

Their first major stop is at the mission station house of the Scottish missionary Mackenzie, who has recreated an English garden in Africa. Stiebel contends that the mission enclosure 'is in microcosm a British paradise in Africa, a British protectorate hierarchically organised and feudally arranged' (70). This mission is fortified by ditch and wall, and a tall tree provides a 'watch tower' (43) to spot savages, specifically the Masai. Mackenzie compliments the visitors that they are 'venturesome people' (47), and this is soon demonstrated. This station is a 'little England' in Africa, as Dryden notes: 'Cleanliness, order, and Protestant hard work dominate Haggard's vision of the white imperialist in Africa' (184). No surprise that, as the missionary comments, 'Nearly all my men have gone down to the coast with ivory and goods' (45). Katz asserts: 'Romance accommodates itself to the politics of imperialism' (50). Religion is supported by trade.

According to Richard Patteson, this situation reflects 'the conflict between missionary and mercantile impulses' often found in imperial romances (114). Later Mackenzie tells Quatermain: 'I am well off; it is thirty thousand pounds I am worth today, and every farthing of it made by honest trade and savings in the bank at Zanzibar, for living here costs me next to nothing' (99).

Throughout the novel, as also in *King Solomon's Mines*, Haggard writes of war and armaments in a style recalling Homer's *Iliad* in its incisive arming and battle episodes. The axe of Umslopogaas, Inkosi-kaas, is discussed in Homeric detail, and the warrior defends violence as inherently part of masculinity: 'I kill in fair fight. Man is born to kill. He who kills not when his blood is hot is a woman, and no man … I say I kill in fair fight' (52–3). This use of Homer, of course, renders the experiences heroic and epical. In later episodes, the River Styx and Charon from Vergil's *Aeneid* Book VI are evoked for similar epic enhancement (114). This epical referencing anticipates the similar use of the *Aeneid* in Conrad's *Heart of Darkness*.

When the missionary's daughter Flossie is kidnapped, Quatermain offers himself in exchange, 'being a timid man; my plan was to see the girl safely exchanged and then to shoot myself' (65). The girl herself writes her parents that if she is not rescued, she will shoot herself, since she always carries a Derringer with her. Mackenzie, though a missionary, gives a speech encouraging war with the kidnappers, calling on God to assist them. As Ridley comments, Mackenzie 'reveals himself as a terrifying fighter with the bayonet' (111).

The missionary party plans a night attack on the Masai camp. As in Homer, the weapons (Martinis and Winchesters) and armour are discussed in detail. Then, so is the battle, again in Homeric fashion, in one of Haggard's famous battle sequences (Chapter 7). The 'slaughter' is 'great and grim, in which no quarter was asked or given' (89).

Victory for the Mission Station forces occurs only when a warrior tries to strike Umslopogaas, who is saved by his chain mail, about which the attackers know nothing. Hence, thinking the Zulu is bewitched, the attackers flee. Flossie is rescued, and the fighters have 'the glorious sense of victory against overwhelming odds glowing in our hearts' (93). When Quatermain learns that Mackenzie is deciding to return to England, he declares: '[Flossie] should receive some education and mix with girls of her own race, otherwise she will grow up wild, shunning her kind' (99). The attraction of 'going native' is especially powerful to women, according to Quatermain, who fears anarchic female freedom.

Wagonloads of dead Masai are thrown into the Tana River: 'The crocodiles must have been well fed that night' (96). Fearing retaliation by the Masai, Mackenzie decides to return to England: 'I have had enough of savages' (99). After this battle, Quatermain and his party survive a pillar of fire and witness a vicious fight among gigantic crabs, nature literally red in tooth and claw.

The men come to the country of Zu-Vendis and its capital city Milosis, where two white queens reign. This is the white race Quatermain sought at the beginning. From this point in the text, the men in *Allan Quatermain* are challenged not by savages but by erotic desire and conflict generated by the two queens. Instead of Africans, two white queens become the Other. Quatermain rhapsodises:

> I have seen beautiful women in my day … but language fails me when I try to give some idea of the blaze of loveliness that then broke upon us in the persons of these sister Queens. Both were young – perhaps five-and-twenty years of age – both were tall and exquisitely formed; but there the likeness stopped. One, Nyleptha, was a woman of dazzling fairness … her hair a veritable crown of gold … . Her twin sister, Sorais, was of a different and darker type of beauty. Her hair was wavy like Nyleptha's but coal-black … The lips were full, and I thought rather cruel. (145–6)

Each woman is a potential *femme fatale*, especially Sorais. Dennis Butts observes in his Introduction to the novel that the text 'may have gained particular intensity from Victorian male anxieties about the emergence of the "New Woman"' (xvi).

Sir Henry and Nyleptha exchange glances, attraction at first sight. Quatermain perceives: 'And I sighed and shook my head, knowing that the beauty of a woman is like the beauty of the lightning – a destructive thing and a cause of desolation' (147). Conflict soon arises. Agon, the High Priest, objects to the men killing some sacred hippos. (The High Priest's name in Greek means 'contest', suitable given his opposition to the invaders.) More problematical, Nasta, 'the greatest lord in the country' (149), aspires to the hand of the blonde queen Nyleptha. The men are taken to a dazzling temple to witness a ceremony in honor of the Sun, for Sun-worship is the religion in Zu-Vendis. Quatermain records an invocation to the Sun written in archaic language intended to evoke epic. The men are then set to be tutored in the native language.

Eventually, Curtis confesses his love for Nyleptha to Quatermain: 'I love Nyleptha. What am I to do?' (188). However, in the interval, Sorais also has fallen in love with Curtis. Sorais, also, is now loved by John Good. Quatermain recognises Sorais' 'ominous smile … I felt terribly afraid … She was at heart bitterly jealous of Nyleptha … It is not easy to read so cold and haughty a woman' (186). 'Sorais was a dangerous woman to be mixed up with either with or without one's own consent' (202).

Proving that all men are susceptible, Quatermain states that even he 'then and there fell in love with [Nyleptha] myself' (192). He remarks about Curtis, 'I could not help being a little jealous of my old friend's luck' (196). Nasta precipitates a crisis by asking Nyleptha's hand in marriage. Here, the women become not only the Other but the disruptive Other. Each of the three English adventurers, Quatermain, Curtis and Good, is drawn into the erotic force field of the two queens. Even for so loyal a group, erotic desire can destabilise strong male friendship.

Masculine identity in the case of all three adventurers is destabilised by erotic desire. Sorais attempts to murder Nyleptha, at first with the aid of the besotted Good, who then prevents the murder. But his betrayal is assailed by Curtis, and Quatermain reflects:

> Though I spoke up for Good, I was not blind to the fact that, however, natural his behaviour might be, it was obvious that he was being involved in a very awkward and disgraceful complication. A foul and wicked murder had been attempted, and he had let the murderess escape, and thereby, among other things, allowed her to gain complete ascendency over himself. In fact, he was in a fair way to become her tool – and no more dreadful fate can befall a man than to become the tool of an unscrupulous woman, or indeed of any woman. There is but one end to it: when he is broken, or has served her purpose, he is thrown away – turned out on the world to hunt for his lost self-respect. (212–13)

This fear of women is part of nineteenth-century British culture. Here it is transported to Africa, threatening masculine identity and destroying men's bonds with each other.

As if to make the situation universal, Umpslopogaas then tells a parable about female wickedness, which, it turns out, is about his own deception by a woman. Then he admits having seen Good accompanying Sorais in her murderous mission. 'I knew that she had bewitched thee and that a true man had abandoned the truth' (218). Good responds: 'I must say … that I scarcely thought that I should live to be taught my duty by a Zulu; but it just shows what we can come to. I wonder if you fellows can understand how humiliated I feel, and the bitterest part of it is that I deserve it all … I let her go and I promised to say nothing, more is the shame to me' (218–19). Sorais declares war against her sister. Both she and Nyleptha echo Vergil's Dido in the *Aeneid*, having to contend with civil war.

When Curtis and Nyleptha marry, it is according to the rites of Zu-Vendis and of Anglican Christianity. 'The white hero does marry a native girl … but he does not bring her back to his own country' (Street 101). Later, Nyleptha is sympathetic to Curtis' attempts to impose Christianity on the country, allowing him to control the country on his terms. Unlike Sorais, Nyleptha is the ideal wife for Curtis, yielding power although she is queen. Quatermain recognises that the male bonds are broken: 'Marriages are supposed to be cheerful things, but my experience is that they are very much the reverse to everybody … They mean the breaking-up of so many old ties … the passing away of the old order … As for the old friends – well, of course they have taken the place that old friends ought to take' (230). Quatermain feels he is in 'second place' (230). Millman observes: 'For the male novel, *no* wedding is natural' (49).

For the ensuing battle between the two queens, Haggard again evokes epic, here in his imitation of epic similes: 'In sank the great wedge, into his heart, and as it cut its way hundreds of horsemen were thrown up on either side of it, just as the earth is thrown up by a ploughshare, or more like still, as the foaming water curls over beneath the bows of a rushing ship' (241). Quatermain is severely wounded. He and Umpslopogaas then race to Milosis, the capital city, to save Nyleptha from being murdered by Nasta and Agon. The Zulu kills Agon and hurls Nasta over a parapet in the ensuing struggle. The Zulu dies after breaking a sacred stone and falling beneath the rubble, still clutching his axe. Sorais will later declare about Umpslopogaas: 'He was *a man*' (270). Although Good offers to marry her, Sorais commits suicide. Low observes: 'The deliberate gendering of the natural world as female, and all human agency as male, means that women who possess agency in Haggard are inevitably punished for it' (48). The wounded Quatermain learns that Curtis is with Nyleptha and comments: 'He might have given me a look' (265). While his side has had a victory, Quatermain nevertheless resents this dissolution of male comradeship, provoked by a woman.

The final chapter, the epical 24, is written by Henry Curtis, who praises the deceased Quatermain 'as a man of action and a citizen of the world' (279). He adds that doctors, not Nyleptha, prevented him from seeing Quatermain during his final days. Curtis is now King-Consort. 'The conflict [of primitivism] with progress is seen in the fact that an Englishman is left to rule the country' (Street 124). In one imperialising strategy, Curtis has decided to impose Christianity on the people of Zu-Vendis, replacing their 'senseless Sun-worship' (281). Katz stresses that 'the Englishmen simply succeed in replacing one religion with another' (74).

Also, Curtis has determined on 'the total exclusion of all foreigners from Zu-Vendis … preserving to this, on the whole, upright and generous-hearted people the blessings of comparative barbarism … I have no fancy for handing over this beautiful country to be torn and fought over by speculators, tourists, politicians and teachers, whose voice is as the voice of Babel … nor will I endow it with the greed, drunkenness, new diseases, gunpowder, and general demoralisation which chiefly mark the progress of civilisation amongst unsophisticated peoples' (281–2). Stiebel observes that 'Curtis is himself a "foreigner" in Zu-Vendis, but because he is an English gentleman he is unquestionably the right person to rule the locals' (75).

As with Quatermain, the suspicion of 'civilisation' remains with Curtis. According to Cherry Wilhelm, 'the new society thus combines primitive grandeur with the best of English culture' (48). Dryden notes that Haggard's heroes never 'go native' like Kurtz in Conrad's *Heart of Darkness* (178). They draw the line between white and black. Haggard's attitude toward civilisation is remarkably ambiguous in *Allan Quatermain*. The novel is supposed to instruct young men to become English gentlemen, yet Good and Curtis find that this model can best thrive in the all-white monarchy of an African city. Throughout the novel, this ambiguity exists. Early in the text, Quatermain thinks: 'It is a glorious country, and only wants the hand of civilised man to make it a most productive one' (57).

In a classic white = right imperialist utterance, Quatermain declares:

> But then that is what Englishmen are, adventurers to the backbone; and all our magnificent muster-roll of colonies, each of which in time will become a great nation, testify to the extraordinary value of the spirit of adventure which at first sight looks like a mild form of lunacy. 'Adventurer' – he who goes out to meet whatever may come. Well, that is what we all do in the world one way or another, and, speaking for myself, I am proud of the title, because it implies a brave heart and a trust in Providence. (101)

Adventuring will be a template for future generations: 'The names of those grand-hearted old adventurers who have made England what she is, will be remembered and taught with a love and pride to little children' (101).

Yet, at the same time, Quatermain also regards achievements as inconsequential: 'What was tremendous enough when one was in it, grew insignificant when viewed from the distance. But is it not thus with all the affairs and doings of our race about which we blow the loud trumpet and make such a fuss and a worry?' (248). On his death-bed, Quatermain asserts: 'Well, it is not a good world – nobody can say that it is, save those who wilfully blind themselves to facts. How can a world be good in which Money is the moving power, and Self-interest the guiding star?' (275). In *Allan Quatermain*, there is a celebration of the white 'civilising' mission coupled with an intense *fin-de-siècle* skepticism about existence. Quatermain appears a fatalist: 'We never know what is going to happen to us the next minute … It is all arranged for us, my sons, so what is the use of bothering?' (114).

The juxtaposition of Zulu and white makes masculine identity a crucial concern in *Allan Quatermain*. Is it better to be a warrior in Zu-Vendis or an Englishman at home? Umslopogaas discusses this issue with Quatermain:

> 'I love not this soft life in stone houses that takes the heart out of a man, and turns his strength to water and his flesh to fat. I love not the white robes and the delicate women … When we fought the Masai at the kraal yonder, ah, then life was worth the living … Mine is a red trade, yet is it better and more honest than some. Better is it to slay a man in fair fight than to suck out his heart's blood in buying and selling and usury after your white fashion … . Thou hast thy ways, and I mine; each to his own people and his own place.' (215)

Quatermain thinks: 'I was much attached to the bloodthirsty old ruffian … He was so wise and yet such a child with it all' (215).

Which is the better man? Wilhelm argues that the Zulu 'is a mighty black warrior, dignified, faithful and full of the pride of the Zulu race. He is in his own way a gentleman, a black Sir Henry Curtis, as their twin positions and roles in important battles show' (49). Sir Henry's chain mail shirt 'fitted the great Zulu like a skin' (79). The Zulu challenges the white man's definition of masculinity, which Quatermain deflects by slotting him in the racist category of child. Still, as Millman comments: 'Haggard has chosen to depict this heroic black man *not* as a foreigner, but as an equal' (76).

Transcending race, however, both men agree in their misogyny. Quatermain approved when the Zulu called the Masai 'women' (260) during the fighting. 'In a world where women exist', Millman writes, 'there is an urgent need for a kinship among men that will combat the forces of femininity … Men must love one another or die at the hands of woman' (67), adding: 'Haggard suggests a full-bodied partnership, an almost democratic dissolution of national characteristics. Men are men the world over … . From Haggard's Manichean point of view, if a character is not a man, then he must surely be a woman' (71, 73). According to Fraser: 'Curtis's eventual accession as King-Consort ensures a reversion to the patrilinear and patriarchal norm' (39), which differs from the previous matriarchy of Zu-Vendis culture.

The novel ends with Henry Curtis' brother George publishing the novel back in England, ending the text where it began, in the metropolis. The fact the brother is named after England's patron saint suggests that even with its ambiguities, *Allan Quatermain* may be a primer for young men of the Empire. Yet, writing as 'Gavin Ogilvy' in *The British Weekly*, J.M. Barrie dissented, declaring that the novel 'tells the adventures of three worthless old men, who go into Africa and slay their thousands of human beings' (218). Barrie recognises that the novel will be a primer for young men: 'So far as I can see *Allan Quatermain* is more likely to make boys bloodthirsty blackguards' (218).

This potential did not prevent the novel from achieving bestseller status. Haggard contended as late as 1923 in a letter to the *Times*: 'The Englishman is by blood and taste a trader, a traveler, a fighting man; all, indeed, that goes to make what is known as an adventurer' (Katz 83).

An extraordinary unsigned article entitled 'Reality and Romance' appeared in the *Spectator* (vol. 61, 28 April 1888). The writer observed that the attack on the mission station in *Allan Quatermain* had been paralleled in actuality by an incident occurring in Africa a week earlier when Arab slave-traders similarly attacked a mission station. The English were victorious in routing the Arabs. The writer stresses the imprinting of masculinity by adventure texts: 'Fortunately, the English race has still a dash of heroism in real life as well as in books, and the prediction need not be withdrawn when we force ourselves to remember that we are not reading a novel [about this incident] … Doubtless all the defenders [of the actual station] were great readers of tales of adventure' (570). In citing the adventure novel as one source imprinting English masculinity, the reviewer concludes that the parallels verify 'Mr Haggard's genuineness' (571). One could not ask for better proof about the formation of masculine identity through a text such as *Allan Quatermain*.

Kipling: *The Man Who Would Be King* (1888)

The Man Who Would Be King is one of the nineteenth-century's greatest tales about imperialism and masculinities. Two white adventurers, Daniel Dravot and Peachey Carnehan, decide to become self-appointed 'kings' in Kafiristan ('land of the unbelievers'), 'a desolate region of north-eastern Afghanistan' (Cornell 299). Their venture ultimately fails when the natives discover they are men, not gods. Dravot is executed by the natives; Carnehan survives crucifixion to return to India. Carnehan relates his tale to an outside frame narrator, a journalist, when, albeit crippled, he makes it back to India.

The issue of masculinities is immediately established when the journalist recounts his first meeting with Carnehan, in an Intermediate carriage of a railway train. The narrator describes himself, and Carnehan, as being of the 'Loafer' class, that is, 'He was a wanderer and a vagabond like myself' (244). As they ride, they discuss 'the politics of Loaferdom, that sees things from the underside' (245). Louis Cornell defines a Loafer as 'any European at large in India with no official attachments or visible means of support, a vagabond' (298). Clearly, being a Loafer especially applies to Carnehan.

Yet given the construction of masculinity, to be a Loafer is not conventionally appropriate. Both the journalist and Peachey Carnehan, then, are unusual in their definitions of masculinity. The journalist can identify to some extent with this footloose existence; Carnehan lives it. Both interrogate masculinity by their attraction to Loaferdom. Peachey regards both of them as enterprising: 'If India was filled with men like you and me, not knowing more than the crows where they'd get their next day's rations, it isn't seventy millions of revenue the land would be paying – it's seven hundred millions' (244–5).

Recognising a fellow Mason in Carnehan, the journalist delivers a message to a red-haired, red-bearded man who turns out to be Daniel Dravot. The narrator reflects that the Native States, where the hatred of the English is intense, 'are the dark places of the earth, full of unimaginable cruelty' (247). This remark anticipates the violence that will erupt in the tale.

One June night, closing an issue of the newspaper, the narrator is visited by two men, Carnehan and his friend Dravot. Dravot does not attempt to conceal their various male identities, noting 'the less said about our professions the better, for we have been most things in our time' (251). Their imperialist motives are evident. Dravot states: 'The country isn't half worked out because they that governs it won't let you touch it' (252). Therefore, they opt to go to Kafiristan, a territory free of bureaucratic interference. 'We will ... go away to some other place where a man isn't crowded and can come into his own. We are not little men, and there is nothing that we are afraid of except Drink ... *Therefore*, we are going away to be Kings' (252).

Their purpose for going to Kafiristan is two-fold: to exploit the area economically and to assert their unique form of masculinity, which by conventional standards is anarchic, including even murder. Jeffrey Meyers asserts: '[They] are uneducated and corrupt adventurers, unscrupulous confidence men, common frauds, blackmailers and drunkards' (712). Dravot states they know the territory from being part of the Second Afghan War (1878–80) under General Frederick Roberts. Their model, he asserts, is Sir James Brooke (1803–68), 'the "White Rajah", an English soldier who in 1841 was made ruler of Sarawak by the Sultan of Borneo as a reward for his military exploits' (298–9). Brooke, however, exhibited none of the unscrupulous conduct of Carnehan and Dravot. Hearing this audacious objective, the journalist declares both men fools embarking on an 'idiotic adventure' (255).

Two years later, Carnehan returns to the journalist's office and relates the outcome of their experiment in masculinity. 'I was the King of Kafiristan – me and Dravot – crowned Kings we was!' (258). Most critics assume that Carnehan is schizoid (Draudt) and mad (Shippey/Short). Carnehan admits at the outset: 'I ain't mad – yet, but I shall be that way soon' (259). Carnehan suffers from hallucinations; for example, he perceives mountains as goats.

Furthermore, although Carnehan is relating the story in the first person, he sometimes refers to himself in the third person as 'Carnehan' or 'he'. Various reasons may explain these shifts: incipient madness, a desire to deny the reality of the events, a refusal to relive the experiences, an effort to distance himself from events or an attempt 'to objectify his fantastic tale' (Draudt 321). The reliability of

Carnehan's narrative therefore is questionable. As a fable of a crisis of masculinity, however, it is revelatory.

Marching into the territory, Dravot and Carnehan begin the violent assertion of their exported masculinity. Dravot kills one man and drives off another to get mules. They join ten men in their fight against twenty others, Dravot declaring: 'This is the beginning of the business' (261). They establish their hegemony: 'Dravot he was the King, and a handsome man he looked with the gold crown on his head and all' (262).

His megalomania now emerging, Dravot exults: 'They think we're Gods' (263). They conquer one village after another. Dravot asserts: 'I am the son of Alexander by Queen Semiramis, and you're my younger brother and a God too!' (265). Dravot informs the populace: 'You are *my* people, and by God … I'll make a damned fine Nation of you, or I'll die in the making!' (267).

However, Dravot's aims enlarge: 'I won't make a Nation … I'll make an Empire. These men aren't niggers; they're English. Look at their eyes – look at their mouths. Look at the way they stand up. They sit on chairs in their own houses. They're the Lost Tribes … Rajah Brooke will be a suckling to us' (269). He determines that after he establishes his Empire, he will turn it over to Queen Victoria, who will give him a knighthood.

Fatally, as winter approaches, Dravot decides he wants a wife, even though he and Peachey had signed a 'Contrack' (254) to forswear women during their imperial adventure. At the marriage ceremony, the 'slut' (274) bites Dravot and draws blood, at which the men of the Empire realise Dravot and Carnehan are mortal, not gods. Dravot is forced to the middle of a rope-bridge, which is then cut. Peachey records: 'I could see his body caught on a rock with the gold crown close beside' (277).

Peachey describes his own punishment in the third person: 'But do you know what they did to Peachey between two pine-trees? They crucified him, sir' (277). As proof of the truth of his narrative, Peachey shows the journalist Dravot's withered head and the gold crown. Two days later, the journalist learns that Peachey has died and the head and crown have disappeared.

Few can believe these men are heroes – they are brutal, mad imperialists. Kipling underscores their false heroism by subtle linguistic devices. As Thomas Shippey and Michael Short note (81), one is the use of 'marked theme' in Peachey's narrative, whereby an object precedes a noun and verb in a sentence: 'Crowned Kings we was! In this office we settled it' (258). As in this example, subject verb agreement is violated. These 'breaches of normal word-order' (Shippey/Short 81) indicate Peachey's lower class status as well as incipient madness. Kipling also has Peachey employ 'gloss-tags' (Shippey/Short 82) to stress this lower class origin: 'The mountains they danced at night … but Dan he held up his hand' (278). The men's initial Contrack, as Meyers notes, derives from one between Huck and Tom in Mark Twain's 1876 *The Adventures of Tom Sawyer* (718).

This text, drawing on the adventure tradition, manages to elevate the subject by its mode of narration. Shippey/Short note: 'The real purpose of [Peachey's] monologue is to provide a different mode of narrative for events which (if related simply) would seem more at home in a boy's adventure-book and would receive easy dismissal' (85).

The megalomaniacal masculine fantasy of these two men is indicated in the strange title of the text, where 'man' and 'king' are aligned in an impossible conjunction of mortal and immortal. As Paul Fussell observes: 'One is obliged to be, and yet one cannot be, man and king at the same time' (217). The key word 'would', signifying an action which a person probably knew was ill-advised, reveals the rashness of the power-mad objective to be immortal on this earth.

What is Kipling's objective in this tale? Clearly he indicts the two men for their methods: the vast killing, the exploitation of the land and people, their use of brute force, their assumed superiority, their blasphemy. Yet, as Edmund Wilson recognised, the story is 'a parable of what might happen to the English if they should forfeit their moral authority' (130). According to Meyers, Kipling does not reject imperialism in *The Man Who Would Be King* but rather the methods of colonising used by Carnehan and Dravot: 'The story … represents the dangers and horrors that would result if the organized governments of civilized powers refused the task of colonialism' (717). He concludes that 'Kipling is essentially sympathetic to their imperialis[t]ic ambitions' (723). It is significant that the frame narrator, the journalist, while skeptical of the men's adventure at the beginning of the narrative, appears to be sympathetic to Peachey's venture at the conclusion, falling for the false analogy of Christ's crucifixion with that of Carnehan.

While such is certainly one way of construing the text, Kipling introduces a complicating element, the tendency of males to veer toward extremism in situations where there are inequities of power. Masculinity in these circumstances becomes a wild card. It can lead to aberrant behaviours of the worst kind, and it can also lead to madness. In this ambiguous narrative, if Kipling endorses the imperial project, he is demanding a great deal by asking for men who would not be kings.

Kipling: *The Light That Failed* (1891)

In nineteenth-century British fiction, Rudyard Kipling's *The Light That Failed* of 1891 is unique in its adoption of the adventure format to chronicle a disastrous erotic affair during a time of war. The narrative concerns battle artist/war sketch correspondent Dick Heldar, who falls in love with a childhood friend, Maisie, who does not requite his love. Rather, Maisie, an aspiring artist herself, represents the aspirations of the New Woman for independence in her career, relationships and personal freedom.

Heldar, strongly identified with male groups and male *camaraderie* as befits a military man, begins to go blind. Finally recognising the futility of his attraction to Maisie and desiring to end his life rather than be blind, he goes to the Sudan and commits combat suicide, dying in the arms of his friend Gilbert Torpenhow. Norman Page has noted about Kipling 'that manliness … is a key concept in discussing his work, and that various models of masculine society are prominent, even dominant, in his fiction' (81).

Kipling is the great chronicler of male homosocial spaces: the barracks, the square, the regiment, the public school, the army, the ship. In this first novel, Kipling juxtaposes in extreme tension the domestic, heterosexual world and the martial, homosocial one. The novel alludes to actual colonial wars such as Kandahar, August 1880 in the Second Afghan War; the breaking of the square at the Battle of Abu Klea on 17 January 1885; Garnet Wolseley's expedition to relieve General Charles Gordon at Khartoum 1884–85; Tel-el-Kebir on 13 September 1882 during the Egyptian War; and the death of General Gordon at Khartoum 26 January 1885. It is on the same day as Gordon's death that Heldar receives a severe head wound in the Sudan.

This wound, which damages his eyes, will eventually lead to his blindness. There is a strong suggestion that this blindness is an act of revenge by the colonised. In his essay on Kipling, George Orwell declared that Kipling 'was the prophet of British Imperialism in its expansionist phase (even more than his poems, his solitary novel, *The Light That Failed*, gives you the atmosphere of that time) and also the unofficial historian of the British Army, the old mercenary army which began to change its shape in 1914' (125).

As its title indicates, the novel concerns blindness in many manifestations. Kipling uses this motif in the initial chapter, when the young Dick Heldar shows Maisie how to shoot a revolver. Accidentally, as Maisie is holding the revolver, it goes off in Dick's face. He tells her: 'You nearly blinded me. That powder stuff stings awfully' (11). Dick tells Maisie: 'You belong to me' (15). The blindness from the shot marks his singular blindness to Maisie's desires. He feels he can possess her at his will.

Thus, the blindness signals the male's loss of power and control, the threat to male dominance in the heterosexual world. In desiring to shoot the revolver, Maisie wants male phallic power, which Dick denies her. Blindness is associated with castration, loss of power, denial of the male controlling gaze and fear of the empowered female. According to Betty Miller, 'the note of aggression, of competitiveness, is sounded at the outset' (4) of the novel. After Dick kisses Maisie in this first scene, 'a gust of the growing wind drove the girl's long black hair across his face … and for a moment he was in the dark – a darkness that stung' (14). Dick is thus blinded once by the revolver and once by Maisie's hair.

In contrast to the heterosexual context of the first chapter, in the second chapter, Kipling moves to the homosocial world of the regiment, and the square, some years later in the Sudan. Kipling describes the brutal fighting inside a breached square. Torpenhow tears out the eye of an Arab opponent and 'rose, wiping his thumb on his trousers'' (25). Dick is cut 'violently across his helmet' (25) and then is rescued by Torpenhow.

Having returned to London, Dick becomes successful enough as an artist to have an exhibition at a gallery. After four years, he encounters Maisie, who is studying to be an artist but without much success. Significantly, she tells Dick when he walks too fast: 'You're out of step … you're always out of step' (47). It soon is apparent that Maisie, a kind of New Woman, is interested in her career rather than in Dick as a lover. She is frank with him: 'I've got my work to do, and I must do it … It's my work – mine – mine – mine! I've been alone all my life in myself, and I'm not going to belong to anybody except myself … Dick, nothing will ever come of it … I knew you wouldn't understand, and it will only hurt you more when you find out' (55–6). Betty Miller goes beyond the New Woman model to declare that Maisie anticipates Sue Bridehead in Thomas Hardy's *Jude the Obscure* (1895) in her 'aversion to the conditions of sexual love' (5).

Dick feels: 'One or other of us has to be broken … . There's everything in that face but love … She knows what she wants, and she's going to get it.' He concludes, nevertheless: 'She's sure to come round; and yet – that mouth isn't a yielding mouth' (57). Kipling's source for this fatal male erotic attraction to a woman was Prevost's 1731 *Manon Lescaut* (Green, ed., *Critical Heritage* 27). In the text, the narrative records: 'Not for nothing is a man permitted to ally himself to the wrong woman' (184). This antagonism between a man and a woman in *The Light That Failed* even suggests the agendas of D.H. Lawrence.

In the same chapter, Kipling describes male comradeship, in contrast to Dick's tormented love for Maisie: 'Torpenhow came into the studio at dusk, and looked at Dick with his eyes full of the austere love that springs up between men who have tugged at the same oar together and are yoked by custom and use and the intimacies of toil. This is a good love' (58). The 'hopeless enslavement' (63) of Dick by Maisie, Torpenhow feels, will destroy him as an artist: 'She'll spoil his hand. She'll waste his time, and she'll marry him, and ruin his work for ever. He'll be a respectable married man before we can stop him, and – he'll never go on the long trail [military campaign] again' (72).

Maisie persists in telling Dick she is not attracted to him. She remarks that when other men cared for her, 'they always worried just when I was in the middle of my work, and wanted me to listen to them … They couldn't understand why I didn't care' (74–5). Maisie repudiates the power of the male gaze and rejects male surveillance, whether in her erotic life or professional life. Miller argues that 'deprived of all initiative in the relationship, Dick is allotted the feminine and subservient role' in the text (5). To Miller, Dick becomes a 'minor Samson' (6) with Maisie as Delilah. On the other hand, Martin Seymour-Smith regards the fracture in the relationship as Dick's responsibility: 'Dick is playing some passionate game in which he is projecting whatever it is he really feels, a burning confusion, on the *figure* of Maisie' (172). To Seymour-Smith, Dick is 'a boastful and violent man' (174).

Dick retaliates, accusing Maisie of being masculine: 'You're so like a man that I forget when I'm talking to you … . Everybody must be either a man or a woman … . You aren't a woman' (81–2). Dick feels threatened and castrated by female power and the female artist, fearing the New Woman and her independence. The ideological tension between Dick and Maisie is so great that Dick finds himself 'yearning for some man-talk and tobacco after his first experience of an entire day spent in the society of a woman' (89).

After this episode, Kipling added an entire chapter (8) to the novel that was not in its original short version. In this chapter, Torpenhow and other male friends are shown in a totally homosocial world of male talk about war and women. Heldar confesses that he painted 'a sort of Negroid-Jewess-Cuban' (98) on a voyage, where he had an affair with her. Torpenhow argues that a woman 'can't [be] a piece of one's life' (103). Dick wonders if 'go-fever' is the solution to his situation, 'urging him to go away and taste the old hot, unregenerate life again – to scuffle, swear, gamble, and love light loves with his fellows' (104). Lionel Johnson, reviewing the novel in the *Academy* in 1891, noted Dick's restlessness: 'His life has been that of an Elizabethan adventurer, in the altered manner of this century: a life of the reckless sort, wild and free, with all the virtues of *camaraderie*, and with few of the more decorous moral excellences' (Green, ed. *Critical Heritage* 89).

Hence, Heldar confronts two kinds of geographies in the novel: that of the colonies and the regiment and that of the metropolis. Each contains its own map, one charting a heterosexual relationship in the metropolis, the other a homosocial space of the regiment where a racial other battles for supremacy. Norman Page stresses Kipling's 'general preoccupation with the male clique, for which the experience of war provided both test and bond' (1979, 88).

When Dick learns he will be blind within a year, his choices become urgent. Torpenhow provides male support: 'Torpenhow's arms were round him, and Torpenhow's chin was on his shoulder … . Torpenhow withdrew his hand, and stooping over Dick, kissed him lightly on the forehead, as men do sometimes kiss a wounded comrade in the hour of death, to ease his departure' (137–8). The homoeroticism of the scene introduces an additional tension into Dick's tormented sexuality. Mark Kinkead-Weekes argues: 'Male love is shown at its deepest at the time of Dick's blindness … Kipling is making this male love a substitute and haven, and the very overtness of his worry over homosexuality shows the pressure that insists on risking it. One can now see why Dick must die in Torpenhow's arms in a conclusion which re-orchestrates this scene' (208). Seymour-Smith also realises the latent homosexuality of the text: 'Blindness here is impotence, lack of creative virility, fear that homosexuality may cripple creativity' (174).

When Maisie sees Dick blinded, she recognises 'he was, indeed, down and done for – masterful no longer' (159). Dick's blindness clearly marks the end of his empowering male gaze, whether this was turned on women in the metropolis or blacks in the colonies. Kipling draws on the precedents of Charlotte Brontë's *Jane Eyre* (1847) and Elizabeth Barrett Browning's *Aurora Leigh* (1856) for the motif of the blinding of a male.

The reader learns that Dick has thought of suicide. Having dismissed Maisie, Dick decides to return to the Sudan to join his male comrades. 'He would find Torpenhow, and come as near to the old life as might be' (202). On the train to the battlefield, Dick urges the British soldiers with their machine guns to give hell to the Arabs. Throughout the novel, the Arabs in revolt are considered vermin, obstructions to the imperial project. Reaching the square, Dick is shot 'with a kindly bullet through the head' (208). Torpenhow cradles Dick's body in his arms in a male pietà. Kinkead-Weekes contends that Kipling wants to demonstrate 'the superiority of male love and the male life of action' (206). Dick's hyper-masculinity can be only an export to a homosocial space.

The textual history of *The Light That Failed* involves two versions. In the earlier version, published in January 1891 in *Lippincott's Monthly Magazine*, Dick and Maisie become engaged, a decision forced on Kipling by the publisher. When the longer version appeared in March 1891, it contained the strongly male homosocial Chapter 8 as well as the conclusion with Dick Heldar dying in the Sudan in the homosocial world of the army. Kipling's intention was expressed in the longer version.

In this light, the novel deploys adventure to express a strongly unstable depiction of male/female relations. John Lyon remarks: 'At the centre of this skittish misogyny are powerful fears of sexual failure, impotence and emasculation – symbolically present in the novel's concentration on blindness' (xxi). Norman Page (1979) stresses 'a recurring strand in Kipling's thought: the association of women with the unmanly, and the implication that it is only in a world without women that worthwhile things can be accomplished' (90).

Yet, the issue of masculine gender is complex in the novel. Preben Kaarsholm argues that the long version of the novel is 'a deeply pessimistic study in aggressive male self-destruction' (217). As an analysis of male self-destruction, the text has no equals except perhaps Hardy's *Jude the Obscure*. Kinkead-Weekes notes that 'there are three kinds of light in the novel ... the light of Love, and it fails ... the light of Art, and it fails too... [and] the desert light ... [of] the Trail ... The novel not only separates Love and the Trail (the life of action and danger), but opposes them' (202). Only the light of the Trail suffices: 'At last, when Love and Art have failed, it is to a dawn attack in the desert that Dick returns, to find merciful release in a man's arms as a bullet finds its mark' (202).

But, as Kaarsholm continues, this agenda is a broad, cultural one: 'Kipling's world-view is a deeply depressed and neurotic one – of a life whose sense is dissolving and only held together by desperate effort and of a society where the trend towards *anomie* and total alienation can only be countered by an authoritarian traditionalism whose most topical form is imperialism' (218–19). The authoritarian impulse links the erotic and military dimensions of the novel following the Roman poet Ovid's classic statement 'militat omnis amans': 'every lover is a soldier' in laying siege to a woman's heart, keeping watch and guarding his beloved.

With its complex representations of genders and imperialism, Kipling's first novel, about a light that failed, did not, as an adventure novel, fail. Kipling maps Dick's desire in two ways, one heterosexual in London, the other homosocial, perhaps homosexual, in Africa. The life-and-death African encounters with their violence introduce Dick Heldar to a fierce masculinity where one male must dominate another. Page concludes: 'Various models of masculine society are prominent, even dominant, in his fiction' (1979, 81). This same impetus to be controlling, however, leads to disaster in London. For Kipling, martial suicide is better than marital self-destruction.

Stevenson/Osbourne: *The Ebb-Tide* (1894)

Robert Louis Stevenson and his stepson Lloyd Osbourne published *The Ebb-Tide* in book form in August 1894, the year of Stevenson's death. As a tale of adventure, it is one of the most probing, even philosophical, in the genre, which is part of its distinction. Jacques Rivière in his essay 'The Adventure Novel' cited it as the model of the adventure narrative:

> In *The Ebb-Tide*, let us read again the scene of the arrival of the three adventurers on the pearl island … Upon reading these pages, I feel my life extending into a sort of infinity, instead of contracting and thickening within me. My blood circulates freely; my breath is quick; and during those moments when nothing is yet happening, when events are still in preparation – not a breath of wind on the deck of the ship – I feel myself quietly growing equal to everything prodigious in the universe. (123)

The story is about three outcast drifters in the South Seas. Robert Herrick is a gentleman who went to Oxford but has declined in the world. John Davis [Brown] is a drunken derelict American ship's captain. J.L. Huish is a vile Cockney clerk.

In the course of their rovings they encounter a Cambridge-educated English gentleman, William John Attwater, who in the end shoots Huish and rehabilitates Davis to his Trinity Hall/Protestant Christianity. Herrick faces being forced to remain at the end on Attwater's island, despising Christianity and loathing himself, hoping to escape. It is Herrick who is the philosophical centre of the novel's existential ideology.

The title of the narrative, suggesting the reflux of the tide toward the sea and figuratively a point or condition of decline, marks all three of the rovers. The fall from a higher to a lower level or from better to worse defines all three men, but it particularly designates the fall of Herrick from promising young university student to castaway trash. 'In the telling South Sea phrase, these three men were *on the beach*. Common calamity had brought them acquainted, as the three most miserable English-speaking creatures in Tahiti … Each had made a long apprenticeship in going downward [and] been shamed into the adoption of an *alias*' (124).

The narrative especially dwells on Herrick's decline or ebb. Jenni Calder (1979) labels him 'the central character' (20). 'Robert Herrick was the son of an intelligent, active, and ambitious man, small partner in a considerable London house. Hopes were conceived of the boy; he was sent to a good school, gained there an Oxford scholarship, and proceeded in course to the Western University. With all his talent and taste (and he had much of both) Robert was deficient in consistency and intellectual manhood' (125). Herrick carries about him a copy of

Vergil's *Aeneid* (124). For Herrick, the irony of his interest in Vergil is marked. In Vergil, the transplanted protagonist assumes a new identity (from Trojan to Roman) and realises the imperial project. In the case of Herrick, he is like Aeneas in being transplanted but is a dismal failure at realising himself in an imperialising context.

Having chosen a clerkship in New York, Herrick's 'career thenceforth was one of unbroken shame. He did not drink, he was exactly honest, he was never rude to his employers, yet was everywhere discharged' (125). 'If Herrick had gone there with any manful purpose, he would have kept his father's name: the *alias* betrayed his moral bankruptcy' (126). Stevenson/Osbourne stress the gendered nature of this fall by referring to Herrick's 'manhood'. This is a masculine decline, a failure to achieve a stable masculine identity. Vergil is connected in Herrick's mind with 'the busy schoolroom, the green playing-fields' (125) and other elements of the male script, now all lost to him.

In fact, Herrick demonstrates the falsity of the penis/phallus equation. He has the penis, but he has no power, authority or control. This is the result: 'Herrick became shy. There were women enough who would have supported a far worse and a far uglier man. Herrick never met or never knew them: or if he did, some manlier feeling would revolt, and he preferred starvation' (126).

Of the other two men, 'the American who called himself Brown … was known to be a master-mariner in some disgrace'. The other [J.L. Huish] is a sadistic 'drawfish person, [with] the pale eyes and toothless smile of a vulgar and bad-hearted cockney clerk … He was totally vile' (127). In his despair, Herrick writes his fiancé Emma: 'I know, had I chosen, that I might have done well; and yet I swear to you I tried to choose … I had not the manhood of a common clerk … Turn the key in the door; let no thought of me return; be done with the poor ghost that pretended he was a man and stole your love' (140). Herrick ruminates: 'I have no pride, no heart, no manhood' (144). The universe is such that 'everybody has a false name in the Pacific' (141).

The three wastrels take control of a ship, the *Farralone*, and decide to commandeer its cargo, which they believe to be full of champagne. Herrick realises 'the gulf where he had fallen. He was a thief among thieves. He said it to himself' (159). Wishing to drown, he asks 'And I'm still living? It's some beastly dream' (160). At the wheel, Herrick is overcome by 'a wave of nausea … [It jarred] his spirit like a file on a man's teeth' (163). To Herrick 'it was thus a cutting reproof to compare the islanders and the whites aboard the *Farralone*' (168). Herrick 'held but a twinkling and unsure belief in any future state … . [He felt] the doom which seemed to brood upon the schooner, a horror that was almost superstitious fell upon him … He had sold his honour' (170). Soon all three men discover they have been deceived in the cargo. In fact, most of the 'champagne' is just water.

In Part II, Stevenson/Osbourne repeatedly mock the three men as 'adventurers' (188, 190, 191). They drift to an island owned by Attwater, who is six feet four and full of 'virility' (191). According to Calder: 'The enclosed world of the schooner encounters the enclosed world of Attwater's island' (21). Davis tells Herrick to get Attwater on ship so he can kill or remove him and get his fabulous collection of pearls. A strong believer in Christianity, Attwater tells Herrick: 'I dislike men, and hate women' (205). He also tells Herrick 'I like you' (205) and that he is 'very attractive' (205). This lure of homosexuality intensifies the investigation into masculine identity in *The Ebb-Tide*.

Herrick does not share Attwater's belief in religion: 'I do not believe. It is living truth to you; to me, upon my conscience, only folk-lore. I do not believe there is any form of words under heaven, by which I can lift the burthen from my shoulders' (207). Robert Kiely believes Attwater represents Stevenson's strict, self-righteous religious father (189), 'the primary reminder of Victorian Britain ... a Protestant Christian [marked by] Puritanism' (181). Kiely contends that Herrick finds in Attwater a fearsome individual: 'What is discovered on the island is something like a whole man, admirable, almost majestic, but with blackness rooted to his soul' (189).

 Having told Attwater that Huish and Davis plan to murder him, Herrick feels 'he had complied with the ebb-tide in man's affairs, and the tide had carried him away' (208). 'O my God, my God, why was I born?' (222). Deciding to commit suicide by swimming, Herrick discovers he 'was one who could not' (228). Reaching shore again, he tells Attwater: 'What I am? A coward ... Here I am. I am broken crockery; I am a burst drum; the whole of my life is gone to water; I have nothing left that I believe in, except my living horror of myself' (230). Of Herrick, Kiely writes: 'There is no need to turn Herrick into Stevenson to see that the author shares with his shabby hero a general disillusionment with the efficacy of open-air adventure in distant lands' (191).

When Davis and Huish launch their attack to kill Attwater on his island, Attwater shoots Huish, who is about to throw vitriol into Attwater's face. Instead, the bottle breaks and it is thrown onto Huish's face. Mercifully, Attwater delivers a second shot which puts Huish out of his misery. Yet, Herrick will discover that Attwater is 'an exploiter, a tyrant obsessed with power; he will accept Herrick if Herrick accepts his authority' (Calder 22).

The ship is burned to destroy evidence. Davis embraces Christianity and pretends to be content to remain on the island. For Jenni Calder, 'Davis in fact survives, but his spirit is annihilated' (22). Herrick is enraged, since he does not accept Christianity. He hopes the approach of a friendly ship will allow him to leave this island prison. Herrick, to Calder, 'resists an alliance with Attwater, whose power and cruelty is not less naked' (22) than the vileness of Huish. Herrick may not want a homosexual relationship with Attwater.

Roslyn Jolly (1999) notes about Stevenson's South Sea tales that 'the anti-imperialism and pro-native sentiments of all the stories clashed with the romance of imperialism' (xxx). She underscores the narrative's 'gritty naturalistic style and frequently sordid subject-matter [which] startled its readers and challenged the current vogue for imperial romances' with its 'uncompromisingly unromantic view of imperialism' (xxvii). The influence of *The Ebb-Tide* probably extends, as

Cedric Watts (1996) has shown, to Conrad's *The Nigger of the 'Narcissus'* and *Victory.*

In her 2006 essay, Roslyn Jolly argues that Ballantyne's *The Coral Island* is a 'literary ancestor for *The Ebb-Tide* … . Stevenson reworked Ballantyne's classic boys' book in his narrative of failed adventure and existential unease' (79). She concludes: '*The Coral Island* established connections between chivalrous masculinity, Christian paternalism, romance and empire in the imagination of the young Stevenson and other boys of his generation. In *The Ebb-Tide*, these connections are undone, and the contradictions of colonialist ideology laid bare' (89).

Even though *The Ebb-Tide* presents despicable white men, as Katherine Linehan argues it still contains a racist attitude toward the native Polynesians who constitute the crew of the men's ship:

> Ironically, however, even while Stevenson rejected white supremacy as a wholesale proposition, he did retain a considerable part of its ideology, recognizable in the recapitulation theory which was extremely popular throughout Europe in the late nineteenth century. This theory argues that human development, whether within individuals or social groups, recapitulates earlier evolutionary stages along the path towards maturity. The proposition that ontogeny recapitulates phylogeny … was thus manipulated to support a view of whites as fully-evolved, brown-skinned people as at a 'childhood' level of development, and African blacks as more hedonistically primitive. (411)

In the text, for instance, an old crew member Uncle Ned tells Herrick 'his simple and hard story of exile, suffering, and injustice among cruel whites' (166). Another, Sally Day, tells Herrick he is a good man, to which Herrick responds: 'He turned, and choking down a sob, shook hands with the negrito. They were kindly, cheery, childish souls … The fact that he was held in grateful favour by these innocents served like blinders to his conscience' (168). Thinking of Polynesians as 'childish' or 'innocent' may be only Herrick's ideas, but in the tale there is a presumption that white men, even as disgusting as this quartet, may still be superior to indigenes.

When the novella appeared in 1894, it was left to Israel Zangwill in his review to stress its uniqueness. First, Zangwill notices that 'Stevenson dispenses with a heroine altogether' in his desire to repudiate the standard contents of English novels (Maixner, ed. *Critical Heritage* 460). He also observes that Stevenson combines here the novel of character and the novel of adventure: 'There are two species of novels, the novel of character and the novel of adventure. Mr Stevenson loves adventure, but he is also a student of character … And so it has naturally occurred to him to combine the two species in one and to have flesh-and-blood figures acted on by incidents, and reacting on them, instead of lay figures buffeted about by the winds of romance' (461). Hence, *The Ebb-Tide* stands against the novel of heterosexual eroticism even as it moved beyond an adventure tale of mere incident.

What *The Ebb-Tide* bequeaths to the adventure tradition, of which Conrad will be so major a part, is the stress on masculinities under siege and in crisis, with a realistic rather than romantic approach to its material. Claire Harman emphasises another element of the story significant to Conrad: 'No one recognised the birth of a new and very modern literary motif in Stevenson's invention of a hidden settlement ruled over by a maverick lone white man' (446), a theme to be deployed by Conrad in *Heart of Darkness* and *Lord Jim.*

While not denying the critique of imperialism in the tale, its great legacy is to interrogate masculinity in a completely existential manner, especially in the figure of Robert Herrick. In this, its genuine legacy is in Conrad's *The Secret Sharer* and *The Shadow-Line.* As a document of the *fin-de-siècle*, there can be no more powerful text of the 'ebb' of a century than *The Ebb-Tide.*

Schreiner: *Trooper Peter Halket of Mashonaland* (1897)

The protagonist of Olive Schreiner's *Trooper Peter Halket of Mashonaland* is a pro-imperialist rapist and murderer who becomes an advocate for humane treatment of blacks by the end of the short tale. Schreiner wrote the novel after the abortive Jameson Raid led by Leander Starr Jameson, a close associate of Cecil John Rhodes, who had made a fortune in diamonds and gold in Cape Colony. The Jameson Raid, 29 December 1895 – 2 January 1896, was an attempt, backed by Rhodes, to annex the gold-rich Boer Republic of the Transvaal for England by overthrowing the government of Paul Kruger. The Raid was masterminded by Rhodes. After the Raid failed, Schreiner denounced him.

The action of *Trooper Peter Halket* is set in Mashonaland (which eventually would be included in what became Rhodesia). Peter Halket is 'an Englishman who idolises Rhodes, is working as a scout in the forces of the British South African Company. They are putting down the 1896 Ndebele and Shona rebellions (which resisted white attempts to annex the land that would eventually be named Rhodesia)' (Boehmer 216). According to Marion Friedman, the text is a 'savage indictment of [Rhodes'] Chartered Company's men. Rape, pillage, atrocity, murder, enslavement: all these charges are brought and the responsibility in large part is laid on Rhodes' (18). The text specifically references the Jameson Raid (65, 99). Halket is the son of a washerwoman and a day labourer, a person of no social distinction.

Not yet twenty-one, Halket finds himself lost on the veldt. There he has an encounter with a stranger, who turns out to be Jesus Christ, who counsels him to reject his brutal ways and embrace a tolerant humanitarian attitude. Moved by the experience, Halket frees a black man and is killed by the captain of his troop. Halket imitates the sacrifice of Christ. The story is a *Bildungsroman* but is unusual because the text has an overt political agenda in its denunciation of Rhodes and the Jameson Raid. Gerald Monsman notes: '[Schreiner] cast Rhodes as the archetype of the white invader, the oppressor less of the colonial Afrikaners than of the natives and the land' (110).

On the top of a kopje, Halket finds himself alone at night. He has found the 'remains of a burnt kraal … where a month before the Chartered Company's forces had destroyed a native settlement … . He had not much fear of the natives; their kraals had been destroyed and their granaries burnt for thirty miles round' (26–7). He and his comrades, he remembers, discuss 'the niggers they had shot or the kraals they had destroyed' (28–9). Halket comes from a 'little English village' (30), where he had not been much of a student. He wishes to make 'a great deal of money … [when] the Mashonas and Matabeles would have all their land taken away from them' (31–2). His attitude is strongly imperialist; he fantasises about wealth and power leading him to a knighthood.

Drowsing before the fire, Halket recalls two recent violent events. 'He saw the skull of an old Mashona blown off at the top, the hands still moving. He heard the loud cry of the native women and children as they turned the maxims on to the kraal; and then he heard the dynamite explode that blew up a cave. Then again he was working a maxim gun … What was going down before it [were] black men's heads' (36). In both these events, Halket was present. The text recurs to the events as it progresses.

The first event was the machine-gunning of black men 'six weeks' (49) earlier; 'two hundred black carcasses were lying in the sun' (95). In the other incident, described by the stranger, two women, one eighty years old, the other younger and pregnant, survive the brutal dynamiting of the cave (61). Halket initially demonstrates no regret for these actions, which only destroyed 'niggers'. The machine gun, named after its inventor Sir Hiram Maxim, is also, as Monsman notes, a 'maxim', 'the symbol of the phallocentric power of Cecil Rhodes and his pack of mercenaries … The stuttering of the maxim gun here embodies raw domination, the power of destruction, imperialism's parodic harvest' (113). Schreiner reveals the details of these two incidents, the machine-gunning of the men and the dynamiting of the cave of the women, in scattered allusions in the text, replicating Halket's mind as it intermittently reflects on his horrific violence.

In his early discussions with the stranger/Christ, Halket is relentlessly racist. 'I had two huts to myself, and a couple of nigger girls. It's better fun … having these black women than whites. The whites you've got to support, the niggers support you! And when you've done with them you can just get rid of them. I'm all for the nigger gals' (42). 'One girl was only fifteen; I got her cheap from a policeman who was living with her, and she wasn't much. But the other, by gad! I never saw another nigger like her … She'd got a nigger husband and two children' (43). The link between male dominant white sexuality and imperialistic economic exploitation is more than evident.

Halket got the women by exchanging liquor for them. At least one of the women is impregnated by Halket, but when they escape, he suspects the woman will abort the foetus: 'I expect they did away with it before it came; they've no hearts, these niggers; they'd think nothing of doing that with a white man's child' (47). He was present when 'three niggers' were hung as spies (50), although, remembering his kind mother, he doesn't like hangings, though 'some fellows think it's the best fun out to see the niggers kick' (51). As for Rhodes, '*he's* death on niggers … With Cecil, it's all right, you can do what you like with the niggers' (52–3). He dislikes blacks, furthermore, because 'these bloody niggers here are rebels because they are fighting against us' (56).

Schreiner is emphatic about this racism to indicate how far Halket must travel to change his beliefs. This alteration is accomplished by the stranger, who turns out to be Christ: he is a Jew, from Palestine, has wounds in his hands and feet, and has spent forty days and nights in the wilderness. Through a series of parables and the recounting of sermons by a little preacher (64–76), Halket is transformed. He tells Christ: 'I would like to be one of your men … I am tired of belonging to the Chartered Company' (80). Halket calls Christ his 'master' (86, 92). Christ sends him back to the ranks to be a prophet of racial tolerance.

When Halket arrives back at his camp, he discovers a black man, regarded by his Captain as a spy, bound to a stunted tree, clearly evoking Christ crucified. Monsman regards this tree as 'the reflection of an imperfect brotherhood of white and black... an incriminating Tree of Knowledge' (120). It might also, Monsman comments, signify 'the strangling control of the conniving Rhodes' (122). This captive black man turns out to be the husband of the woman Halket had made his mistress. A colonial soldier tells an Englishman that the reformed Halket objected to this viciousness: 'Oh, [Halket] started, how did we know this nigger was a spy at all … And then [Halket] broke out that, after all, these niggers were men fighting for their country … They're fighting for freedom … All men were brothers' (106–7). Halket's espousal of racial equality will doom him.

The Captain orders that Halket will shoot the black man the following day. With the exception of an observing 'Englishman' (119), the men are completely racist. 'What's one nigger more or less … They don't feel, these niggers, not as we should, you know … They've no feeling, these niggers' (110). Then men regard Halket as crazy since his time alone out on the kopje. Halket frees the black man. The Englishman finds Halket's dead body, with two wounds. The Captain has shot Halket for enabling the black man to escape. This execution causes the Englishman to state: 'There is no God in Mashonaland … There is no God' (121).

At the beginning of the tale, Halket is described as having 'lost his way' (26). However, this losing the way enables the transformation of his masculinity, as he loses his racist self and embraces tolerance. *Trooper Peter Halket* evokes a Platonic dialogue, and specifically the *Crito*, where the justice of Socrates' sentence is debated. Like Socrates, the captive black man's ankles bleed from the restraints: 'The riems had cut a little into his ankles; and a small flow of blood had made the ground below his feet dark' (117).

According to Monsman: 'The distance between Peter's seeing the natives first as totally other and then at the end as like himself has been the result of his new encounter with Christ's morality' (115). 'The murderous Peter now embodies a prototypical humanity' (122). While one reading of the novel certainly can establish this evolution, there is the disturbing reference by the Englishman at the conclusion that God no longer exists. In his transition to a masculine identity, Halket has been brutally transgressive, engaging in rape and murder. Is his alteration a one-off model, seeing that from one perspective God does not exist and therefore the model of Christ cannot be perpetuated?

At one point in the text, the image of Christ is associated with Halket's memory of his kind mother. 'I've been wondering ever since you came, who it was you reminded me of. It's my mother! You're not like her in the face, but when your eyes look at me it seems to me as if it was she looking at me' (48–9). Christ is an androgyne. Hence, Halket's identification with him is a radical reformation of masculinity. Halket rejects the violent brutal masculinity of his Captain, Jameson and Rhodes. He accepts this androgynous reconception of masculinity in Christ, an androgynous male Schreiner had already delineated in the figure of Gregory Rose in *The Story of an African Farm* (1883).

Halket's rite of passage in *Trooper Peter Halket* is radical. His extreme violence at the beginning of his passage through life represents a brutal imperialist conception. His end, which is his death, might only relate to him, yielding no paradigm. Two years later, the second Boer War began. That violent conflict appears to establish Peter Halket as disturbingly unique.

The texts examined in this chapter show various reactions to encountering, knowing and mapping 'other' cultures. According to Peck: 'When the hero is away from home he might be tempted by or yield to the way of life that he seems to be opposing; he might be seduced, or more commonly in the masculine world of the sea story, he will meet violence with violence' (13). In each of the texts examined in this chapter, violence and sometimes seduction elicit the mapping of the 'other' culture, whether this is with the narratives in Africa of Haggard, Schreiner and Kipling (*The Light That Failed*), or in Asia of Kipling (*The Man Who Would Be King*), or in the South Seas of Stevenson. Violence in these texts is inextricable from masculinities, be they English or foreign. In the next chapter, this violence will become part of stories of imperial adventures involving economic initiatives entailing invading.

Russell West, writing about Conrad, discusses masculinity and geography in terms which apply to many of the texts discussed in this chapter and the next:

> One effect of leaving behind civilised Europe for the perils of the colonies [is] a polarisation of men. Travel to the tropics either makes of them mythical heroes ... or ruins them, stripping them of their dignity and manly attributes ... . The geographical translation ... inevitably entails some sort of danger for men, a test of their mettle. Crossing borders puts masculinity under the spotlight, reinforcing it on the one hand, so as to produce narratives of masculine prowess ... or, conversely, weakening it ... . The disturbance of male identity implicit in leaving the civilised world [is] a *revelation* of a masculinity inherently unstable. (11, 14)

West notes an additional context, particularly relevant to Chapter 4 of this study: 'That men fail as a direct result of their entanglements with foreign women has a great deal to say about the nature of European masculinity itself' (13). Change in geography, a component of all the texts in this study, dictates that to cross borders is to transport, transfer, and/or transform masculine identities.

Chapter 3

Invading

During the late nineteenth century, adventure fiction was inextricably involved with imperialism. Many of the texts examined here offered representations of Englishmen exploring to assert white superiority or functioning in the colonies in economic contexts, these often being exploitative. Texts such as *King Solomon's Mines, Allan Quatermain* or *Typhoon* show whites as ostensibly superior to Asians or Africans. Economic exploitation figures in texts such as *Prester John* or *The Man Who Would Be King*. Because imperialism often involved war, some adventure texts, such as *The Light That Failed* or *Trooper Peter Halket of Mashonaland*, engage explicit military contexts. Other texts use foreign locales for existential encounters, as in *The Ebb-Tide* or *The Shadow-Line*. These cases of 'invading' for imperialising reasons deeply engage masculinity. Norman Vance has commented: 'The alliance of manliness with imperialism … represents an extension of the mid-Victorian combination of manliness and patriotism' (195).

Edward Said (1993) defines imperialism as 'the practice, the theory, and the attitudes of a dominating metropolitan center ruling a distant territory' (9). Said continues that colonialism, 'which is almost always a consequence of imperialism, is the implanting of settlements on distant territory' (9). Adventure fiction is especially important as part of the 'ideological formations' which sustain imperialism and colonialism, as Said argues: 'Neither imperialism nor colonialism is a simple act of accumulation and acquisition. Both are supported and perhaps even impelled by impressive ideological formations that include notions that certain territories and people *require* and beseech domination, as well as forms of knowledge affiliated with domination' (9). When a text such as *Heart of Darkness* or *Trooper Peter Halket of Mashonaland* critiques such ideology, it becomes part of that ideological discourse.

This emphasis on imperialising contexts in adventure texts is a legacy of such exhortations as John Ruskin's 'Inaugural Lecture' as Slade Professor at Oxford University, delivered in 1870. Ruskin informed his audience:

> There is a destiny now possible to us – the highest ever set before a nation to be accepted or refused. We are still undegenerate in race; a race mingled of the best northern blood. We are not yet dissolute in temper, but still have the firmness to govern, and the grace to obey … This is what [England] must do, or perish: she must found colonies as fast and as far as she is able, formed of her most energetic and worthiest men; – seizing every piece of fruitful waste ground she can set her foot on, and there teaching these her colonists that their chief virtue is to be

fidelity to their country, and that their first aim is to be to advance the power of
England by land and sea. (17–18)

Ruskin's assumptions of white superiority, moral prerogative and religious
authority in this lecture impelled imperialism a decade later. The declaration of
the Queen as 'Empress of India' in 1876 by the Royal Titles Act signalled a new
aggressive impetus in imperial efforts.

The great number of imperial military campaigns demonstrates the degree
to which war dominated Victorian consciousness. Some of these battles were
victories: Kandahar [1 September 1880, Second Afghan War], Ulundi [4 July 1879,
Zulu War] and Omdurman [2 September 1898, Egyptian Campaign]. Some were
narrow successes, such as Rorke's Drift [22 January 1879, Zulu War] or Tamai [13
March 1884, Sudanese War]. Others were dreadful defeats: Gundamuck [January
1842, First Afghan War], Isandhlwana [22 January 1879, Zulu War], Majuba Hill
[26–27 February 1881, First Boer War], El Teb [9 February 1884, Sudanese War],
and Khartoum [26 January 1885, Sudanese War]. Some adventure fiction, such as
The Four Feathers or *The Light That Failed*, stressed military conflicts.

Imperialism and war stressed masculinity, often, as with voyaging and initiation,
in homosocial spaces. According to Peter Stearns: 'For men, the nineteenth
century, effectively launched and ended by major wars, was a militant, indeed
military century. A greater percentage of European men served in the military,
even in peacetime, than ever before' (68). Imperialism and war reveal masculinity
as constantly under negotiation, as Peter Stearns continues: 'Masculinity is not
simply a position of power that puts men in comfortable positions of control … .
If we understand masculinity as a constant contradictory struggle rather than just
the privileged position within a power disequilibrium, we come closer to a full
definition of gender studies' (108). Kaja Silverman notes 'the centrality of the
discourse of war to the construction of conventional masculinity' (68) but observes
that death and dismemberment often confound such masculinity. Henry Newbolt
in his poems, such as 'Vitaï Lampada', 'The School at War', 'The Schoolfellow'
or 'Clifton Chapel', celebrated the valour elicited by warfare or commemorated
those who died fighting, but adventure fiction exhibits much greater complexity
about allegiances than Newbolt's poems suggest.

In the texts considered in this chapter, imperialism catalyses not only
confrontation with the colonised but also with the self. In 'An Outpost of Progress'
this encounter leads to suicide; in *Heart of Darkness* to limitless alienation; in *The
Four Feathers* to a survivor's recuperation of the self; in *Green Mansions* to self-
exile; in *Prester John* to economic success; and in *The Shadow-Line* to a recovered
sense of selfhood. Hence, the record of these texts verifies Stearns' emphasis on
masculinity as struggle and contestation.

John Peck suggests that a key component of sea stories is exploration for the
sake of economic success, embodied in the tale of Jason and the Argonauts. Jason
succeeds in his enterprise, returning home with the Golden Fleece. Peck writes:
'The story of Jason emphasizes opportunity, the potential for trade and the benefits

that can accrue from exploration' (13). Each of the texts examined in this chapter entails an explicit or implicit agenda of economic exploration and frequently exploitation. The settings may vary from Africa to Asia to South America, but the potential for being Jason underlies these narratives.

In 1872, Benjamin Disraeli urged his countrymen to embrace imperialism:

> The issue is not a mean one. It is whether you will be content to be a comfortable England, modeled and moulded upon Continental principles and meeting in due course an inevitable fate, or whether you will be a great country, an Imperial country, a country where your sons, when they rise, rise to paramount positions, and obtain not merely the esteem of their countrymen, but command the respect of the world. (cited in Dryden, 5)

The texts which follow reveal that this respect could be quite elusive.

Conrad: 'An Outpost of Progress' (1897)

Joseph Conrad's 'An Outpost of Progress', written rapidly in 1896, was serialised in 1897. An excoriating critique of imperialism, it appeared in the same year as the Diamond Jubilee of Queen Victoria. It is set at a European ivory trading station in the Congo 'on the banks of the Kasai River, a tributary of the Congo' (Boehmer 454). It concerns two traders, Kayerts, chief of the station, who is there to fund a dowry for his daughter Melie; and Carlier, his assistant, 'an ex-non-commissioned officer of cavalry' (84), a lout whose brother-in-law got rid of him by securing him an appointment to the Great Trading Company. (As A.T. Tolley notes [316] Conrad uses the names of two men he disliked from his African experiences.)

A black man, 'a Sierra Leone nigger, who maintained that his name was Henry Price' (83), yet is called Makola by the natives, is their assistant. He acts as their bookkeeper. He 'despised the two white men' (83). As Lothe argues, 'the narrator is not only removed from the characters in time and space; he is also capable of entering their minds and explaining what they themselves do not comprehend' (48). The 'real administrator' at the outpost is the black Makola, not the two white men (Lothe 54).

Makola trades the ten black station men for ivory, selling them into slavery. The Kayerts/Carlier station is three hundred miles from the nearest trading-post. In their intense isolation, Kayerts and Carlier quarrel over some sugar. Kayerts accidentally shoots Carlier. Hearing the return of the Managing Director's steamship, Kayerts commits suicide.

Graver recognises that 'An Outpost of Progress' has affinities with Kipling's *The Man Who Would Be King*: 'Both stories describe the breakdown of two European egoists who had hoped to get rich quickly in a primitive society, and both end with scenes of slaughter and crucifixion' (13). These resemblances confirm the use of the adventure paradigm for analysis of masculinities in imperialising contexts at the end of the century. Conrad is 'attempting to interrogate Western hegemony at the extreme limits of its confrontation with distant, alien cultures' (Hamner 175).

The Director thinks of Kayerts and Carlier as 'two imbeciles ... I always thought the station on this river useless, and they just fit the station!' (85). They are already, in other words, failures as white males. The omniscient narrator comments: 'They were two perfectly insignificant and incapable individuals' (85). In fact, they lack 'all independent thought, all initiative, all departure from routine' (87). According to Andrea White, the tale 'presents deliberate subversions of the generic hero in the figures of Kayerts and Carlier' (153). The men exhibit 'a moral vacuousness ... . Unlike the genre's adventure heroes before them, they will fail to emerge from the wilderness intact' (156–7). There can be no 'progress' as the ironic title would appear to advertise. Such a tale as this demonstrates that 'Conrad's fiction challenges notions of confident Empire and the assumptions of white superiority' (Dryden 8).

In a Darwinian universe, then, these men, ignorant and vulnerable, cannot survive. The narrator then reflects that most men are kept moral, confident and law-abiding only 'in the safety of their surroundings ... But the contact with pure unmitigated savagery, with primitive nature and primitive man, brings sudden and profound trouble into the heart ... To the negation of the habitual, which is safe, there is added the affirmation of the unusual, which is dangerous; a suggestion of things vague, uncontrollable, and repulsive, whose discomposing intrusion excites the imagination and tries the civilised nerves of the foolish and the wise alike' (86). 'No two beings could have been more unfitted for such a struggle ... They could only live on condition of being machines' (87) the narrator informs the reader. Daniel Schwarz (1980) declares that 'these men can only function within highly organised bureaucratic structures in which individuality has lost its meaning' (26).

At first, the two men get 'on well together because of their stupidity and laziness ... and in time they came to feel something resembling affection for one another' (88). When black, naked warriors come to trade, Kayerts and Carlier, with white racist superiority, regard them as 'brutes' or 'animals' or a 'herd' (89). It is 'a dog of a country' (89). This racism appears in such comments as the following: 'The nigger had had too much palm wine' (94). The two men 'understood nothing, cared for nothing' (90). Kayerts reads a home newspaper trumpeting imperialism 'in high-flown language. It spoke much of the rights and duties of civilisation, of the sacredness of the civilising work, and extolled the merits of those who went about bringing light, and faith and commerce to the dark places of the earth' (90).

Carlier raves that civilisation will eventually transform the station in a hundred years. Such boasting is absurd. The narrator labels the two men, ironically, 'the two pioneers of trade and progress' (9). Conrad exposes the insanity of the project and its executants by his mocking, as Fraser notes, of 'contemporary journalese' (157). The title of the tale is absurdly ironic. Lothe remarks that at this wretched outpost, 'civilization does *not* follow trade' (53).

One morning a knot of armed traders from the coast emerges from the jungle. During the night, Makola, 'a civilized nigger' (97), trades the station men for ivory. Kayerts is enraged at first: 'You have sold our men for these tusks!' Makola, whose alternative white name 'Price' now takes on a new significance, rebukes him: 'I did the best for you and the Company ... Why you shout so much? Look at this tusk' (98). Soon, Kayerts and Carlier are helping Makola to weigh and store the ivory for the advent of the Director.

The narrator demonstrates the hollow nature of Kayerts and Carlier when they mouth platitudes about the evil of slavery:

> They believed their words. Everybody shows a respectful deference to certain sounds that he and his fellows can make. But about feelings people really know nothing. We talk with indignation or enthusiasm; we talk about oppression, cruelty, crime, devotion, self-sacrifice, virtue, and we know nothing real beyond the words. Nobody knows what suffering or sacrifice mean – except, perhaps the victims of the mysterious purpose of these illusions. (99–100)

Schwarz (1980) regards the narrator as 'Conrad's self-assured surrogate ... [He] is the major figure of the tale' (26) who delivers a scathing indictment of Kayerts and Carlier. The men's empty rhetoric masks the ruthlessness of the project of exploiting the natives. 'They condone the exchange of their African labourers for ivory because they had taken little ivory and thus their profits were low' (Killam 93).

Conrad makes an ironic point about white 'civilising' in the narrative by showing three different kinds of blacks, as Tolley observes (318). The first group, represented by the local tribe and its chief Gobila, are 'natives in their original state', believing in dark gods and not understanding the white men. The second group, the armed traders from the coast, have learnt the worst of white commercialism, bearing arms and willing to engage in slave-trading. The third kind of black is represented by Makola/Price, who, the most 'civilised', is a bookkeeper and translator. He turns out to be ruthless in exchanging station hands, to be enslaved, for ivory. He has been totally corrupted by adopting the practices of white economic imperialist exploitation represented by the Company.

The weeks pass into months of waiting. We learn that the Director has decided to visit 'all the important stations on the main river. He thought that the useless station, and the useless men, could wait' (103).

Carlier becomes argumentative and then insubordinate. Carlier advocates 'the necessity of exterminating all the niggers before the country could be made habitable' (102). This remark anticipates the famous outburst of Kurtz in *Heart of Darkness* two years later, 'Exterminate all the brutes!' Carlier's irritation reaches a climax when he demands sugar, rationed by Kayerts, for his coffee. Faced with this insolent assistant, Kayerts realises: 'It seemed to Kayerts that he had never seen that man before. Who was he? He knew nothing about him. What was he capable of?' (103). Carlier then strips the veneer off 'civilisation' and 'progress': 'You are a hypocrite. You are a slave-dealer. I am a slave-dealer' (104).

Tearing through their residence, the two men collide and Kayerts' revolver accidentally discharges, killing Carlier. Claude Maisonnat argues that Kayerts shoots Carlier not because Carlier is a rebel but because he reveals Kayerts' otherness, that he is 'a failed colonizer, a failed pilgrim of progress, a slave-dealer and eventually a murderer' (122). Before dying, Carlier demolishes the ideology of the penis/phallus equation. The killing is especially grim because it turns out Carlier was unarmed. Schwarz (1980) believes that 'the outpost of progress quickly becomes an outpost of savagery. Rather than being agents of change, these men are changed: like Kurtz [in *Heart of Darkness*], they gradually regress to savagery' (27).

This transgression leads to brutal self-confrontation, as Kayerts ponders: 'He had plumbed in one short afternoon the depths of horror and despair, and now found repose in the conviction that life had no more secrets for him: neither had death! He sat by the corpse thinking; thinking very actively, thinking very new thoughts. He seemed to have broken loose from himself altogether. His old thoughts, convictions … appeared in their true light at last!' (107). The role-playing of the white male script is terminated.

Kayerts and Carlier become each other's double: 'Then he tried to imagine himself dead, and Carlier sitting in his chair watching him … He became not at all sure who was dead and who was alive … By a clever and timely effort of mind he saved himself just in time from becoming Carlier' (108). Fog and mist appear, reflecting this moral hell of unstable identities, 'the mist white and deadly, immaculate and poisonous' (108). When Kayerts 'breaks loose from himself', his self-confrontation is both individual and cultural indictment: white manhood has no might and is not right.

Kayerts then hears the sharp sounds of the steamer's whistle as the Director reaches the station. The narrator describes these whistles 'like the yells of some exasperated and ruthless creature' (108). Conrad had first written 'fabulous' for 'ruthless' in this sentence. He decided to make this reference fearsome rather than fantastic. 'Progress was calling to Kayerts from the river. Progress and civilisation and all the virtues' (108). But Kayerts also realises that with the corpse he will be judged 'so that justice could be done' (109).

Instead, Kayerts hangs himself from the cross marking the grave of the predecessor who had been chief, who had died of a fever. When the Director finds him, Kayerts 'was putting out a swollen tongue at his Managing Director' (110). The ideology of 'progress' cannot mask economic exploitation. Its penalty is self-destruction. Mark Wollaeger regards this suicide at the call of 'progress' in the whistle of the steamship as excessively ironic, with Conrad too under the influence of Guy de Maupassant (25). While one might agree, it is also the case that Kayerts has reached a true dead-end: die now by his own hand or die later after being condemned a murderer.

According to Lawrence Graver, 'An Outpost of Progress' is 'a classic revelation of bourgeois stupidity and pretension' (11). It is a brutal exposure of the fallacy of the penis/phallus equation. Despite being mediocre, Kayerts and Carlier assumed their superiority over any black on the African continent. To these two men, black masculinity would be an oxymoron. However, in a text saturated with irony, black males, some treacherous, reveal that whites do not own manhood any more than they own ivory.

Conrad's tales of imperialising draw from the adventure tradition. Millman, for example, contends: 'Joseph Conrad had much to learn from a novelist like Haggard, who wrote unperturbedly of dark journeys and hollow men. Conrad responded to Haggard's model and transformed it into art. The popular male novel supplied Conrad with the conventions he needed in order to examine horrors very alien indeed to what one finds in the drawing rooms of the great Victorian novels' (80).

Conrad: *Heart of Darkness* (1899)

Joseph Conrad published *Heart of Darkness* in *Blackwood's Magazine* from February to April in 1899. Influenced by the adventure narratives of Haggard and Stevenson, Conrad deploys the adventure genre to include not only explorations of territory but also explorations of the self. In Marlow's words, the exploration offers 'the chance to find yourself' (31), a journey into the self, as Schwarz notes 'a spiritual voyage of self-discovery' (64). Marlow elaborates: '[The steamboat] had given me a chance to come out a bit – to find out what I could do. No, I don't like work. I had rather laze about and think of all the fine things that can be done. I don't like work – no man does – but I like what is in the work – the chance to find yourself. Your own reality – for yourself – not for others – what no other man can ever know' (31). The search is for a masculine identity which may apply only to the man who seeks it, not to others: 'what no other man can ever know'.

But adventure presents dangerous psychological hazards, as Marlow recognises when he encounters the Russian 'harlequin' figure at Kurtz's compound, 'the absolutely pure, uncalculating, unpractical spirit of adventure' (55). Conrad 'recasts the tale of imperial adventure in terms of a psychological quest' (Simmons 91). For G.D. Killam, the 'voyage Marlow describes is a spiritual voyage of self-discovery' (86). Hence, within the text, Marlow both deploys the discourse of adventure and in the figure of the Russian reveals the absurd chaos of adventure. Conrad as author brilliantly exploits the adventure genre while simultaneously condemning its ruthless content. Hunter describes adventure in this novella as 'institutionalized adventurism … imperialism in the Belgian Congo' (133) as the focus of the text. However, Conrad convincingly represents both 'institutionalized' and personal adventurism in *Heart of Darkness*. The Russian harlequin figure stands for the madness of the imperialism of the Congo project, as M.M. Mahood argues, because his 'patchwork clothing [is] reminiscent of the multi-coloured map [of Africa] in the Brussels office' (22).

The title of the novel has biblical overtones. It echoes Psalms 74:20: 'For the dark places of the earth are full of habitations of cruelty.' It echoes as well the titles of Henry Stanley's *In Darkest Africa* (1890), his account of his final African adventure of 1887–89, and William Booth's *In Darkest England and the Way Out* (1890). Of particular interest, as Hugon claims, is that Stanley's mission was to 'rescue a German explorer' (90). Marlow's pursuit of Kurtz is a failed rescue.

Heart of Darkness illustrates the validity of Lee Horsley's ideas about Conrad and the adventure genre:

> Conrad's novels are often included in studies of adventure tales because his rewritings of adventure motifs, though they are in many respects sardonic reversals of the genre, are at the same time powerful expressions of the virtue inherent in heroic assertion. His narratives of loss and ironic disillusionment depart from popular versions of the adventure form … The most difficult trials the Conrad hero faces are, of course, moral and psychological rather than physical: he is a carrier of strongly positive values, but, instead of facing the straightforward choices confronting a Haggard adventurer, he must cope with unsettling self-doubt, anxiety and uncertainty. (26)

The novella concerns the excursion of Charles Marlow as captain of a steamship to a remote trading outpost in the Congo Free State, though Conrad does not name it to give the narrative greater universality. There he encounters Kurtz, who as an ivory trader manages the Inner Station upriver. Killam advises that 'ivory was the most readily transportable form of wealth' (88). Kurtz is deteriorated beyond Marlow's belief. He dies as Marlow attempts to bring him back to 'civilisation'. The story is multivalent in its significance: a critique of imperialism, an epic journey, an exposure of the id, an analysis of the consequences of 'going native', a representation of existential hell, and an investigation of coruscating alienation.

It is also an analysis of masculinity, where a received template of penis = phallus is proved false, delusive and self-destructive. Marlow goes up the Congo expecting to meet 'a remarkable man' (61). He instead confronts a male wreck in the figure of Kurtz. This disjunction is evident in Kurtz's name. Although it derives from the German for 'small' or 'short', Kurtz turns out to be rather tall. Nothing is contiguous; it is all contingent.

Another hint of this incongruity is the fact that Marlow captains a steamship, not a sailing ship. Steamships do not allow for the same reliance on the male community as do mercurial sailing ships, subject to the vagaries of nature. So, both the name and the equipment signal fragility in the masculine system.

There are three central males in *Heart of Darkness*: the first unnamed narrator; the second narrator, Marlow; and Kurtz, the idealist who goes native and self-destructs in the Congo. The heart of *Heart of Darkness* is the interrogation of a male paradigm, the transmission of Marlow's novel to the first narrator, and the corrosive effect of men on each other and their inability to establish a male identity in an existential hell.

Conrad signals his focus on masculinity by his narrative structure, which involves a first or outside male narrator, who listens to Marlow as second narrator recount the story of his venture/adventure to an all-male microcosmic community aboard the yawl *Nellie*, which is anchored in the River Thames at sunset. These men are The Lawyer, The Accountant, The Director of Companies, Marlow, and the unnamed first narrator. Each of the first three represents the legal and economic nexus which drives imperialism. The men are waiting for the ebb tide, that is, the outgoing tide, the path to imperialising. On the other hand, the ebb symbolically marks a decline or fall. At the conclusion, the men have 'lost the first of the ebb' (76). There is no movement but rather an ominous stasis, a suspension, a question. Furthermore, it could well be that Conrad is paying homage to the motif of decline and failure in Stevenson's *The Ebb-Tide* of 1894.

According to Joseph Bristow, 'this redoubling of first-person narrative perspectives was, to say the least, uncommon in fiction in the late 1890s' (156). The result is that this tale of masculinities epitomises in its narrative structure the crisis of masculinity observed by Elaine Showalter. Bristow continues: 'Given that the story is set within a complex narrative frame (with one first-person narrator enclosing another), the putative authenticity of the inset narrator, Marlow, is constantly drawn into question' (156). Marlow is immediately set apart: '[He] sat cross-legged right aft, leaning against the mizzen-mast. He had sunken cheeks, a yellow complexion, a straight back, an ascetic aspect, and with his arms dropped, the palms of hands outwards, resembled an idol' (7). The first narrator labels him a 'wanderer' and 'not typical' (9).

The waterway suggests epical journey, the exploration of the interior of the self and the rite of passage which will be recounted. In 'Youth' Conrad had depicted Marlow as a young man first experiencing the East. That tale ends with optimism. Here, Marlow, now older, narrates a tale of far more challenging aspect. The first narrator has already thought deeply about masculinity. He recalls the names of Sir Francis Drake and Sir John Franklin, 'knights-errant of the sea' preoccupied with 'conquests' (8), who embodied 'the dreams of men, the seed of commonwealths, the germs of empires' (8). Masculinity and economics are inextricable. The first narrator accepts these models of masculinity at the outset of the narrative.

Marlow utters the first words of dialogue 'And this also ... has been one of the dark places of the earth' (9). Not only Africa is dark. The legacy of its distribution at the Berlin Conference of 1885, conquest and exploitation, has reached the Thames. There is no separation between the metropolis and the colony. Yes, the story is supposedly about a Belgian territory, but in effect it is about all such territories colonised by Europeans. It entails 'the fascination of the abomination' (10): white men cannot stay away.

Marlow is a circumspect apologist for this attitude. He believes that imperial ventures are redeemed by the coloniser's 'efficiency' and the loftiness of the 'idea' behind such ventures, that is, bringing light, civilisation, improvement, sanitation, money, and development to those conquered and appropriated territories. He admits that 'taking it away from those who have a different complexion ... is not a pretty thing when you look into it too much' (10). Yet the 'idea' exists 'at the back of it ... something you can set up, and bow down before, and offer a sacrifice to' (10).

Marlow recounts that when he was younger, he believed in these exploits. He was taken with 'the glories of exploration' and he determined that he would go to these 'blank spaces', including the North Pole (11). When he goes to the Company's offices in the unnamed Brussels, Marlow is pleased to see a map of Africa with 'a vast amount of red – good to see at any time because one knows that some real work is done in there' (13). That is, it is good to see the civilising mission being accomplished in territory governed and owned by Britain. There is a bit of purple (German). Marlow is destined for the yellow (Belgian) of the Congo. This mapping underscores the European desire for power over the 'other' in Africa.

Marlow early in his narration alludes to the Romans coming to Britain in centuries past: 'Imagine [the commander of a trireme] here – the very end of the world ... nothing but Thames water to drink' (9–10). Conrad uses this recollection to give his novella the substructure of epic, especially as practised by Vergil in the *Aeneid*. Lillian Feder has enumerated many of these epical elements in *Heart of Darkness*, including: the journey as a descent into hell (following *Aeneid* Book VI), the voyage of the hero, the querying of imperial power, the pervasive gloom, the rites and rituals necessary for passage (Marlow confronting the two women in the office as Aeneas must pass the Cumaean Sibyl), the occupants of hell (the natives like shades), the loss of a helmsman (Aeneas loses Palinurus, Marlow his helmsman), the combat with indigenous populations, the Congo River similar to Acheron and Styx, and the catalogue of ships (in Conrad the *Erebus* and *Terror*).

These epic elements all contribute to the investigation of masculinity even as in Vergil the focus is on the transformation of masculinities, as Aeneas alters from a Trojan to a Roman man. Feder contends that *Heart of Darkness* 'has three levels of meaning: on one level it is the story of a man's adventures; on another, of his discovery of certain political and social injustices; and on a third, it is a study of his initiation into the mysteries of his own mind' (290). These same levels Feder finds in the *Aeneid*.

This epical focus compels the reader to recognise the parallels between Vergil's and Conrad's intentions: to chronicle the alteration of masculine identity. As Aeneas must alter from Trojan to Roman, Marlow changes from the narrator of 'Youth' to the narrator of *Heart of Darkness*. As in Vergil, in Conrad this alteration is accompanied by confronting 'other' masculinities: Turnus in the *Aeneid*, the blacks in *Heart of Darkness*.

On his journey, Marlow encounters the enslaved blacks. In language racist now and disturbing then, Marlow and others describe blacks as 'grotesque' (17) men, 'savage/s' (19, 38, 51, 60), 'nigger/s' (12, 26, 28, 65), 'poor devil' (38). Kurtz will designate them 'brutes' (51). Chinua Achebe's essay 'An Image of Africa', and the rebuttals which followed, chronicle this racism. Yet, Marlow's encounters with blacks are also encounters with 'other/othered' masculinities. There are dancing, rituals and killings. Some are 'fine fellows – cannibals – in their place' (36).

Marlow even asserts: 'No they were not inhuman. Well, you know that was the worst of it – this suspicion of their not being inhuman … What thrilled you was just the thought of their humanity – like yours – the thought of your remote kinship with this wild and passionate uproar … Yet, it was ugly enough, but if you were man enough you would admit to yourself that there was in you just the faintest trace of a response to the terrible frankness of that noise' (37–8). At this point in the narrative, Marlow does not realise that this alternative black masculinity is the one which mesmerised Kurtz who, 'going native', goes to extremes.

Finally meeting the actual Kurtz, his potential alter ego, Marlow eventually realises that Kurtz 'had taken a high seat amongst the devils of the land' (49). His behaviour has become megalomaniacal, murderous and cannibalistic. 'His nerves went wrong' (50), Marlow states in a sublime understatement. 'Many powers of darkness claimed him for their own' (49). Marlow recognises that 'all Europe contributed to the making of Kurtz' (50) by its imperial ambition. The results are devastating. Kurtz in a report wishes to 'Exterminate all the brutes' (51), the native population. Marlow observes: 'The wilderness had found him out early, and had taken on him a terrible vengeance for the fantastic invasion. I think it had whispered to him things about himself which he did not know' (57).

The violence underlying the imperial venture is especially devastating in *Heart of Darkness*, because, as Jerome Thale has demonstrated, there is, in addition to the epical palimpsest, a second form of narrative precedent in the novella, 'the story as a grail quest' (159). Thale details some of these elements: 'As in the grail quest there is the search for some object, and those who find and can see the grail receive an illumination. Marlow, the central figure, is like a knight seeking the grail, and his journey even to the end follows the archetype … . And in the journey itself there are the usual tests and obstacles of a quest' (159–60).

If the pervasive 'gloom' (8) alludes to the *Aeneid*, the grail motif adds another tier of meaning to the text in Thale's view: 'The grail motif is of course connected with the profuse – and somewhat heavy-handed – light-darkness symbolism' (160). The idealism associated with the grail motif, however, is demolished by the revelation of violence in Kurtz's beliefs and practices. Marlow is compelled, in an awful illumination, to realise his own potential to become a violent man. Thale observes: 'Kurtz is the grail at the end of Marlow's quest' (166).

Kurtz's example proves a turning point for Marlow, as Kurtz and Marlow elide. Marlow declares: 'If anybody had ever struggled with a soul I am the man … His soul was mad. Being alone in the wilderness, it had looked within itself and, by Heavens I tell you, it had gone mad. I had … to go through the ordeal of looking into it myself' (65). 'It was written I should be loyal to the nightmare of my choice' (64). Kurtz's death-bed final words, 'The horror! The horror!' (68), perhaps reveal his recognition of his own degradation. They may also indict the imperial project, or they might not. They might more generally apply to Africa itself. Patrick Brantlinger suggests a final interpretation of these words, a nihilistic philosophy: 'Kurtz's heroism consists in staring into an abyss of nihilism so total that the issues of imperialism and racism pale into insignificance' (270).

These words certainly characterise the existential situation, the void of existence, in which Kurtz and Marlow find themselves, as Marlow summarises: 'Destiny … is … that mysterious arrangement of merciless logic for a futile purpose. The most you can hope from it is some knowledge of yourself … It is his extremity that I seem to have lived through' (69). Marlow concludes that Kurtz achieved some kind of 'victory' (70) at his end. "That is why I have remained loyal to Kurtz to the last' (70).

Marlow preserves this masculine bond with Kurtz when he tells Kurtz's fiancée, the Intended, that Kurtz's dying words were her name. This is a lie, but Marlow remains true to his allegiance to Kurtz, even though earlier in the text he claims to abhor lies. But he also sustains a male code of 'protecting' or 'shielding' women from the truth, of concealing reality to reinforce male prerogatives of superiority and control: 'I could not tell her. It would have been too dark – too dark altogether' (76). This reference to the Intended specifically ignores Marlow's generalising misogynist rant earlier in the text when he noted: 'It's queer how out of touch with truth women are!' (16).

Marlow would have lied, presumably, to any woman. Jefferson Hunter defines this lying procedure as Marlow's 'furnishing her with a conventional adventure story rather than the truth' (141), that is, the lie perpetuates a romantic conception of undying love. Marlow conceals the truth via a conventional adventure ploy in a text which subverts the conventions of adventure fiction.

Marlow reinforces the male code and male solidarity. John Batchelor notes Marlow's 'maleness, his generous virility' (42) and argues that 'Conrad is a *macho* novelist in this story as in much of his other work' (43). To Marlow, the women are unimportant: 'They – the women I mean – are out of it – should be out of it' (49). Batchelor concludes: 'As Marlow here implies, the important relationships are between men' (43). While Conrad does deal brilliantly with women in works such as *Chance*, *Victory*, or 'Amy Foster', all-male universes prevail in this novella or narratives such as 'Youth' or *Typhoon*. Batchelor even argues that the width of the gun barrels in *Heart of Darkness* changed from ten inches in the manuscript to eight inches in *Blackwood*'s to six inches in the final text (44), revealing anxiety about sexual potency but also stressing the phallus as masculine signifier. In many of his texts, Millman observes, 'Conrad's world is indisputedly [sic] a male world … If given the choice, Conrad's heroes would just as soon dwell in an altogether womanless world' (80–81).

But the first narrator grasps the futility of this attempt to prop up a failed male code and to rehearse a tired male script: 'I raised my head. The offing was barred by a black bank of clouds, and the tranquil waterway leading to the uttermost ends of the earth flowed sombre under an overcast sky – seemed to lead into the heart of an immense darkness' (76). Marlow has revelations which he attempts to camouflage, although he is honest with the male microcosm on the yacht about the lie.

The novella concludes as it began with the male homosocial group on board the boat. Conrad's title *Heart of Darkness* has been construed by many critics. Some of these significances would include: the Congo, Africa itself, Africans themselves, the evil within mankind, the processes of colonisation and existential alienation. These are all legitimate. However, the constant references to 'darkness' in the novella assume one additional connotation from the setting, that the male rite of passage is a dense journey through psychological darknesses.

The unnamed first narrator senses the destruction of the dominant fiction of masculinity. He acknowledges the destabilisation of masculinity which, to him as a man, is darkness. This unnamed narrator makes a point of asserting: 'The others might have been asleep, but I was awake' (30). It is he who interprets Marlow's narrative as a text about the fallibility of received constructions of masculinity and the imperial idea, a revelation Marlow himself avoids and evades. At the beginning of the novella, the first narrator had noted: 'We were fated, before the ebb began to run, to hear about one of Marlow's inconclusive experiences' (11). However, if Marlow avoids, evades and lies (as in his false account to the Intended), the first narrator at the end does none of these.

The first narrator's initial adulation of heroic masculine models such as Drake and Franklin is proved impossible to sustain. Transformed, he now knows what 'no other man can ever know'. The text then becomes this first narrator's message that he has rejected these paradigms. For what others, we do not know. Conrad himself experienced 'a disillusionment that bordered on nihilism' (Mahood 18) about his own Congo experiences. In this text, darkness is pervasive at its conclusion.

Mason: *The Four Feathers* (1902)

A.E.W. Mason's *The Four Feathers* was one of the great Edwardian best-sellers. 'In its first forty years of publication, it sold close to a million copies in England alone' (Hoppenstand xxiii). It has been filmed at least six times. The novel recounts the rite of passage of Harry Feversham, whose ancestors and whose father have had distinguished military careers. On the eve when his regiment is to ship out to the Sudan, Harry resigns his commission because of his engagement to Ethne Eustace. In reality, he is also confronted 'not by fear, but by the fear of fear – and finding, when it seems too late, that his is that finest bravery of all which can endure danger and pain in spite of the vivid imagination which urges him to run away' (Green 89).

Three brother-officers, Willoughby, Trench and Castleton, send him three white feathers as a sign of his cowardice. His fiancée Ethne Eustace adds a fourth feather from her fan. In the course of the novel, Harry redeems himself by daring exploits in Egypt and the Sudan during the wars begun in 1882.

Mason's knowledge of the Sudan was based on experiences during his travels beginning in January 1901 to the region. He went to Khartoum and Omdurman. At Omdurman, he saw the infamous prison the House of Stone, which figures in the novel. Mason spoke with the Austrian Slatin Pasha (Rudolph Slatin), who had been imprisoned in the House of Stone and who had been shown Gordon's decapitated head. He also heard the story of Sir Reginald Wingate, Director of Intelligence, who had managed to escape the prison with the aid of a Beja tribesman who dropped four matches as a sign of the plans for his escape (Green 87–8). Mason also deploys this episode in his novel.

The effect of sexuality in Harry's decision was clarified by Mason in a letter to Alexander Korda during the making of the 1939 film. Having noted Harry's fear of fear, Mason continued: 'That fear is immensely increased when, at the moment of going upon active service, he becomes engaged to a girl whom he loves; for if he proves himself a coward, he will bring shame upon her too. He resigns his commission and receives from three of his brother officers three white feathers. That is the first motive' (in Green 91). The interconnection between the heterosexual love Harry bears Ethne and the homosocial identification with the regiment is stark.

If Feversham's love for Ethne is part of the first motive, her reaction to seeing the first three feathers compels the second motive, according to Mason: 'The second [motive] is that the girl to whom he is engaged, being young and ignorant, adds a fourth feather to the other three – and it is this fourth feather, which inspires in Harry Feversham a resolve to make his three brother officers take their feathers back in the hope that in the end the girl will take hers back too. These two motives are the mainsprings which have kept this story alive' (in Green 91).

Harry Feversham's close friend from Oxford, Jack Durrance, who is eventually blinded by sunstroke, recalls engagements and battles of the Egyptian and Sudanese wars very specifically, a device by which Mason grounds his adventure text *The Four Feathers* in historical actuality (60). These include: Kassasin, 28 August 1882, during the Egyptian Revolution; Tamai 31 March 1884 during the Sudan Campaign; Tel-el-Kebir 13 September 1882, a victory over the Egyptians; Tokar, relieved by British forces in March 1884; the death of Charles Gordon at Khartoum 26 January 1885; and the breach of Sir John McNeill's zariba 20 March 1885. This same series of engagements is quoted again in the final paragraph of the novel.

Mason's purpose is to evoke the militaristic masculinity of men who have no doubts about the imperial mission or their own masculine identity. These references frame the story of Harry Feversham's rite of passage, appearing in Chapter 7 before he emerges in disguise in Egypt and then in the concluding chapter and paragraph, when Feversham has married Ethne and been 'redeemed' and restored by his heroic deeds in the Sudan. Mason's purpose is not merely to deal with exciting events in foreign territories, therefore. In addition, he interrogates masculine codes and the penis/phallus equation through Harry Feversham's tortured evolution of a masculine identity. Howarth notes how unusual is Mason's hero: 'Mason might have been expected in the climate of the time in which he wrote … to create heroes who sauntered through all dangers unflinchingly. In fact the hero of *The Four Feathers*, Harry Feversham, is a man with doubts, particularly doubts about his own courage in the face of physical danger' (126).

The origins of this tormented masculine identity are stressed in the first chapter of the text. On 15 June 1869, his birthday, aged fourteen, young Harry is allowed to dine with his father and his father's friends at one of their 'Crimean Nights' at Broad Place, where the veterans of the Crimea meet and rehash their deeds in that war. The first to arrive is Lieutenant Sutch, who limps across the hall from an old wound. Poor and disregarded, Sutch had once loved General Feversham's wife and Harry's mother, Muriel Graham, a woman of imagination.

Sutch still wonders 'that for some mysterious reason she had married this man so much older than herself, and so unlike to her in character. Personal courage and an indomitable self-confidence were the chief, indeed the only qualities which sprang to light in General Feversham' (6). Sutch is 'interested to see whether the lad [Harry] took after his mother or his father – that was all' (7).

Hearing these tales, Harry experiences them as if they were 'happening actually at that moment and within the walls of that room. His dark eyes – the eyes of his mother – turned with each story from speaker to speaker … It seemed to Sutch the lad must actually hear the drone of bullets in the air … . For this, after all, was Muriel Graham's boy' (7). Sutch recognises the 'queer sickly smile' (8) on Harry's face, one he had seen in the faces of soldiers going into an engagement to face death. However, no one except Sutch looks at Harry. When his father allows him to remain for an additional hour, claiming it would not make any difference, Harry looks at his father 'with a curious steady gaze', to Sutch's mind silently asking the question of his father 'Are you blind?' (9).

Harry then listens 'with all his soul' (9) to the stories told by his father and a surgeon-general of two men who buckled under the stress of battle. Lord Wilmington, who ought to have had 'a voice to bid him play the man, if only in remembrance of his fathers' (9), refused to take a message over the battlefield. In the end, he 'slunk back to London … and blew his brains out' (10). The other coward is a surgeon who committed suicide in India during a war. Harry's father believes Harry cannot understand these two cases of cowardice: 'Harry understand! … How should he? He's a Feversham' (11). He again looks at his father as if to ask 'Are you blind?' Harry thinks 'never had he heard an untruth so demonstrably untrue' (11).

Having his mother's imagination, Harry can envision himself in the stories of Lord Wilmington and the suicidal surgeon. Left to the 'peril of his thoughts' (11), Harry walks through the portrait gallery filled with images of his military ancestors with 'the steel-blue inexpressive eyes; men of courage and resolution, no doubt, but without subtleties, or nerves, or that burdensome gift of imagination … . men rather stupid, all of them, in a word, first-class fighting men, but not one of them a first-class soldier' (12). Todd Willy (1982) observes: 'Even so popular a fictionalist of English imperialism as A.E.W. Mason in his best selling *The Four*

Feathers of 1901, had begun by then to portray suicides by practicing imperialists as complex and unhappy psychological tragedies rather than as exemplary and exquisitely satisfying deeds' (196).

Sutch recognises that Harry is 'set apart ... no less unmistakably in mind as in feature from his father and his father's fathers' (13). Alone, Harry 'saw that the face of the broken officer and the face of the dead surgeon were one; and that one face, the face of Harry Feversham' (14). The father's paradigm of masculinity is not transmitted to the son. The second chapter occurs thirteen years later, in June 1882, when Feversham is twenty-seven. He is shown in his flat with three fellow officers. Captain Trench is small and balding; Willoughby is a man 'of invincible stupidity ... born stubborn as well as stupid [with] crippled thoughts' (15–16). The third man is Harry's closest friend, Durrance: 'Both men were securely conscious of [their friendship]; they estimated it at its true strong value ... Both men were grateful for it, as for a rare and undeserved gift' (17).

The link between Feversham and Durrance at the moment is Ethne Eustace. Harry has announced his engagement to her, and it was Durrance who introduced them. Harry determines to go to Ethne's home in Donegal, Ireland. He receives a telegram which disturbs him. It is notification that the regiment is to ship out to Egypt and the Sudan. The cause for this telegram is the fundamentalist revolt being led by two men in the Sudan: Mohammed Ahmed, who has declared himself the Mahdi, who aims to expel foreigners from the land; and Arabi Pasha, who wants to wrest Egypt from foreign control. Harry and his friends are sent to address these 'rebellions' and 'revolts.'

Durrance receives orders to accompany General Gerald Graham to Egypt. Durrance declares he would be content to die in active service, 'to die decently was worth a good many years of life' (24). Durrance recognises he has always been restless. In contrast, Harry has resigned his commission. He sees Durrance off. Feversham goes to Ireland to visit Ethne, who blames herself for keeping Harry away from the war, depriving him of a chance for distinction.

While with Ethne, a package arrives with three white feathers from Willoughby, Castleton and Trench, who regard his resignation as an act of cowardice. Harry admits to Ethne they were justly sent. He reflects: 'He had no thought of denial or evasion. He was only aware that the dreadful thing for so many years dreadfully anticipated had at last befallen him. He was known for a coward ... He stood as he had once stood before the portraits of his fathers, mutely accepting condemnation' (34).

Harry's resignation reflects his childhood experiences:

> 'All my life I have been afraid that some day I should play the coward, and from the very first I knew that I was destined for the army. I kept my fear to myself. There was no one to whom I could tell it. My mother was dead, and my father – ... My father ... could never have understood. I know him. When danger came his way it found him ready, but he did not foresee. That was my trouble always. I foresaw ... I foresaw the possibility of cowardice.' (36)

He tells Ethne about the disgraced officer and surgeon he had heard of at the Crimean Night and the oppression of the portraits in the gallery. Getting the telegram, 'I took the chance it seemed to offer, and resigned' (37). He tells Ethne she had nothing to do with it, but in fact he feared to disgrace her as well as his father. She breaks off the engagement and gives him a fourth feather from her fan. 'She wished to make an end' (38).

These deathless chapters are not melodramatic. Rather, Feversham is oppressed by out-dated male paradigms which he cannot accept. It is not a question of fear, which everyone else seems to think. Instead, he despises the military and his father. If he fears anything, it is killing, killing following a masculine model he loathes. Rarely has a novelist so caught the brutal oppression of masculine modelling on its inheritors. It is an act of Oedipal revolt, but it is a rejection of all the cultural fathers who transmit these paradigms. To any observer it is cowardice; to Harry it is principle. Sutch, discussing the situation with Feversham, remarks: 'Brute courage? Women make a god of it' (48), conditioned by the culture to equate brute courage with masculinity. Harry reiterates he could not bring disgrace on Ethne. Sutch recognises that 'the uncomprehending father and the relentless dead men on the walls had done the harm. There had been no one in whom the boy could confide' (49).

Feversham shows Sutch the four feathers: 'To you they are the symbols of my disgrace. To me they are much more. They are my opportunities for retrieving it … What if I could compel Trench, Castleton, and Willoughby to take back from me, each in his turn, the feather he sent? … To be in readiness for that moment is from now my career. All three are in Egypt. I leave for Egypt to-morrow' (51). Brian Street observes: 'It is a commonly held view in the writings of the period that under-developed countries provide scope for character training and physical toughness' (38).

In the text, three years pass to May 1885. According to Street, Mason 'describes rapid movement from England to the Sudan, thus making the foreign land less permanently alien, and he shows how what happens thousands of miles away may affect individual lives at home. Thus distant countries are brought within the world view of those who have never seen them' (26).

Harry Feversham, disguised as a Greek, surfaces in Suakin, where he hears about lost letters of Charles Gordon, killed earlier that year at Khartoum. 'After three years of waiting one of Harry Feversham's opportunities had come' (61). Harry contacts Abou Fatma, Gordon's body servant, for assistance in locating these letters in the town of Berber, demolished and rebuilt. Harry travels disguised as a Dervish with a patched jibbah 'over his stained skin, his hair frizzed on the crown of his head' (80). He knows if he is caught he will be mutilated. Nevertheless, in this first enterprise, he travels as the enemy, as indeed he is. He has rejected group militarism in favour of making his own decisions about his masculine identity, choosing time and place. Durrance reads that some man (Feversham) has succeeded in recovering letters exchanged between Gordon and the Mahdi. These have been turned over to Willoughby.

This balance of power and honour begins to change after Harry's first daring deed. He has shown the brute Willoughby what genuine heroism is. Two years later, staggered by Harry's deed, Willoughby returns the white feather to Ethne, saying he has 'withdraw[n] my accusation' (118). In Chapter 15 Willoughby recounts to Ethne Harry's retrieving of the letters in Berber. He is forced to admit that 'Feversham felt no fear' (126). This heroism is set in a context of 'religious fanaticism' which 'foments political revolt' (Street 141).

Then it is learned that Jack Durrance has been blinded by sunstroke when he ran into the desert to retrieve his helmet. The optic nerve is destroyed. Having in the interval told Ethne he loved her, Durrance now realises he cannot inflict his damaged body on her. Durrance presents an aspect frightening to the Victorian world of the narrative and the Edwardian world of its publication. The damaged male body indisputably shows the falsity of the penis/phallus equation. The echoes of Dick Heldar's body damaged by blindness in Kipling's 1891 *The Light That Failed* are evident.

Durrance recognises this result. He is a man 'trained to vigour and activity … a man, too, who came to the wild, uncitied places of the world with the joy of one who comes into an inheritance' (98). 'I have lived out of doors and hard, and that's the only sort of life that suits me' (100). Hence, a second masculine template, after that of Feversham Sr, proves inadequate. Durrance's white body is wrecked; Harry Feversham's body is preserved by being disguised as a Greek or an Arab. '[Durrance] was by birth the inheritor of the other places, and he had lost his heritage' (106). 'Durrance saw ever so much more clearly now that he was blind' (111). Back in England, however, Durrance 'dreamed himself back into his inheritance' of the East (168).

Piecing the background of Harry's resignation together, Durrance finds that this decision, 'when every manly quality he possessed should have been at its strongest and truest, remained for Durrance, and, indeed, was always to remain, an inexplicable problem' (188). Durrance recognises that Harry is engaged in retrieving his honour on his own terms. Durrance tells Sutch: 'The shock of the disgrace is, after all, his opportunity … It's his opportunity to know himself at last. Up to the moment of disgrace his life has all been a sham and illusion; the man he believed himself to be, he never was, and now at the last he knows it' (203). There can be few more clear statements about masculinity entailing the performance of false scripts. The 'sham' in Feversham's name indicates the false masculine scripts forced upon him.

By August 1887, Harry deliberately gets himself captured as a spy to be taken to Omdurman, where Trench is imprisoned in the House of Stone, which Mason had seen in 1901. 'He had his allotted part to play' (172). Disguised, he assumes a role, testing another masculine model. The House of Stone is a 'foul and pestilent hovel [where] the prisoners were packed, screaming and fighting' (221). Colonel Trench, imprisoned for three years, thinks 'that the imagination of God could devise no worse hell than the House of Stone on an August night in Omdurman'(223).

When Trench and Feversham meet in the prison, Trench is filled with remorse about the incident of the feathers, which he had initiated five years ago. After seven months of this hellhole, during work detail a box of matches is dropped, indicating their imminent escape. Finally, Abou Fatma escorts them from the area to freedom. When Trench reaches out his hand to thank Harry, Harry refuses to take it, claiming 'I served myself from first to last' (258). When Trench takes back his feather, Feversham shakes his hand. For Feversham, 'his six years of hard probation had come this morning to an end' (260).

Mason makes this rite of passage explicit: 'There had been a timidity in his manner in those days, a peculiar diffidence, a continual expectation of other men's contempt, which had gone from him. He was now quietly self-possessed; not arrogant; on the other hand, not diffident. He had put himself to a long, hard test; and he knew that he had not failed' (264). Eventually, Feversham marries Ethne.

Durrance returns to the East, very much imitating Dick Heldar in Kipling's *The Light That Failed* in arriving at Port Said. As his name suggests, Durrance endures his blindness and his restlessness. Like Feversham, Durrance is an innovation in adventure fiction. Howarth notes that 'there is a delicacy in Durrance which is not far below the surface' (128). This delicacy sets him apart from the conventional Newbolt Man of courage and dauntlessness: 'Perhaps Newbolt Man does emerge here to some extent, but it is in a rare, three-dimensional form. It was not the least of Mason's distinctions that in *The Four Feathers* he was able to achieve characterization in depth' (128).

Yet Feversham at the conclusion is writing a history of the Sudan War. Mason surely intends that this history will involve 'his-story' as a vantage point, that is, that its martial history will also be a new version of masculinity. Robert Giddings argues that the film versions of the novels provide 'models of maleness' (215), but the novel itself provides these. As Gary Hoppenstand (2001) suggests, the text reveals that 'battlefield bravery is stupid bravery' (xix).

Margery Fisher claims about the narratology of *The Four Feathers*:

> A first-person narrative would have been disastrous with such a subject. Harry Feversham's doubts and perplexities, his quiet tenacity and endurance, could only have seemed mawkish and artificial if these and other changes in him had been made the matter of soliloquy. As it is, the narrative ranges freely from one important character to another so that the central dilemma is seen first from one point of view and then from another. (190)

By this strategy, Mason allows the discourse about masculinity to be multi-faceted.

The novel is about masculinity and how it is learned in various dimensions: 1. Harry cannot accept his father's version of masculinity, with complete alienation on both sides; 2. Sutch is an alternative father; 3. Durrance proposes the model of male friendship; 4. Males constantly test each other; 5. Women misjudge masculinities; 6. The wounded male body is threatening. In *The Four*

Feathers, these inflections elevate the text to a high rank in the use of adventure fiction to interrogate masculinities. Jefferson Hunter rightly compares this study of cowardice with that in Conrad's *Lord Jim* published two years before: 'A confessional scene between Feversham and an older, wiser lieutenant [Sutch] mimics the long colloquy between Marlow and Jim, but afterward the novels part company, as Feversham goes forth to the wars and in the course of time redeems himself, returning the feathers one by one' (132).

To Sutch, Harry 'saw the underside of it' while on his mission (282). But revision will be difficult. This conflict in *The Four Feathers* between models of English maleness is part of a tradition recognised by J.S. Bratton: 'The tension between Old England, its beauty and cultivated fertility, its security, its beloved associations with family or sweetheart left behind, and the new lands of promise, which are exciting but also hard and masculine, dangerously unfamiliar, lawless and lonely, is a deep structural polarity in the fiction of the second half of the nineteenth century' (87). At the conclusion, Feversham Sr proposes to start the Crimean Nights again. The text is filled with details about Oedipal scenarios: Durrance's blindness, Sutch's limp leg, Harry's rejection of his father's brand of masculinity. It will be left to Harry, as a 'New Man', to confute the failed masculinities of the past by advocating that every man must individually carve his masculine identity.

Hudson: *Green Mansions* (1904)

W.H. Hudson's *Green Mansions* was published in 1904 after its author, born in Argentina, had come to England in 1874. Hudson became one of the great naturalist writers in English. A success when published, the novel was reissued in 1916 with a Foreword by John Galsworthy, who defended the author vigorously. 'Of all living authors – now that Tolstoi has gone – I could least dispense with W.H. Hudson' (v). Of the novel, Galsworthy declared: 'In form and spirit the book is unique' (viii).

Galsworthy aligned Hudson with the emerging ecological/environmentalist attitude: 'All Hudson's books breathe this spirit of revolt against our new enslavement by towns and machinery' (ix). In its focus on the purity of its Venezuelan 'green mansions' and their destruction, Hudson has written a story where environment, pristine at first, is destroyed for reasons of revenge, superstition and racial fear. In this focus on environmentalist attitudes it anticipates Henry De Vere Stacpoole's *The Blue Lagoon* four years later. Fairchild (357) and Tomalin (118) both note that Hudson had no firsthand knowledge of the Venezuelan forest, yet, as Tomalin remarks this 'wild paradise is painted, fern by fern, leaf by leaf, shadow on shadow, through the eyes of the hero Abel' (118).

Hudson's narrative concerns Abel Guevez de Argensola, a young man who flees a failed revolution in Caracas and eventually comes to the hills of Parahuari in the Venezuelan province of Guayana. There, a political exile, he intermittently lives with a tribe of Indians, whose chief is Runi. 'Mr Abel' at first befriends Runi's nephew Kua-kó, who will later become his enemy. Abel invades a forest, across the savannah, which he will designate as the 'green mansions' (41): 'I dropped on my knees and kissed the stony ground, then casting up my eyes, thanked the Author of my being for the gift of that wild forest, those green mansions, where I had found so great a happiness!' (41).

In the green mansions, Abel meets an old man, Nuflo, and his putative granddaughter Rima (a contraction of Riolama, named after her birthplace), an other-worldly young woman of seventeen whose main mode of communication is through a bird-like language, in Carlos Baker's (1946) words 'a nature-goddess' (252). Ian Duncan in his Introduction to the novel notes Rima's descent from mythological women like Philomela and Procne (xiii). Baker (1946), Hoxie Fairchild and Rudolph Landry argue that Rima and incidents in *Green Mansions* derive from multiple sources, including Rousseau, Shelley and Wordsworth. At the end of the narrative, Rima is destroyed by fire by the hostile Indians, who regard her as the daughter of the monster Didi. Abel leaves the destroyed 'green mansions'. John T. Frederick summarises his character: 'He is vain, crafty, curious, brave, vengeful, capable of deep love and murderous hate' (53).

Abel narrates his tale to an external narrator, a British civil servant who lives in Georgetown, British Guiana, around 1887, where Abel, though 'an alien, a Venezuelan' (3) has been accepted by the populace. The external narrator comments: 'This feeling brought us together, and made us two – the nervous olive-skinned Hispano-American of the tropics and the phlegmatic blue-eyed Saxon of the cold north – one in spirit and more than brothers' (5).

This use of the frame narrative, as David Miller has noted (92), incorporates elements of confessing, witnessing and narrating. These processes are crucial to the text of *Green Mansions* because the text concerns the 'intersecting of the paradisial with a symbolism of "darkness" or evil' (92). Miller regards this 'darkness' as 'ontological before it is moral' (89) in the novel. That is, Abel's life describes an inextricable evil at the core of existence. Miller regards both the Indians and Abel as part of this universal evil: 'The Indians who kill [Rima] are motivated by a sort of blind malignity, while Abel enters into a different kind of evil, a moral insanity' (91). The frame narrative evokes the similar device in *Heart of Darkness*, and the focus on existential evil, as Miller notes, 'is just as central to Conrad as it is to Hudson' (105).

Abel is the quintessential self- and politically-exiled adventurer. In the first three paragraphs of his narration, he uses the word 'adventure/s' three times, each with a different inflection: first in reference to his sojourn 'among the savages' (7); second in reference to political revolt (7); and third in reference to his failed revolt and his outcast status (8).

Abel is soon revealed as a classic imperialist. He describes his fascination with the 'countless unmapped rivers' of the jungle (8). He talks with men who 'had travelled in the interior to trade with the savages' (10). He ostensibly wishes to 'collect information' (10). These are all characteristic of whites who conquer indigenes by mapping, trade and ordering. Abel wishes to achieve fame by writing a journal of his experiences. He also wishes to find gold to fund another insurgency movement which would avenge his father, killed by traitors in the revolution. Both of these objectives fail: the journal is destroyed by rain; there is no gold.

Abel's racism is evident from his early comments about Indians: 'They were a set of hollow bronze statues that looked at me, but I knew that the living animals inside of them were tickled at my singing' (21). 'I listened to them as to stories invented to amuse a child' (25). Embraced by Runi, Abel thinks: 'It was the first and last embrace I ever suffered from a naked male savage, and although this did not seem a time for fastidious feelings, to be hugged to his sweltering body was an unpleasant experience' (19).

Although the Indians of Guayana initially accept Abel, he regards them as his inferiors: '[The Indians] were savages, with ways that were not mine; and however friendly they might be towards one of a superior race, there was always in their relations with him a low cunning, prompted partly by suspicion, underlying their words and actions. For the white man to put himself mentally on their level is not more impossible than for these aborigines to be perfectly open, as children are, towards the white' (36–7).

When Kua-kó offers his sister in marriage to Abel, Abel reflects: 'This was that young sister of his, whose name was Oalava, a maid of about sixteen, shy and silent and mild-eyed, rather lean and dirty; not ugly, nor yet prepossessing. And this copper-coloured little drab of the wilderness he proposed to bestow in marriage on me!' (47). He is suspicious of her brother: 'It would, of course, have been a great mistake to suppose that my savage was offering me a blow-pipe and a marketable virgin sister from purely disinterested motives' (48). Later he comments about Oalava, the Indian maiden, 'whose physical charms needed no description since they had never been concealed' (91). Being female and brown is degradation enough in Abel's eyes; being naked as well underscores her low status of civilisation.

Rima's foster-grandfather Nuflo, a white man who had saved her mother, shares Abel's racist sentiments: '[The Indians] are infidels, and therefore the good Christian must only hate them. They are thieves … murderers' (61). He conceives a diabolical method of destroying the Indians: 'Why should they remain living so near us as to be a constant danger when a pestilence of small-pox or some other fever might easily be sent to kill them off?' (130). For Hudson, genocide is potentially a realistic if horrific alternative in the world of *Green Mansions*.

Abel decides to penetrate the forest, the 'green mansions' alone, when the Indians will not go there for fear of the daughter of the Didi, a river-spirit. He is drawn by a mysterious voice, a bird-song/language, he hears in the forest. He believes 'that in this wild and solitary retreat some tremendous adventure was about to befall me' (33). Finally he sees the 'bird-girl', who is petite, 'not above four feet six or seven inches in height, in figure slim, with delicately shaped little hands and feet' (44). On a subsequent visit, Abel is threatened by a snake. The girl, Rima, fearing Abel will kill the coral snake, approaches him as an avenging 'wasp' (51), revealing her own ferocious allegiance to animals and her opposition to invaders.

Rima's body is analysed by Abel as it would be for a collector: 'It was her colour that struck me most, which indeed made her differ from all other human beings. The colour of the skin would be almost impossible to describe … . It was not white, but alabastrian, semi-pellucid, showing an underlying rose-colour' (53). The hair is marked by 'its extreme fineness and glossiness' (54). 'She was a wild, solitary girl of the woods, and did not understand the language of the country in which I had addressed her' (54). Abel attempts to embrace her as a conqueror: 'I took her arm in my hand, moving at the same time a little nearer to her … . I slipped my arm around her slender body to detain her' (55). At that moment, avenging Nature and the environment and Rima, the snake bites Abel.

Rima takes Abel to Nuflo's hut, where he is nursed back to health. However, Rima's demeanour in the domestic locale is markedly different from her freedom in the forest: 'The face also showed the same delicate lines, but of the brilliant animation and variable colour and expression there appeared no trace. Gazing at her countenance, as she stood there silent, shy, and spiritless before me, the image of her brighter self came vividly to my mind, and I could not recover from the astonishment I felt at such a contrast' (63). That is, once in the domestic space assigned to women by patriarchy and under the gaze of two men, Nuflo and Abel, Rima loses all her proto-feminist independence. Abel soon acknowledges her 'double personality' (65) of retiring servant to men in a domestic space and an angry independent fearless woman in the forest of the 'green mansions'.

When Abel commands Rima to look into his eyes, she is reluctant, for she knows the male gaze is dominating: 'There is a pool in the wood, and I look down and see myself there. That is better. Just as large as I am – not small and black like a small, small fly' as she would appear in his eye (73).

In these passages, Rima speaks in the Spanish she learned from colonising priests. When she exclaims to Abel 'And you ask me to talk to you!' (77), Abel ascribes this to 'sudden petulance' (77), when clearly she recognises Spanish as the language of the conqueror. Miller notes 'the stilted quality of some of Rima's dialogue' (155), which could be ascribed to the fact that Spanish is not her first language.

From his position of superiority, Abel never makes any effort to learn Rima's language, even though he is sensitive to poetry and music. '[Her] mysterious speech died down to a lisping sound' (72). 'When I listen to Rima's voice, talking in a language I cannot understand, I hear the wind whispering in the leaves' (77). 'She had always spoken [Spanish] somewhat reluctantly' (94). 'Not one [person] would understand the sweet language you speak' (104). When Abel declares he understands Spanish, Rima replies: 'Oh, that is not speaking … . To you that do not understand, what can I say? … You are you, and I am I; why is it – do you know?' (119). Later she remarks of their conversations in Spanish: 'I can tell you, but it will not be telling you' (156).

Abel finally realises 'what my inability to understand her secret language meant to her … And so long as she could not commune with me in that better language, which reflected her mind, there would not be that perfect union of soul she so passionately desired' (155). Despite his love for Rima, however, Abel never learns her language, retaining his white imperialist superiority.

Other methods Abel uses to maintain white superiority are naming and mapping. He describes to Rima the Cordilleras and the great mountains Cotopaxi and Chimborazo (102–3). Abel admits, like Marlow in *Heart of Darkness*, that he always had an attraction to maps: 'Since boyhood I had taken a very peculiar interest in that vast and almost unexplored territory we possess south of the Orinoco, with its countless unmapped rivers and trackless forests; and in its savage inhabitants, with their ancient customs and character, unadulterated by contact with Europeans. To visit this primitive wilderness had been a cherished dream' (8).

Abel has a strong discussion about mapping with Rima. When she asks about the border of Guayana and desires to go there, Abel responds: 'It is all a savage wilderness, almost unknown to men – a blank on the map.' She rejoins: 'The map? – speak no word that I do not understand … If it is a blank … then you know of nothing to stop us' (105). Rima will commune with her mother, in the earth, about Abel: 'He marked out and named all the countries of the world … He named the mountains of Riolama' (112).

However, Rima has her revenge. When Abel leaves the forest after Rima's destruction, the traumatised Abel records: 'When I try to retrace my route on the map there occurs a break here – a space on the chart where names of rivers and mountains call up no image to my mind' (198). The space of desire and domination he 'mapped' with Rima has become psychologically desolate.

Abel's dominant male stance is demonstrated in his attitude to women in general. Of a past relationship in Caracas, he comments:

> And the woman I had loved, and who perhaps loved me in return – I could forget her too. A daughter of civilisation and of that artificial life, she could never experience such feelings as these and return to nature as I was doing. For women, though within narrow limits more plastic than men, are yet without that larger adaptiveness which can take us back to the sources of life, which they have left eternally behind. (88)

Later Abel is 'thinking, thinking, thinking now of the woman I had once loved, far away in Venezuela, waiting and weeping and sick with hope deferred' (92). This tactic of abandoning a woman who loves recurs in Conrad's 'A Smile of Fortune' several years later.

Wounding women by his absence, Abel tries the same sadistic strategy with Rima. 'I did not consider that I had sufficiently punished Rima for her treatment of me. She would be anxious for my safety, perhaps even looking for me everywhere in the wood. It was not much to make her suffer one day after she had made me miserable for three' (83–4). He revels in his power over Rima: 'The poor girl in her petition had unwittingly revealed to me the power I possessed, and it was a pleasing experience to exercise it' (113). In his hallucinations of the spirit of Rima after her death, Abel recognises his abuse: 'It was, indeed, Rima returned to tell me that I that loved her had been more cruel to her than her cruelest enemies; for they had but tortured and destroyed her body with fire, while I had cast this shadow on her soul – this sorrow transcending all sorrows, darker than death, immitigable, eternal' (194).

Abel's first erotic (kissing) encounter with Rima occurs when she is unconscious and he fears she is dying as he holds her in his arms. 'At last, bending lower down to feel her breath, the beauty and sweetness of those lips could no longer be resisted, and I touched them with mine. Having tasted their sweetness and fragrance, it was impossible to keep from touching them again and again. She was not conscious – how could she be and not shrink from my caress?' (151–2). Again, he takes advantage of her illness, her passivity allowing him to be completely dominant.

When Abel returns to the forest after the journey to Riolama, he discovers that the Indian tribe, while he is away, under Runi and Kua-kó has burned Rima in a tree, at the top of which she fled to escape. Other Indians had seen Rima as a woman on her fatal excursion to Riolama and had informed Runi that she was not a spirit. As Carlos Baker notes in his Introduction to the novel (1962), 'the long taboo is accordingly destroyed' (xx). Runi's tribe can now invade her sanctuary and kill her. Nuflo is likewise dead.

In revenge, Abel involves Runi's rival Managa and his tribe to kill all Runi's tribe after Abel himself has killed Kua-kó. He fancies that Kua-kó thinks he can beat 'any white man' (176), but Abel kills him: '[I] drove my weapon to the hilt in his prostrate form ... I experienced a feeling of savage joy' (176). Miller asserts that this act of revenge underscores 'Abel's blood-lust, degradation and insanity' (104). According to Duncan, 'the massacre of Runi's clan will be merely the next stage in a long historical process of extermination – long enough, and fateful enough, to be rationalized as a process of natural history' (xxi). This is a pattern in adventure narrative of having the indigenous young woman die: Ustane in Haggard's *She* or Foulata in Haggard's *King Solomon's Mines* come to mind.

Echoing Job, Abel rejects God after his killing of Kua-kó: 'I cursed the Author of my being and called on Him to take back the abhorred gift of life ... . I would hate Him' (177, 179). Degenerating after acknowledging his murderous self, Abel has lost his identity: 'I, no longer I, in a universe where *she* was not, and God was not' (191). Chapters 21 and 22 are startling, as they record a male's total mental collapse and nervous disintegration – in the form of a personal confession. On arriving in Georgetown, 'in rags, half-starved and penniless' (201), Abel decides: 'That is my philosophy still: prayers, austerities, good works – they avail nothing, and there is no intercession, and outside of the soul there is no forgiveness in heaven or earth for sin ... In that way I have walked ... self-forgiven and self-absolved' (202).

Abel's invasion of the the province of Guayana, impelled by personal, political, economic and erotic motives, displays the highly inflected nature of imperialism. Duncan notices 'that Abel's crime bears the historical burden of European perfidy and violence in the Americas' (xxi). Although at the beginning of his narrative he glances at 'the great American tragedy' (10) perpetrated by whites in the Americas, he does nothing but conform to its worst practices. Baker (1962) observes: 'By his very entry into her forest, Abel sets in motion the events that must destroy the girl he loves' (xx).

In this process, Hudson suggests, the power of the matriarchy is destroyed by Abel's patriarchal agendas. Throughout the text, Rima calls on her mother, whom she regards as living pantheistically in the earth. She tells Abel: 'Her body is in the earth and turned to dust' (70). Rima cries 'Mother – mother – mother!' (71). Rima later demands to 'go and seek for my mother's people' (104). As has been noticed, Abel, in patriarchal fashion, responds: 'We cannot go there. It is all a savage wilderness, almost unknown to men – a blank on the map' (105). The patriarchy regards the location where mother and daughter originated as of no significance, repudiating the claims of the matriarchy.

When Rima discovers Nuflo's treachery in keeping her ignorant of her birthplace, she calls on her mother to avenge her against the patriarchy: 'O, mother, mother, listen to me, to Rima, your beloved child … All these years I have been wickedly deceived by grandfather – Nuflo – the old man that found you' (110). Both Nuflo and Abel represent the oppressive patriarchy that has effectively destroyed the matriarchate. It is a modification of the myth of Demeter searching for her lost daughter Persephone. In *Green Mansions* it is the daughter, searching for the protecting mother, who is destroyed.

In mapping, naming, loving and killing, Abel manages to destroy the paradise of his green mansions. It is significant, however, that it is a British civil servant who transmits the text to the public, endorsing the colonial project. Although the protagonist is named Abel, he recognises the Cain within himself and becomes Ashasuerus/The Wandering Jew (201) at the conclusion, an outcast adventurer and intruder. He has recorded his self-destruction in this confession, identifying with his nemesis: 'For were we not alone together in this dreadful solitude, I and the serpent, eaters of the dust, singled out and cursed above all cattle?' (193), with its evocation of the Book of Genesis. Abel's narrative, nevertheless, sustains a white male paradigm which records one more stage in a process of extermination in South America. Mapping geography and mapping desire are conjoined in *Green Mansions*.

Buchan: *Prester John* (1910)

In September 1901, at the age of twenty-six, John Buchan sailed to South Africa as Private Secretary to Alfred, Lord Milner, the British High Commissioner for South Africa. He returned to England in August 1903. In the intervening years,

Buchan gathered information and mastered the terrain which would figure in one of his greatest novels, *Prester John*, published in August 1910. Andrew Lownie notes it was his 'first real success as a novelist' (111). It is one of the finest novels in the English adventure tradition and one of the most disturbing in terms of race and imperialism. As Stephen Gray observes, 1910 was 'the year of Union between the four provinces of South Africa, the year of consolidation of territory under the British flag' (127).

As a *Bildungsroman*, *Prester John* is different from other stories of initiation by Conrad, for instance, where the sea plays so important a part. Its ancestry is more in the land adventures of writers like Haggard in *Allen Quatermain* and *King Solomon's Mines* and Stevenson in *Kidnapped*. The story is narrated by 19-year-old David Crawfurd, who goes to the Transvaal and encounters a native uprising by Zulus led by the Reverend John Laputa, who invokes the legend of Prester (or Priest, Presbyter) John, a Christian king of Ethiopia (Abyssinia) during the fifteenth century (71), to reinforce his rebellion against whites in the Transvaal.

Crawfurd witnesses 'the connection between native religion and nationalism' (Street 141) as a colonist. The history of *Prester John* is recounted to Crawfurd by the British secret-service agent James Arcoll in Chapter 7 of the novel. Gray labels Laputa's revolt as 'one last suicidal bid to drive the English back into the sea from which they came' (128). This Ethiopianism of black revolt had begun on the continent in the 1870s, and it is significant, as Street stresses, that when Buchan arrived in South Africa in 1901, 'the "Ethiopianism" scare was at its height and there were many examples of secessionist churches led by black ministers' (143). Brian Street adds that *Prester John* 'perpetuates only the alarmist fears of the settlers in South Africa in the early 1900s' (145). For Lee Horsley Laputa represents 'a great primitive force which threatens to undermine Western colonialism' (73), a pan-African repudiation of white domination.

After many escapades, and in alliance with James Arcoll, a British secret agent, the revolt is subdued. Following a final confrontation with Crawfurd, Laputa hurls himself into a void wearing the famous necklet of rubies worn by the Queen of Sheba, which had symbolised his authority. Crawfurd returns to Scotland enriched by massive wealth in diamonds and gold. Craig Smith contends: '*Prester John* celebrates a frontier mythology, the freedom of the (white, British, male) individual, that is at once imperial fantasy, nostalgia, propaganda, and education' (176), 'a virtual handbook for the budding colonial' (177).

The novel begins when David Crawfurd is thirteen at Kirkcaple in Scotland. Crawfurd and two friends, Archie Leslie and Tam Dyke, rebelling against attending church, wander along the shore at night. Tam tells his friends that a black man had preached at his church: 'A nigger … a great black chap' (9), noting that the preacher has said 'a black man was as good as a white man in the sight of God and he had forecast a day when the negroes would have something to teach the British in the way of civilization' (9). Tam advises: 'If I were the minister I wouldn't let a nigger into the pulpit' (9).

Minutes later, the boys see the black minister, 'who had shed his clerical garments' by the shore 'practising some strange magic alone by the sea. I had no doubt it was the black art … . Here we were … a few yards from a savage with a knife' (13). Street recognises that throughout *Prester John* Crawfurd 'follows [Laputa's] progress and takes great interest in his different roles, each symbolised by a change of clothing … . Laputa's rejection of Western civilisation, then, is partly intellectual, and his changes of clothing are conscious and political' (117–18).

Crawfurd describes Laputa thus: '[His face] was black, black as ebony, but it was different from the ordinary negro. There were no thick lips and flat nostrils; rather … the nose was high-bridged, and the lines of the mouth sharp and firm. But it was distorted into an expression of such a devilish fury and amazement that my heart became like water' (14). These remarks by Tam Dyke and Crawfurd establish a racialised matrix that endures throughout the text. Tam finishes off this litany by calling the minister 'the big black brute' (16), associating blacks with animals rather than humans, a touch away from King Kong.

When Crawfurd's father dies, he leaves university. As in *Treasure Island*, the death of the father frees the son to go on adventures to seek his fortune and identity. It also involves finding a new father, in this case, albeit fleetingly, even a black man. Crawfurd is asked to go as an assistant storekeeper at Blaauwildebeesstefontein in the far north of the Transvaal. Thus, from the beginning, Crawfurd's mission is associated with materialism, economics and exploitation. On the ship to the colony, Crawfurd meets Mr Wardlaw from Aberdeen, sailing to be a schoolmaster. He tells Crawfurd: 'It sounds like a place for adventure, Mr Crawfurd. You'll exploit the pockets of the black men and I'll see what I can do with their minds' (21). On the ship, Crawfurd also sees Henriques, a Portuguese who will be associated with Laputa, but only to exploit the rebel. Also on the ship is Laputa, who preaches to the passengers: 'Some of us were hurt in our pride in being made the target of a black man's oratory' (23).

Crawfurd, however, is also fascinated, praising the man's figure and voice. Again racism permeates his commentary about Laputa: 'He had none of the squat and preposterous negro lineaments, but a hawk nose like an Arab, dark flashing eyes, and a cruel and resolute mouth. He was as black as my hat' (23). At this point, Buchan introduces the tropes of detection, mystery and clues, pervasive throughout the text, which will render young Crawfurd an amateur Sherlock Holmes. 'I was on the trace of some mystery of which I alone had the clue' (23) he declares, since he remembers the man from the encounter back in Scotland.

Crawfurd remarks on his 'assiduous toil of the amateur detective' (24). The Durban manager of the firm, Colles, tells Crawfurd: 'I want you to keep your eyes skinned, and even write privately to me if you want any help … You're sure to get on the track of something' (26). Crawfurd encounters his pal Tam Dyke, who again labels Laputa a 'black brute' (27). Crawfurd records: 'My mind being full of mysteries, … I felt that at last I had got to foreign parts and a new world' (27).

From Aitken, the Scottish landing-agent for a company on the Rand, Crawfurd hears about I.D.B., 'illicit diamond broking' (28). By such trading, Laputa and his associates, including Henriques, hope to finance the revolt. This information only spurs Crawfurd's detective instincts: 'I was going to a place with a secret, and I meant to find it out' (29). Without calling Africa the 'Dark Continent' here, the novel turns the continent into a place where the white man must decipher the geography, resources and inhabitants. Tam Dyke wants to be included if there is going to be 'fun' or a 'row' (30), classic terms of adventure espionage.

Arriving at the store, headed by Peter Japp, Crawfurd's economic sense is on the alert immediately, as he realises there could be 'a profitable export in tobacco' (34). He also recognises that he is being subject to 'espionage' (37) and is constantly under surveillance, 'perpetual spying on myself' (39). He discovers that Japp is involved with I.D.P. Ever enterprising, Crawfurd builds a store at Umvelos, 'taking my courage in both hands' (45).

Crawfurd begins to explore surrounding territory, complete with rituals such as swimming naked in a nearby lake, a male purification rite very marked in Childers' 1903 *The Riddle of the Sands*. This bathing recalls Crawfurd's bathing with his friends as a lad back in Scotland. Also, though 'hemmed in by barbarism' (58), 'I had grown no beard, having a great dislike to needless hair' (59). Beardless, Crawfurd confronts the bearded barbarians. The words 'clue' and 'evidence' permeate the text as Crawfurd pursues his civilising 'detective work' (64).

The schoolmaster Wardlaw tells Crawfurd he is fearful of another black rising should a leader like Shaka (ruled 1816–28) arise again. Blacks' 'have only just ceased being a warrior race' (53). They might 'organize a crusade against the white man' (54). Wardlaw fears the Ethiopianism ('Africa for the Africans' 73) movement emanating from the African continent and the United States. The motto 'Africa for the Africans' as Lownie notes, 'had been coined by a missionary-educated African, Joseph Booth, in 1897' (112). Crawfurd becomes wary and tries to gather 'evidence' (56) about potential black revolt.

One of the most unusual features of Buchan's novel is the number of times when Crawfurd records his fears, dropping his masculine imperialist masquerade. 'I was really scared, more out of a sense of impotence than from dread of actual danger. I was in a fog of uncertainty' (57). 'I was horribly afraid, not only of unknown death, but of my impotence to play any manly part' (61). 'The sense of impotence is stifling … I was in the second stage of panic, which is next door to collapse. I tried to cry, but could only raise a squeak like a bat … Things were very bad with me' (108–9). 'There were tears of weakness running down my cheeks' (162). 'I was in a torment of impotence' (163). After Laputa's death, 'I wanted to sit down and cry' (182). These are remarkable admissions. While they serve to increase Crawfurd's eventual heroism as imperialist and adventurer, they also demonstrate that Buchan can question the penis/phallus equation and interrogate the masculine script. Smith argues that 'the white man's fear and hatred of the black man equals a fear of impotence' (189). Buchan sees masculinity as destabilised.

Crawfurd is jolted back to his mission by James Arcoll, the British spy agent in the Transvaal, who confirms that the illicit diamond trade is funding the Zulu uprising, with the Portuguese Henriques as 'the chief agent' (69) of this trade. Arcoll informs Crawfurd of the Matabele wars of 1893 and 1896 as examples of dangerous insurgency. Arcoll admits that '[The Zulus] have had plenty of grievances, and we are no nearer understanding them than our fathers were. But they are scattered and divided. We have driven great wedges of white settlement into their territory' (73). Tim Couzens (43–4) suggests that other events, such as the Ndebele-Shona Rising in Rhodesia 1896–97 and the Bambata Rebellion in Natal of 1906, are evoked in the text. Gray suggests the latter is 'the recent historical precedent' (128) for the revolt.

Arcoll tells Crawfurd that Laputa presents himself to his followers as the 'incarnated spirit of Prester John' (75), asserting he possesses the ruby necklet, the 'Great snake', that belonged to his legendary predecessor. Arcoll declares: '[Laputa is] an educated man, but he is also a Kaffir. He can see the first stage of a thing, and maybe the second, but no more. That is the native mind. If it was not like that our chance would be the worse' (76). Crawfurd is revived when Arcoll labels him 'plucky': 'Since I'm in this thing, I may as well see it out' (78). 'Fear had gone from the establishment, now that we knew the worst' (79). Crawfurd can label this challenge 'fun' and claims: "I was strung up to the gambler's pitch of adventure' (80).

Yet, Crawfurd remains conflicted when he confronts Laputa: 'I explained that I was fresh from England, and believed in equal rights for all men, white or coloured. God forgive me, but I think I said I hoped to see the day when Africa would belong once more to its rightful masters' (84). Like Jim Hawkins in the apple barrel in *Treasure Island*, Crawfurd in the cellar of his store overhears Laputa and Henriques plotting. Here spying and mercantilism are one.

In Chapter 10, 'I Go Treasure-Hunting', the economic motives become explicit in this imperialist assertion:

> There was hid treasure ahead of me – a great necklace of rubies … This cave of the Rooirand was the headquarters of the rising, and there must be stored their funds – diamonds, and the gold they had been bartered for. I believe that every man has deep in his soul a passion for treasure-hunting … I lusted for that treasure of jewels and gold. Once I had been high-minded, and thought of my duty to my country, but in that night ride I fear that what I thought of was my duty to enrich David Crawfurd … . Behind my thoughts was one master-feeling, that Providence had given me my chance and I must make the most of it. At any rate, I was a fatalist in creed … I looked on the last months as a clear course which had been mapped out for me … I believed I saw the workings of Omnipotence. (95)

Crawfurd has moved from impotence to a feeling of omnipotence under God. Rarely in imperial fiction has a passage been so blatant and so conflicted. Though

Crawfurd has some anxiety about being greedy, economics triumphs, as does the exploitative ethos of imperialism. Then in a classic move, justifying imperialism, this greed turns out to be sanctioned by God. That Crawfurd be wealthy is a divine mandate. Even he recognises: 'Perhaps the Calvinism of my father's preaching had unconsciously taken grip of my soul' (95).

Breaking into the cave of the Rooirand, Crawfurd witnesses a religious ritual ceremony of purification inaugurating Laputa as the leader of the revolt. 'Laputa stripped off his leopard skin till he stood stark, a noble form of a man' (100). He sees the Great Snake ruby necklet: 'I had never seen such a jewel' (103). Crawfurd is mesmerised: 'He had some of the tones of my father's voice, and when I shut my eyes I could have believed myself a child again … There was a tone of arrogant pride … I understood that here are men born to kingship' (104). Laputa tells stories of 'white infamy': 'What have ye gained from the white man? … A bastard civilization … has sapped your manhood … Ye … are now the servants of the oppressor' (105). Laputa promises that the 'alien' will be overthrown and that 'another Ethiopian empire would arise' (105).

The most amazing element, however, is that Crawfurd is powerfully attracted to the man as almost a second father:

> By rights, I suppose, my blood should have been boiling at this treason. I am ashamed to confess that it did nothing of the sort. My mind was mesmerized by this amazing man. I could not refrain from shouting with the rest. Indeed I was a convert … I longed for a leader who would master me and make my soul his own, as this man mastered his followers. I have already said that I might have made a good subaltern soldier, and the proof is that I longed for such a general … . I had to struggle with a spell which gripped me equally with the wildest savage. (105–6)

Horsley writes: 'The standard role of the Buchan hero is to thwart the plans of fanatical, Nietzschean rebels against the established order … . Crawfurd embodies a more thoroughgoing ambivalence towards the charismatic villain than is evident in any of Buchan's other novels' (74–5).

This extraordinary admission shows the overwhelming inclination to identify with the colonised, to transgress, to 'go native', to betray one's country, to find a new and better father, and to submit to a master. Gray notes: '[Crawfurd] is constantly filled with … affection and admiration for Laputa, played out in a father-son bonding … It is a far more personal affair than a matter of colonial conquest – it is the obliteration of the father whom the stripling has to overturn in order to survive' (130). The cave marks Crawfurd's 'entry into manhood' (131).

In addition to this father/son affiliation/contestation between Laputa and Crawfurd, Maria Davidis argues that the focus on Laputa's naked strong physique at several points in the text suggests that Laputa is a 'homoerotic object' in the Greek erotic tradition of the older male and younger man: Laputa is both 'older homoerotic object and priestly father figure' (233), albeit these 'Platonic undertones may not be intended by Buchan' (234). Crawfurd's transgressive admiration of Laputa may include a homoerotic element that intensifies Laputa's threat to Crawfurd's imperial mission, with the dangerous possibility of 'mingling sexual and political conversion' (234). It is certainly the case, as Davidis argues, that Laputa is 'both a hypermasculine object and potential dominator' (231).

Crawfurd is captured. When he confronts Henriques, Crawfurd steals the necklace and escapes. He becomes a white Laputa: 'I took the rubies and stowed them below my shirt and next my skin' (125). He recognises this identification: '[I] stripped to the skin. I emptied my boots and wrung out my shirt and breeches, while the Prester's jewels were blazing on my neck. Here was a queer counterpart to Laputa in the cave!' (129).

But this identification with Laputa does not last: 'I was approaching my own country. Behind me was heathendom and the black fever flats. In front were the cool mountains and bright streams, and the guns of my own folk' (129). 'White men and civilization – all gave me new life and courage' (131). 'If [Laputa] drove out the white man, he should not clasp the Prester's rubies on his great neck' (134). He analogises this situation to playing football: 'Playing football, I used to notice how towards the end of a game I might be sore and weary; … but when I had a straight job of tackling a man my strength miraculously returned. It was even so now' (135).

When Crawfurd and Laputa meet again, Crawfurd rebukes him in the language of defenders of imperialism: 'What in God's name are you doing in this business? You that are educated and have seen the world, what makes you try to put the clock back? You want to wipe out the civilization of a thousand years, and turn us all into savages' (151). Laputa defends his revolt: 'It is because I have sucked civilization dry that I know the bitterness of the fruit. I want a simpler and better world, and I want that world for my own people … Will you not give me leave to be a patriot in turn?'(151). Gray observes that Crawfurd will not entertain the 'supposition that civilization could, in fact, be savage' (132).

Crawfurd embraces a new manliness: 'I was always a fatalist, and in that hour of strained body and soul I became something of a mystic. My panic ceased, my lethargy departed, and a more manly resolution took their place … . I had played a master game' (162). Moving toward the final confrontation with Laputa, Crawfurd admits he 'had forgotten all about patriotism. In that hour the fate of the country was nothing to me … My one idea was that the treasure would be lost, the treasure for which I had risked my life' (171).

Crawfurd acknowledges both maturation and severe testing: 'These last four days had made me very old' (172). 'I marched up the path to the cave, very different from the timid being who had walked the same road three nights before. Then my terrors were all to come: now I had conquered terror and seen the other side of fear. I was centuries older' (174).

In the cave of the Rooirand, Crawfurd sees Laputa, wounded by Henriques, for the last time. Laputa tells him that 'I am dying, and there will be no more kings in Africa.' Crawfurd regards him as 'great': 'I was hypnotized by the man. To see him going out was like seeing the fall of a great mountain' (177). Laputa, however, recognises that Crawfurd is materialistic and imperialistic. When Crawfurd sees the coins and diamonds, Laputa comments: 'Once it was the war chest of a king, and now it will be the hoard of a trader' (178). Crawfurd admits Laputa's doom is 'a fall like the fall of Lucifer' (179).

Telling Crawfurd 'my race is doomed', Laputa strips naked, puts Prester's Collar around his neck, and pitches himself into the gulf of the cave. David Daniell believes that Buchan presents 'the majestic powers of Laputa' (107) in the novel, but the text presents rather his destruction for imperial motives. Daniell believes that Laputa represents 'a lost leader' and 'a loved father' (113).

The white imperialist Crawfurd has it all: 'I wanted to live now ... I had won. Laputa was dead and the treasure was mine ... I had only to be free again to be famous and rich' (183). 'I felt like a runner in the last lap of a race ... Daylight was only a few steps ahead, daylight and youth restored and a new world' (184).

In a symbolic rebirth, Crawfurd manages to leave the cave. 'Here was a fresh, clean land, a land for homestead and orchards and children. All of a sudden I realized that at last I had come out of savagery' (189). Crawfurd plans to recreate Scotland in the Transvaal. Arcoll admits that 'our job now is simple, for there is none of his breed left in Africa ... .You will be a rich man ... . You've saved this country, Davie, and I'm going to make sure that you have your reward' (194). Certainly the cave echoes Plato's *Republic*, where the ascent from the cave marks an individual's rising to the light of reason.

Arcoll recognises that this achievement involved transgression: 'I think for about four days you were as mad as they make. It was a fortunate thing, for your madness saved the country' (199). The imperial mission has succeeded. Arcoll tells the assembled blacks about the 'power of the white man ... claiming for the king of England the right of their old monarchs' (196).

In this imperial project, Crawfurd is entrusted with 'the work of settlement' (197):

> It was an experience for which I shall ever be grateful, for it turned me from a rash boy into a serious man. I knew then the meaning of the white man's duty. He has to take all risks, recking nothing of his life or his fortunes, and well content to find his reward in the fulfilment of his task. That is the difference between white and black, the gift of responsibility, the power of being in a little way a king. (197–8)

Stiebel, while noting the obvious influence of Haggard on Buchan's text, comments: 'Buchan's imperialism (and racism) is far more categoric than Haggard's earlier visions of Noble Savagery superimposed onto the Zulus. Buchan, like Crawfurd, is a firm believer in "the white man's duty"' (109).

Crawfurd embraces this justification for white domination over black: 'So long as we know this and practice it, we will rule not in Africa alone but wherever there are dark men who live only for the day and their own bellies ... I learned much of the untold grievances of the natives, and saw something of their strange, twisted reasoning' (198). Crawfurd accepts the idea that imperialism is benevolent and that white is right. This conclusion, according to Stephen Gray, is in marked contrast to the writings of Haggard: 'The difference between a Haggard and a Buchan is that in Haggard we have a man who, like Quatermain, raided but finally retreated; in Buchan the flag is there to stay … In Buchan the white men have prevailed' (128).

After being away from Scotland for only eighteen months, Crawfurd gets diamonds and coins. He remains ever the careful man of economics. 'I found that I had a very considerable fortune. The whole of my stones I sold to De Beers, for if I had placed them on the open market I should have upset the delicate equipoise of diamond values. When I came finally to cast up my accounts, I found that I had secured a fortune of a trifle over a quarter of a million pounds' (200). The business manager Aitken 'laid down a big fund for the education and amelioration of the native races … training [the Kaffirs] to be good citizens of the state' (202).

This process eliminates native culture to make black white: 'There are playing-fields and baths and reading-rooms and libraries just as in a school at home' (202). The schoolmaster informs Crawfurd that the Kaffir farms are controlled by a curfew. 'Though it is peace nowadays we mean to keep all the manhood in them that they used to exercise in war … We have cleaned up all the kraals … It's a queer transformation we have wrought' (203). Crawfurd thinks he will return to the Transvaal, at least for a visit. His attitude is summarised by his statement: 'Then I knew that, to the confusion of all talk about equality, God has ordained some men to be kings and others to serve' (103). Gray observes that the novel 'happens to have been first published in 1910, the year of Union between the four provinces of South Africa, the year of consolidation of territory under the British flag which had waved all the way from the Cape, if not to Cairo, at least up to Mashonaland' (127).

Buchan's template for masculinity in *Prester John* is male superior and white dominant. Crawfurd destroys black opposition to the colonial project, getting wealth in the process. According to Couzens, 'Buchan's ideal is a kind of Club, a small elite ruling over Uncle Tom's Lodge' (61). Couzens credits the novel with 'the transmission of general prejudice … . For Buchan, the North-Eastern Transvaal was a combination of importing his prejudices and of finding a reality to conform with them' (54). Despite the appearance of altruism as a camouflage and his fleeting vulnerabilities, in reality Crawfurd is racist and materialistic, an imperialising model for young men, finding all the venture in adventure. 'The theme of [Crawfurd's] own maturation is transposed into an unshakeable political axiom' (Gray 131). Smith contends that the novel 'is an instruction manual for British youth' as well as 'a proto-allegory of genocidal apartheid' (189).

However, according to Lownie, the novel 'was also making a prophetic statement about black nationalism. *Prester John*, which anticipated the very similar Nyasaland Rising of the Reverend John Chilembwe in 1915, was supposedly a favourite of black nationalists such as Jomo Kenyatta' (112). If Crawfurd has no doubts about his imperial manhood, then, perhaps Buchan does. He did not title the novel *David Crawfurd* but *Prester John.*

Conrad: *The Shadow-Line* (written 1915; published 1916–17)

Joseph Conrad's *The Shadow-Line* was written in 1915 and serialised 1916–17 before appearing as a book in 1917. Published with the subtitle *A Confession*, the novella draws on Conrad's own experiences in January 1888 in Singapore. He had signed off the *Vidar* on 4 January 1888 and then was offered the command of the *Otago*, which he assumed on 19 January 1888. In Singapore, like his protagonist in the novella, Conrad had stayed in a sailors' home. Owen Knowles and Gene Moore cite letters to the effect that Conrad acknowledged using autobiographical elements in *The Shadow-Line*, albeit these were transmuted by artistry to a more universal tale than just an autobiographical record.

Like its predecessor of 1910, *The Secret Sharer*, *The Shadow-Line* records a rite of passage. It is a reminiscence narrated by an unnamed mature skipper in a retrospective tale about his first command as a young man. The narrator addresses 'no identifiable narratee' (Lothe 122). This novella, however, does not involve the figure of the double as had its predecessor *The Secret Sharer*. Furthermore, in this narrative, unlike its 1910 predecessor, there is considerable space devoted to the narrator's experience ashore as well as on ship. Conrad states in his 'Author's Note' that he originally called the tale 'First Command' (xxxviii).

The young man resigns as first mate of a steamship where he served under Captain Kent, gets a first command on a sailing ship after attempts to thwart him and faces challenges which test his manhood and maturity: being becalmed, a raging fever among the crew and the disappearance of quinine from his ship. He also makes two major mistakes: he takes his ill first mate, Burns, with him on the ship; and he fails to check the quinine personally, accepting a doctor's statement that it is fine.

The title refers to the transition from youth to adult manhood. Lawrence Graver notes that at this period Conrad is especially concerned with 'the psychological or moral aspects of masculine self-knowledge' (178). On the first page, the narrator asserts the theme: 'The very young have, properly speaking, no moments. It is the privilege of early youth to live in advance of its days … One goes on. And the time, too, goes on – till one perceives ahead a shadow-line warning one that the region of early youth, too, must be left behind' (3). Later passages underscore the theme of initiation. This transition takes place 'in an Eastern port', unnamed (4). As D.C.R.A. Goonetilleke remarks, as in 'Youth' and *The Secret Sharer*, *The Shadow-Line* indicates the Far East 'as an area having a psycho-moral significance for the European foreigner' (40).

The narrator refers to 'that twilight region between youth and maturity … [in which] one is peculiarly sensitive to … insult' (26). 'I was still young enough, still too much on this side of the shadow-line, not to be surprised and indignant at such things [the attempt to thwart him]' (37). 'Youth is a fine thing, a mighty power – as long as one does not think of it. I felt I was becoming self-conscious' (55). 'I don't know what I expected. Perhaps nothing else than that special intensity of existence which is the quintessence of youthful aspirations. Whatever I expected I did not expect to be beset by hurricanes' (83). Edward Said (1966) believes the tale 'portrays … that moment when the youthful visions of the narrator can no longer sustain him; unfortunately, the placidity of old age is also far beyond him' (170).

The Shadow-Line stresses the viciousness of males toward each other. The young sailor in the novella is confronted by villainous men. While he is at the Officers' Sailors' Home, a letter arrives offering him the command of the sailing ship. The Chief Steward at the Home at first conceals the letter, hoping the arrogant and evil fellow-resident Hamilton, who has not paid his bill, will apply for the position and leave. As Jacques Berthoud (1986) remarks, the narrator will learn that 'mankind dwells in enemy territory' (13), 'an existential apprehension of the world' (10).

When the new Captain discovers the deception, he remembers it as a turning point in his life: 'It was the first instance of harm being attempted to be done to me – at any rate, the first I had ever found out' (37). Later, on board the steamer *Melita* sailing to assume command of his ship in Bangkok, the narrator meets its captain, who treats him roughly: 'He was the first really unsympathetic man I had ever come in contact with. My education was far from being finished, though I didn't know it. No! I didn't know it' (47).

The narrator owes his command to Captain Giles, 'an expert … in intricate navigation' (12) who is staying at the Home. Giles had advised the young man that 'things out East were made easy for white men. That was all right. The difficulty was to go on keeping white' and that 'some of them do go soft mighty quick out here' (14). Clearly, the narrator is being advised to avoid damaging masculine paradigms.

The fact that the tale is set in 1887, during the Golden Jubilee celebrations for Queen Victoria (16), makes the advice pertain to the challenging business of policing the Empire. But if the narrator as a young man was part of the Empire, he is also in a bizarre position in the ship he abandons before assuming his new command. 'It was in an Eastern port. She was an Eastern ship, inasmuch as then she belonged to that port. She traded among dark islands on a blue reef-scarred sea, with the Red Ensign over the taffrail and at her masthead a house-flag, also red, but with a green border and with a white crescent in it. For an Arab owned her, and a Syed at that. Hence the green border on the flag' (4). The narrator describes the British Empire as 'complex' (4). This complexity exists because the Arab 'had to employ white men in the shipping part of his business' (4). He is 'an old, dark little man blind in one eye, in a snowy robe and yellow slippers' (4). Hence, the juxtaposition of white and 'non-white' is essential to the functioning of the economic apparatus of which the narrator is a part. As an imperialist he is an invader; as a trader he himself is invaded. He is transported to his new ship in Bangkok. His nightmarish experiences will occur in the becalmed sea of the Gulf of Siam. At the end of the novel, he heads to the Indian Ocean. Hence, it is in Asia, where he has 'invaded', that he will experience a psychological invasion.

Giles' conversation initially upsets the young man: 'The whole thing strengthened in me that obscure feeling of life being but a waste of days, which, half-unconsciously, had driven me out of a comfortable berth, away from men I liked, to flee from the menace of emptiness ... and to find inanity at the first turn … . A great discouragement fell on me. A spiritual drowsiness. Giles' voice was going on complacently; the very voice of the universal hollow conceit' (22–3). The young skipper's ennui is existential: he does not understand his decision to abandon a secure position. He makes a choice, but in a meaningless universe.

The narrator's early dislike of and even dismissal of Giles only proves his immaturity and misjudgement, as it is the supportive Giles who sends him to Captain Ellis, the Harbour Master, 'the deputy-Neptune for the circumambient seas' (30). Ellis informs him he is the right man for the job and that others 'are all afraid to catch hold ... Afraid of the sails. Afraid of a white crew. Too much trouble. Too much work. Too long out here. Easy life and deck-chairs more their mark' (31). Only a sailing ship is a genuine test of manliness.

Therefore, in embracing the command of a sailing ship rather than a steamship, the narrator is accepting a genuine challenge. The narrator's being given the command enchants him: 'I was very much like people in fairy tales' (40). He considers this a rite of passage: 'A sudden passion of anxious impatience rushed through my veins and gave me such a sense of the intensity of existence as I have never felt before or since. I discovered how much of a seaman I was, in heart, in mind, and, as it were, physically – a man exclusively of sea and ships; the sea the only world that counted, and the ships the test of manliness, of temperament, of courage and fidelity – and of love' (40).

Although the Captain refers to his ship in the female gender (40, 49–50), the ship/microcosm is part of a world without women. In his Introduction to the novel, Jeremy Hawthorn cites the manuscript where the phrase 'like the women in it' appears after the second reference to 'ships' in the previous second quotation ('the ships [like the women in it,] the test of manliness'), but Conrad cancelled the phrase to render the text even more exclusively homosocial (xxii). The genuine testing of a man does not involve women in this narrative. 'One is a seaman or one is not. And I had no doubt of being one' (44). Finally on board his ship, the narrator reflects: 'I stood, like a king in his country, in a class all by myself' (62). Jeremy Hawthorn (2007) concludes: 'Conrad's slight-of-hand allows for a manliness that magically excludes both women and effeminacy' (133).

The challenges, however, are only beginning. Sitting in the saloon of his ship, the narrator believes he is the first in a long line of successful skippers: 'A succession of men had sat in that chair … a sort of composite soul, the soul of command' (52–3). He believes he has 'his place in a line of men whom he did not know' (53). Seeking to be part of a patriarchal succession, the Captain soon learns this is not a completely desirable fraternity. Allan Ingram regards this line of men as an insidious 'shadow-line' in the narrator's life (225).

In fact, the narrator is becoming estranged from himself. He stares at himself as if in a mirror: 'I stared back at myself with the perfect detachment of distance ... both as if he were myself and somebody else' (53). The narrator has internalised the shadow-line: he is his own dangerous shadow, his own other. A warning is sounded after he meets Burns, the chief mate: 'I became aware of what I had left already behind me – my youth' (55).

Burns informs the skipper-narrator that the mad old villainous captain, his predecessor, had died in that chair, not a paradigm to be embraced. He learns that his predecessor had played his violin night and day and furthermore had a ferocious mistress, 'an awful, mature, white female with rapacious nostrils and a cheaply ill-omened stare in her enormous eyes ... A professional sorceress from the slums' (59). The narrator's education about masculinity continues: 'That man had been in all essentials but his age just such another man as myself. Yet the end of his life was a complete act of treason' (62). As Mark Thomas stresses, 'the act of resisting the doubling is part of the narrator's initiation' (231). Soon the fever prostrates the steward and then Burns. Burns believes the fever is a legacy of the evil previous captain, whose malevolent influence extends beyond the grave. The ship is becalmed. The fever plays havoc with the crew.

According to Paul Newman, many of the events in *The Shadow-Line* echo those of Coleridge's 'Rime of the Ancient Mariner', including the becalmed sea, the compulsion to narrate, the narrator's guilt, the Life-in-Death fever and the pervasive evil. The Captain then faces a nightmare similar to the Ancient Mariner's when he discovers that the quinine is actually some useless powder; he experiences 'a mental shock' (89), one of the most brutal moments of his maturation. He tells Burns: 'I feel as if I were going mad myself' (93).

This fear of madness, according to Ingram (229), is one of many allusions ('despair, inactivity') to *Hamlet*, which are amalgamated in the text with references to the Ancient Mariner. Ingram notes 'the shadow-line in the human mind between sanity and madness' (237) as one more inflection of the title. Burns informs the skipper he believes the insane captain had sold the quinine. The narrator is devastated: 'The person I could never forgive was myself. Nothing should ever be taken for granted. The seed of everlasting remorse was sown in my breast' (95). Burns tells the narrator that his predecessor was 'an evil brute ... just downright wicked ... . Sooner call a shark brother' (118–19). The narrator must overcome this frightening Oedipal father.

Like the Ancient Mariner, the narrator experiences overwhelming guilt. The climax of this growth of self-awareness is recorded in the narrator's diary: 'I feel as if all my sins had found me out ... My first command. Now I understand that strange sense of insecurity in my past. I always suspected that I might be no good. And here is proof positive. I am shirking it, I am no good' (107). Ingram asserts that the diary constitutes yet another 'shadow' in the narrator's existence (226). 'The seaman's instinct alone survived whole in my moral dissolution ... . I stood amongst [the crew] like a tower of strength, impervious to disease and feeling only the sickness of my soul' (109). The narrator's alienation reaches existential proportions: 'He [the helmsman] was alone. I was alone, every man was alone where he stood' (113). Soon after the narrator accepts responsibility, rain and wind arrive to grace his rite of passage.

Finally the ship reaches Singapore after a total of three weeks at sea. When the narrator sees Captain Giles again, he admits: 'I feel old' (131). Giles advises: 'The truth is that one must not make too much of anything in life, good or bad ... . A man must stand up to his bad luck, to his mistakes, to his conscience, and all that sort of thing ... . You will learn soon how not to be faint-hearted ... . Precious little rest in life for anybody. Better not think of it' (131–2).

According to John Peck, *The Shadow-Line* has an 'extra dimension' in Conrad's work because it is 'the first work Conrad published after the start of the First World War. At a time when it really mattered, a traditional standard of conduct and a man's readiness to be tested are positioned directly at the centre of Conrad's novel [with] a straightforward emphasis on the interdependence of men' (183). Conrad does assert some traditional standards here, but the novel is not without its complications and is more complex than Peck argues.

One can agree with Albert Guerard that the narrator is suffering from depression and engages in a 'night journey' into the self (31). The young Captain-narrator, surviving the challenges of fever and a mad predecessor's legacy, has achieved wisdom, self-knowledge and maturation. Said, however, argues this is an 'uncertain maturity' (177), that the skipper has crossed 'the line of shadowy, unrealized ambitions into a sort of restricted, terrible reality' (186). Berthoud notes that 'the qualified affirmation with which *The Shadow-Line* concludes is purchased at the cost of a succession of disillusionments' (19).

According to Daniel Schwarz (1982), the challenge for Conrad is 'how to dramatise two separate selves, the younger self and a mature speaker who has successfully completed his rites of passage' (89). In dealing with the younger self of a mature man, *The Shadow-Line* bears resemblance to the mature Marlow narrating his tale about his past experiences in 'Youth' and *Heart of Darkness*. As in both of those narratives, the narrator 'selects and arranges the past events to create a self-image' (Schwarz 83), a self-image which may cater to narcissistic wish-fulfilment rather than to reality. The narrator's initial condescension to Captain Giles recalls the sneering contempt of Jukes directed at his captain, MacWhirr, in *Typhoon*. In *The Shadow-Line* the narrator must contend with several Oedipal fathers: Giles with 'his big paternal fist' (27); Burns the chief mate; and the mad captain who was his predecessor. Josiane Paccaud-Huguet notes that the sale of the quinine 'is the sign of complete betrayal by a father-figure, who has sold the quinine at the request of the Other, the rapacious female companion' (163).

The narrator also has a strong desire for sexual solitude. Early in the story he describes 'rash actions' as symbolised by 'getting married suddenly' (4). His second engineer on his first ship, 'a sturdy young Scot', replies when the narrator said he is leaving the ship: 'I've been thinking it was about time for you to run away home and get married to some silly girl' (6). The narrator describes this second engineer, John Nieven, as 'a fierce misogynist' (6). The narrator regards

Nieven's response as 'the most crushing thing he could think of' (6). When Burns discusses his wife and child in Sydney and contends that the young skipper may some day have a family, the narrator reflects: 'I had no family. As to the wife-and-child (some day) argument it had no force. It sounded merely bizarre' (70). The narrator occupies a hyper-masculine solitary position.

According to Ian Watt, 'we can find no warrant for believing that the shadow-line is crossed once and forever' (165), an opinion shared by Schwarz (1982): 'In a sense the shadow-line has to be continually met' (91). At one point in the narrative, Burns refers to the previous captain as the 'Flying Dutchman' (94), perpetually condemned to roam the earth as an exile. F.R. Leavis (1969), in a landmark essay on the novel, declared it 'a profound work, and complex in its profundity ... . [It is] central to Conrad's genius' (109–10).

The epigraph 'D'autres fois, calme plat, grand mirror/De mon désespoir' (3) is taken from Charles Baudelaire's poem 'La musique' ['Or else there is a flat calm, the giant mirror of my despair']. How does this reference relate to the young skipper? It may represent the becalmed ship which was the locus of his hellish experience in the Gulf of Siam. It may signify a process he is still undergoing. It suggests the existential void he might still inhabit. It may stand for his disillusionment. It might represent the early shadow he has passed after crossing the line.

Certainly there is considerable disillusionment during the process of this transition. This situation is most clearly indicated in the skipper's references to enchantment and fairy tales about his forthcoming experiences in his new command. For example, the narrator at the beginning regards the state of being a young man as entering 'an enchanted garden' (3). Soon, however, he experiences his first disenchantment and decides to leave the steamship: 'One day I was perfectly right and the next everything was gone – glamour, flavour, interest, contentment – everything' (5). He continues: 'The past eighteen months, so full of new and varied experience, appeared a dreary, prosaic waste of days. I felt ... there was no truth to be got out of them' (7). He was trying 'to flee from the menace of emptiness' (23) when he left his position. He gives up this berth in the hope of rebirth.

But this first phase of existential ennui does not prevent the skipper from indulging in fantasies of enchantment when he gets notice of his first command: 'Here I was, invested with a command in the twinkling of an eye, not in the course of human affairs, but more as if by enchantment ... I was very much like people in fairy tales' (39–40), he admits. He thinks of Captain Ellis as 'a fierce sort of fairy' and the ship he commands as 'an enchanted princess' (40). He regards the sailing ship as a test 'of love' of a chivalric kind, far preferable apparently than any woman.

Of course, these fantasies of a fairy-tale existence are brutally dispelled as he crosses 'the shadow-line': hence the mood of despair emphasised in Baudelaire's poem, for in the text he twice undergoes profound disillusionment, once when leaving the steamship and again when taking command of the sailing ship. Said (1966) contends that the young skipper 'is going on to become a ship's master, an imperialist serving a heartless code' (177), which may bring another siege of despair. Said believes he has 'an uncertain maturity' (177).

Hence, the disturbing myth of the Flying Dutchman enhances the genius of *The Shadow-Line*. Even if this achieved manhood will be tested constantly, the experience recorded here is a first if not final stage of a powerful transformative male rite of passage. Like the Flying Dutchman, the narrator-skipper will roam and invade at will in a constant search for his masculine self: having just touched shore, he informs Giles 'I shall be off at daylight to-morrow' (132). He is off to the Indian Ocean.

According to John Peck:

> It can be said that three elements compete for attention in sea stories: there is the individual sailor, who more often than not will display distinctively masculine qualities; the sea and the other shore as places of danger, where challenges have to be met; and thirdly, the social, economic and political dimension, that the ship is a product of technology, that it has been built for a purpose, and that there is a practical aspect to every sea voyage. (14)

This chapter has concentrated on the third, economic, dimension of adventure texts, but the individual explorer and the other shore are components of this economic agenda. In Conrad and Buchan, the protagonists are in foreign locales for evident economic motives. In Hudson, the protagonist foreshadows economic exploitation of indigenous populations. In Mason, control of the Sudan serves British economic purposes. An additional element of this presence on foreign shores is sexuality, where males, liberated from the constraints of the home country, confront their sexual identities, the subject of the next chapter.

Chapter 4
Loving

Arthur Conan Doyle described the adventure novel as 'the masculine novel' in his essay of 1890 about Robert Louis Stevenson. Doyle argued that the adventure novel de-emphasised love and marriage, which for Doyle had too long constituted the subject of the realistic English novel. He notes that for a man 'Love will often play a subordinate part in his life' yet he also asks 'How many go through the world without ever loving at all?' (652). Doyle, then, recognises that few human lives involve no love at all. He leaves open the issue of sex and love in adventure fiction. Indeed, it is a question of the proportion of a narrative devoted to sexuality that Doyle queries. In some of the texts considered in this book, such as *Trooper Peter Halket of Mashonaland*, *Prester John*, *Treasure Island*, *Captains Courageous* or *The Secret Sharer*, heterosexual relationships scarcely or never appear, giving way to homosocial spaces.

In others, however, sexuality, especially transgressive sexuality in the form of miscegenation (racial or ethnic) features importantly in the text. In *King Solomon's Mines*, for example, Foulata, loved by John Good, dies declaring that nothing would have come of a black/white alliance. In *The Man Who Would Be King*, Dravot's desire to father a line of kings entails an ethnic transgression for which he pays with his death on the rope bridge.

Other sexual relationships, while not involving miscegenation, are crucial to the narratives. *The Light That Failed* represents a protagonist who commits combat suicide because of physical and psychological forces that prevent him from having any strong sexual relationship. In *The Four Feathers* it is a woman's power to inflict pain which spurs the protagonist to seek his manhood. In *Green Mansions* a man's involvement with an ethereal woman leads to her death and to his exile, prefiguring the ruin of the native population.

These texts involve power in its relationship with sexuality. In many of these narratives, the white male has a superiority based on race, as in *King Solomon's Mines* or in *Green Mansions*. Issues of power and gender in *The Light That Failed* lead to conflict and the dissolution of relationships. In *Heart of Darkness,* Marlow lies to the Intended for several reasons, one of which is to preserve male solidarity with the dead Kurtz.

Woman is often the gendered, racial or ethnic other in adventure texts such as those described above. However, some texts, such as those considered in this chapter, engage heterosexual relationships in situations where power is more equivocal than in those cited above. In Haggard's *She*, Leo Vincey abandons Ustane for the Queen herself, who by virtue of her power controls him. In Stevenson's 'The Beach of Falesá' the protagonist eventually marries a native woman and remains with her. The protagonist of 'The Planter of Malata' destroys himself as a result of the corrosive effects of power in his sexual relationship. In *A Smile of Fortune* a man leaves a woman when she learns to love him. In a radical way two cousins become lovers and parents in *The Blue Lagoon* in a remote geographical location. A remote location also serves the protagonist and the Princess in *The Prisoner of Zenda*.

Hence, Doyle is correct to label these texts 'masculine' narratives, and yet there is clearly a desire on the part of these writers *not* to exclude sexuality from their narratives. In this respect, many of the texts in this study incorporate sexualities, even if the emphasis is on other masculine agendas such as initiation or economics. But it can legitimately be argued that in several of these tales, such as *Green Mansions*, *The Blue Lagoon* or 'The Planter of Malata', sexuality is the most significant experience for the protagonists, leading to a transformation of masculine identies. John Peck notes of sea stories that 'taking control of and dominating one's environment' (5) is a constant component. In the texts examined in this chapter, part of this control and domination involves sexuality. In all these texts, but particularly those by Conrad, Stacpoole and Stevenson, the sea enables these sexual encounters. As Peck observes, however, 'there is such an obvious gap between the social (and especially sexual) arrangements of those at sea and the arrangements of those on land' (29). All the texts in this chapter explore this 'gap' in the sexual experiences of the un- or up-rooted adventurer when he leaves the sea for the shore.

Haggard: *She* (1887)

After the great success of *King Solomon's Mines*, Rider Haggard began writing its sequel, *Allan Quatermain*, continuing the adventures of his hunter-narrator. At the same time, Haggard conceived an extraordinary legend of an empowered woman who reigned as queen in Africa for 2,000 years and finds her reincarnated lover in a young man, twenty-five year old Leo Vincey, who travels to her land with his companions, Ludwig Horace Holly, a Cambridge don who is his guardian, and Job, their man-servant. This tale, narrated by Holly and sent to an external Editor, became *She: A History of Adventure*. The story, as Showalter remarks, is part of the genre of 'the male quest romance' (81), a genre marked by 'allegorized journeys into the self' (82). In the case of *She*, this is particularly the journey of Leo Vincey.

Haggard's subtitle aligns the text with the adventure genre, but unlike *King Solomon's Mines* or *Allan Quatermain*, where the erotic is not particularly stressed, the subject of *She* is eroticism. Hence, Haggard deploys the adventure genre in a revolutionary manner by this emphasis. In a comment applicable to all three texts, Mazlish asserts that Africa provides a place to draw from 'the Dark Continent of the mind, the underground kingdom of the unconscious'; imperialism is 'a way of dealing with repressed impulses' (742). Imperialism allows 'the working out of unconscious drives, as well as those of state' (742). Unlike in *King Solomon's Mines* or *Allan Quatermain*, however, in *She*, as Etherington notes, 'This time the identification of present European man with an African past is made literal' (194) in the tale of Leo Vincey.

In his notorious essay 'About Fiction' published in *The Contemporary Review* (February 1887), Haggard declared: 'Sexual passion is the most powerful lever with which to stir the mind of man' (176). He makes it clear he is going to give men what they want. He decries the 'namby-pamby nonsense' of current British fiction, which must be written for sixteen-year-old girls. He asks: 'Why do *men* hardly ever read a novel? Because, in ninety-nine cases out of a hundred, it is utterly false as a picture of life … The ordinary popular English novel represents life as it is considered desirable that schoolgirls should suppose it to be. Consequently it is for the most part rubbish, without a spark of vitality about it' (177).

In other words, Haggard is creating a kind of 'male novel' here, ignoring the restrictions that the publishers' female audience mandated. Andrew Lang, a friend of Haggard and a defender of the 'romance' genre, stated in his review of *She* in the *Academy*: 'The book is a legend, not a novel … The whole story is an allegory of the immortality of love' (36), while recognising that the violence would repel some readers. The journal *Public Opinion* (14 January 1887) declared *She* 'far more fascinating' than Flaubert's *Salammbô* (38), arguing: 'We have found it almost as fascinating as Mr Stevenson's *Treasure Island*, and greater praise than that we can scarcely give it' (38). The reviewer in *Blackwood's* (February 1887) labelled Haggard 'the new *avatar* of the old story-teller, with a flavour of the nineteenth century and scientific explanation, but at the same time a sturdy and masculine force of invention' (302). The reviewer noted that, in his focus on Africa, Haggard had a 'distinct sphere which is his own' (302). Commenting on 'the art of the story-teller, which, perhaps, had fallen a little out of repute', the reviewer added that Stevenson and Haggard had 'brought it back' (302).

Hence, in the text there is constant emphasis on the spectacularity of the male body. The young explorer, Leo Vincey, has a god's body, which is noted repeatedly throughout the text. The Editor labels him 'the handsomest young fellow I have ever seen. He was very tall, very broad, and had a look of power and grace of bearing that seemed as native to him as it is to a wild stag … . That fellow is like a statue of Apollo come to life. What a splendid man he is!' (1). Vincey is called 'the Greek god' as a nickname, 'the handsomest man in the University' (2). His guardian is the don Holly, who is 'as ugly as his companion was handsome' (2). Millman notes of adventure texts: 'In these novels descriptions of manly beauty occur often, having an almost magical function: a good appearance replaces and *is* psychology, a sure sign of inner worth' (13). The focus on the beautiful male body as erotic object, to both men and women, distinguishes this 'male novel'.

It is fortunate that Leo Vincey has a god's body, for several reviewers deplored mundane references and Leo's colloquialisms in the novel. According to the *Athenaeum* (15 January 1887): 'The conception is weird, fantastic, and certainly fascinating, but the treatment is lamentably unequal … It would, in fact, seem that [Haggard] has essayed a task beyond his natural powers ... [Compared with *King Solomon's Mines*] there is more of downright commonplace' (93). William E. Henley (writing as H.B.) in the *Critic* (12 February 1887) noted about the novel: 'The invention is, to my thinking, admirable; but the writing, the taste, the treatment, are often beneath criticism. And the worst is, there is no hope of better ... It is hardly to be doubted that [Haggard] will go on writing ill and inventing well until he is exhausted' (78).

Holly signs his letters 'L. Horace Holly', the first letter indicating his being the physical obverse of his young charge. Holly admits he is branded, like Cain, a person of 'abnormal ugliness ... Women hated the sight of me' (8). Leo, according to John Moss, evokes Adonis, Osiris and Dionysus, the latter two resurrected according to mythology (30).

Vincey's father gives Leo in charge to Holly, instructing him to open an iron box on the young man's twenty-fifth birthday. Holly takes the child, refusing to find a nurse, so Leo is raised in an all-male environment: 'I would have no woman to lord it over me about the child, and steal his affections from me. The boy was old enough to do without female assistance, so I set to work to hunt up a suitable male attendant' (19), who is Job. Hence, this erotic novel, replete with an obsessed young man and an obsessed queen, really espouses, like Jason in Euripides' *Medea*, a world without women. Showalter notes that by this adoption 'Holly thus miraculously achieves virgin fatherhood', with the book catering to 'the fantasy of male reproductive autonomy' (84).

Holly is overwhelmed by Leo's beauty: 'Leo at twenty-one might have stood for a statue of the youthful Apollo. I never saw anybody to touch him in looks' (21). Later Holly recognises Leo's 'clear-cut Grecian face' (80). David Bunn claims that 'from an early age Leo is an instrument of male revenge: he is a sort of blonde [sic] Eros, fatally attractive to women'. Leo represents 'the archetypal urge towards revenge against women' (17). Throughout the narrative, according to D.S. Higgins, Holly remains the 'proficient voyeur' (95).

When Leo is twenty-five, the iron box is opened. In it, there are a letter from Leo's father, a Greek potsherd, parchment rolls and a scarab with an inscription. The potsherd records the tale of Kallikrates by his wife Amenartas. Kallikrates was slain by a jealous white queen when Kallikrates did not return her love. Amenartas wants her son or a descendant to slay the murderous queen. Not for nothing is the Vincey name derived from Vindex, 'the Avenger'.

Leo is the re-embodiment of Kallikrates, whose name means 'The Strong and Beautiful, or, more accurately, the Beautiful in Strength' (10), as a footnote defines. Hence, this erotic story is a revenge tale against a woman. Leo, Holly and Job are enroute to Zanzibar three months later. Job soon despises 'these blackamoors and their filthy, thieving ways. They are only fit for muck' (51). Leo is imperilled by an attack by whales which, as Evelyn Hinz asserts (426), suggests the belly of the whale, that is, re-birth.

The men are saved from being slain by the command of She, later identified as Ayesha, She-Who-Must-Be-Obeyed, the queen of this East African land who resides in the city of Kôr. Her subjects have a different notion of gendered behaviour, as Holly records when one of the women, Ustane, rushes up and kisses Leo: 'It then appeared that, in direct opposition to the habits of almost every other savage race in the world, women among the Amahagger are not only upon terms of perfect equality with the men, but are not held to them by any binding ties. Descent is traced only through the line of the mother … . Among the Amahagger the weaker sex has established its rights' (81, 89). Holly comments as well: 'Job, like myself, is a bit of a misogynist' (88). With descent being matrilineal, males have a less dominant role in Kôr. As Etherington (1984) notes, 'local custom makes women the aggressors in sexual affairs. Marriages are sealed with a kiss and as easily dissolved' (46).

These gendered attitudes in Kôr are disturbing to misogynists: '*She* was obeyed throughout the length and breadth of the land … To disobey her was to die' (90). Etherington (1984) labels Ayesha 'a Diana in jack-boots who preaches materialism in philosophy and fascism in politics' (47). She espouses Social Darwinism, declaring: 'Those who are weak must perish; the earth is to the strong, and the fruits thereof. For every tree that grows a score shall wither, that the strong ones may take their share. We run to place and power over the dead bodies of those who fail and fall; ay, we win the food we eat from out the mouths of starving babes. It is the scheme of things' (203).

She's preferred mode of execution is to put a hot pot on a person's head. As critics have noted, the male fear of castration is evident in this detail (e.g., Showalter 86). Billali, She's retainer, tells Holly: 'In this country the women do what they please. We worship them, and give them their way, because without them the world could not go on; they are the source of life' (114). However, he adds, once in a while they kill the old women 'as an example to the young ones, and to show them that we are the strongest' (114). Holly's mind remains 'full of dear Leo' (138), representing his androcentric ideology. He thinks: 'I was an Englishman, and why, I asked myself, should I creep into the presence of some savage woman as though I were a monkey?' (140).

When Holly does meet She/Ayesha, she is a veiled erotic object: 'The wrappings were so thin that one could distinctly see the gleam of the pink flesh beneath them … a tall and lovely woman, instinct with beauty in every part, and also with a certain snake-like grace' (142). Ayesha is thus Lamia, *femme fatale* and Cleopatra in one. According to Sandra Gilbert and Susan Gubar (1989): 'She was in certain ways an entirely New Woman: the all-knowing, all-powerful ruler of a matriarchal society … She was a mythic figure, a classic femme fatale … . [She represents] the primordial female otherness, which may have been the real source of male anxieties about New Women' (6–7).

Later, in line with these models, Holly declares: 'This woman was very terrible' (145). When Ayesha unveils herself to Holly, this serpentine motif recurs. She has a 'serpent-like grace … About the waist her white kirtle was fastened by a double-headed snake of solid gold … Only this beauty, with all its awful loveliness and purity, was *evil*' (155). Later, when Ayesha marks Ustane with her fingers, it is with a 'snake-like movement' (208). For one example of Ayesha's violence, in rituals at Kôr, mummies are used for torches.

Men may gaze all they wish. In response, Ayesha alludes several times to the myth of Actaeon, who gazed and was destroyed: 'Like Actaeon, thou hast had thy will; be careful lest like Actaeon, thou too dost perish' (156). Calling Ayesha a Circe, Holly wonders: 'Curses on the fatal curiosity that is ever prompting man to draw the veil from woman … It is the cause of half – ay, and more than half, of our misfortunes. Why cannot man be content to live alone and be happy, and let the women live alone and be happy too?' (159). To confirm Holly's suspicions, Ayesha states that she rules 'by terror' (175). Millman asserts that *She* is 'a massive compendium of the attitudes the Victorian male took toward the Victorian female' (41).

Leo chooses to accept that he is the reincarnated Kallikrates, rejecting Ustane and becoming Ayesha's beloved. As Higgins notices (94), there is an 'overt sexuality' in *She* that is not so evident in *King Solomon's Mines* or *Allan Quatermain.* Holly comments: 'Leo was not too strong-minded where women were concerned' (222). What is surprising is that Holly becomes in love with Ayesha too. Many critics have noted that an incestuous triangle is thus formed (e.g., Showalter 87). The older Holly (the father), wants the mother (Ayesha, who is a few years older than Leo), and he must exclude the son (Leo) from committing incest. Etherington (1984) emphasises: 'There is a case to make for Ayesha as the disguised embodiment of an unfulfilled desire for a forbidden love, a son's incestuous longing for his mother' (88). Just before She enters the fire, she kisses Leo on the forehead, a kiss which to Holly 'was like a mother's kiss' (291).

Holly's capitulation before Ayesha is complete: 'But then and there I fell upon my knees before her, and told her … that I worshipped her as never woman was worshipped, and that I would give my immortal soul to marry her' (190). Leo, Holly's 'my more than son' (160), becomes Holly's rival for Ayesha. When Ayesha kisses Leo, Holly bitterly acknowledges he was 'jealous' (200).

The woman's returned empowering gaze has the ability to empower her. In Chapter 20, Ayesha secures Leo to herself. Declaring him 'Kallikrates reborn, come back' (228), Ayesha, figured as both Venus and Galatea, 'fixed her deep and glowing eyes upon Leo's eyes, and I saw his clenched fists unclasp … beneath her gaze … her sweet and passionate gaze' (229). Holly is 'rent by mad and furious jealousy' (229). Here, father and son contest over the mother's body.

Leo is conscious of his dangerous sexual attraction, but he cannot resist, as he confesses to Holly: 'I am a degraded brute, but I cannot resist that … awful sorceress … In my mind, I hate her – at least, I think so. It is all so horrible; and that – that body [of the dead Kallikrates]! What can I make of it? It was *me*! I am sold into bondage, old fellow, and she will take my soul as the price of herself!' (241). Holly thinks: 'In uniting himself to this dread woman, he would place his life under the influence of a mysterious creature of evil tendencies, but then that would be likely enough to happen to him in any ordinary marriage … Leo was plunged in bitter shame and grief, such as any gentleman would have felt under the circumstances' (242–3). In his own degradation, Holly admits 'I am in love with Ayesha myself to this day', adding 'any *man*' would be (243).

In a fascinating twist, this eroticism has global implications. Ayesha tells Leo they can 'cross to this England of thine' (254). Holly is aware:

> She had evidently made up her mind to go to England, and it made me absolutely shudder to think what would be the result of her arrival there … . In the end she would, I had little doubt, assume absolute rule over the British dominions, and probably over the whole earth, and, though I was sure that she would speedily make ours the most glorious and prosperous empire that the world has ever seen, it would be at the cost of a terrible sacrifice of life. (256)

Etherington (1977) designates this process as 'imperialism in reverse' (194). In no other adventure text does gynephobia reach such heights. Ayesha is feared like Cleopatra. Bruce Mazlish notes that in *She* 'the love-hate feelings toward women are overpowering' (734). Ironically, *She* was published in the year of Queen Victoria's Golden Jubilee.

Having crossed a chasm with a plank, Ayesha guides Leo to the Place of Life. She encourages Leo to stand in the Pillar of Flame, which, she contends, will grant him immortality, as it had granted her. Gilbert (1983) comments: 'This perpetually erect symbol of masculinity is not just a Freudian penis but a Lacanian phallus, a fiery signifier whose eternal thundering return bespeaks the inexorability of the patriarchal Law She has violated in Her Satanically overreaching ambition' (448). When She enters it, She shrivels into an old hag and then into a monkey, a reversal of the human evolutionary process, a devolution. Etherington (1991) writes that 'the idea that not all evolution is progressive runs like a thread of arsenic through Haggard's tale' (xxvii). Millman declares that 'Haggard's link between women and monkeys makes women seem disreputable' (58).

Holly thinks it was the 'finger of Providence' which caused Ayesha's death, for she 'would have revolutionised society' (295) had she lived. Also, the incest taboo would have been violated. With all this at stake, Job drops dead. Leo's golden hair turns grey at the sight: Leo's mythic quest has led to a transformation of his masculinity, a knowledge of himself and his ancestry, evoking the search for identity marked in ancient epic, especially in Vergil's protagonist Aeneas.

Returning from the Place of Life, Leo saves Holly at the chasm. They both reach the Zambesi and then return to England, having been on their 'quest' (316) for two years, three weeks of which were spent in Kôr (Hinz 418). The narrative ends with questions about whether Leo was the reincarnated Kallikrates or whether Ayesha was deceived in believing it. Holly wonders what Kallikrates' beloved Amenartas will do when 'that *final* development ultimately occurs' (316).

The novel *She* took on another life when Sigmund Freud published *The Interpretation of Dreams* in 1900. Freud recounts a dream he had, which he recognises as inspired by Haggard's novel. Freud imagines he is on a dissecting table, viewing his own pelvis and legs; the pelvis is eviscerated. Then he is on a journey where he has to cross a chasm by two wooden planks. When a patient asks for something to read, Freud gives her *She*, 'a *strange* book, but full of hidden meaning … the eternal feminine, the immortality of our emotions' (429). One recognises here the extreme castration fear in the loss of pelvis and legs. The use of the plank to cross the chasm, the phallic column of fire, all attest to male power, yet, as Haggard suggests at the conclusion of the novel, the tale replete with sexual fears will continue.

It is Ayesha who guides the men across the chasm, appropriating phallic power in deed as she had in gaze. Dead, she lives. Her realm is named Kôr, evoking the Greek *kore*, meaning both young woman and an alternative name for Persephone, bridge of the God of Death, Dis (Gilbert and Gubar 16). Gilbert and Gubar, in their analysis of the novel, note that Ayesha was the name of Mohammed's second wife, and Kôr suggests the *Kor-an*, dual markers of Otherness as figured in Islam (28). In terms of late Victorian culture, this Otherness suggests that Ayesha, with her power and independence, reflects the New Woman, whose presence caused much anxiety for men. Hinz also observes that the novel gives the lie to Victorian beliefs in meliorism: 'Haggard's theme is that progress is an illusion' (429), particularly, one might add, because of male erotic desire.

Etherington (1977) contends that 'the layered personality which Freud conceptualised as superego, ego, and id is Haggard's major theme.' When Haggard's explorers go on the road, 'the layers are progressively stripped away. First to go is the top 5% of official civilisation … Below the layer of civilisation brothers are always rivals, sisters are sworn enemies … Beneath this layer of personality lurks still another, more elemental and horrific, which is literally unconscious' (197).

An additional component of this emphasis on the unconscious is the fact that Holly finds many situations impossible to describe. He remarks at various points: 'It is quite impossible for me to describe its grim grandeur' (128); 'surpass my powers of description' (163); 'To describe it is quite impossible' (219); 'I wish that it lay within the power of my pen to give some idea of the grandeur' (259); 'I only wish that I could describe' (273). Language is inadequate to narrate the unconscious.

When *She* was published, an unsigned review in the *Pall Mall Gazette* evidenced disappointment: 'It is not easy to adjust with precision the praise and disparise due to Mr Rider Haggard's new romance. It certainly rises above the commonplace, and it as certainly falls short of excellence. At times we are inclined to think it very cheap work after all' (5). The reviewer could not deny the power of the novel: 'The conception, indeed, is so powerful that we rebel with a sense of injury against the many defects of execution' (5). Andrew Lang, a supporter of Haggard's *King Solomon's Mines*, declared in the *Academy*: 'People are pretty sure either to admire *She* very hotly, or to condemn the fair enchantress with extraordinary vigour … . The more impossible it gets, the better (to my taste) Mr Haggard does it … [He] makes the most impossible adventures appear true' (36). Even Lang, however, claimed that some would fault the extreme 'scenes of savagery' and the length of Ayesha's long 'discourses' (36).

Both Gilbert and Murray Pittock perceive certain parallels between *She* and Conrad's *Heart of Darkness*. Gilbert claims that 'just as Leo and Holly must pass through the matriarchal territory of the Amahagger', so Marlow must pass the antechamber ruled by the two old women/fates (452). Pittock notes such similarities as the journey, the meeting of a mysterious character, the sense of 'the mystery of Africa' (207), 'the technological superiority of modern culture' (207), the witnessing of secret rites and the megalomania of both She and Kurtz.

In *She* male desire dominates individuals, leading to self-realisation even if it leads to self-destruction. Male desire evokes both longing and dread. Etherington (1991) asserts that 'Haggard's treatment of Ayesha reinforces sexual stereotypes even as it seems to challenge them' (xxxi). This conflicted situation is reflected in Leo and Holly. The adventure damages both men. Holly acknowledges: 'Having once looked Ayesha in the eyes, we could not forget her for ever … We both loved her now and for always, she was stamped and carven on our hearts, and no other woman or interest could ever raze that splendid die' (299). Few novels connect so well *eros* and *thanatos*, desire and death, so starkly as does a novel where the undead queen reigns.

Stevenson: 'The Beach of Falesá' (1892)

Robert Louis Stevenson first published 'The Beach of Falesá' in 1892. It was revised in 1893. Together with such stories as *The Ebb-Tide*, it constitutes a group of South Sea tales resulting from his new residence at Vailima after he left Scotland in 1890 for Upolu, Samoa. A first-person narrative, the tale is told by a rough, working class trader named John Wiltshire, who is transferred by his company to the island of Falesá.

There Wiltshire meets Case, a rival trader, who arranges a fake marriage with a native Polynesian, a Kanaka woman, Uma. Starting to care for her, Wiltshire arranges for a Christian marriage with the missionary Tarleton. Eventually, Wiltshire discovers Case has turned the natives against dealing with him by making him and Uma taboo. Case does so by raising superstitious beliefs based on a phony devils'-den shrine Case sets up in the jungle. Wiltshire and Case eventually fight it out to the death (of Case) and Wiltshire settles into his new life with Uma and their three children, a son and two daughters.

Stevenson was proud of the story, as he explained to Sidney Colvin:

> It is the first realistic South Sea story; I mean with real South Sea character and details of life. Everybody else who has tried, that I have seen, got carried away by the romance, and ended in a kind of sugar candy sham epic, and the whole effect was lost – there was no etching, no human grin, consequently no conviction. Now I have got the smell and look of the thing a good deal. You will know more about the South Seas after you have read my little tale than if you had read a library. (ed. Jolly, xxvii)

Stevenson's objectives for the tale lead to an unusual narrative, as Harman declares: '[It] unsettles the reader from the outset by offering no absolute standards of any kind: those of the islanders are uninterpretable, and those of the whites a matter of relativity, with the narrator, a trader called John Wiltshire, the poor best of a very bad lot' (417).

'The Beach of Falesá' deploys adventure motifs (island, tropical locale, violence) with domestic elements (wife, children, household economy), giving the tale a hybrid identity as both adventure text and domestic narrative. And just as the text is a hybrid genre, the subject is about hybridity: 'miscegenation and racial contamination' (Jolly 472). Unusual in an adventure story, 'sexual attraction initiates the plot' (Jolly 472).

The tale is significant for a number of reasons. It addresses the economic exploitation of the natives by white traders. It also presents an inter-racial relationship between Wiltshire and Uma. The tale is complex in its treatment of white racist attitudes toward natives. Wiltshire sometimes rejects this labelling process, but not always. The famous final paragraph is ambiguous about his racial ideas.

The title uses the word 'beach' in a specific sense, that is, the 'place where whites lived and traded on Pacific islands; also taken metaphorically to mean the whites themselves' (Jolly 259). Hence, the tale is about white males in groups. Often these groups, as in *The Ebb-Tide*, are disreputable, immoral and anarchic. The 'beach' is populated by white men and half-castes. The Captain of the ship tells Wiltshire the last man sent there, Vigours, fled this white community. Hence, at first Wiltshire is attracted to Case since he 'was sick for white neighbours' (4). Case 'would have passed muster in a city … He was of English speech; and it was clear he came of a good family and was splendidly educated … He had the courage of a lion and the cunning of a rat … . Case used me like a gentleman and like a friend, made me welcome to Falesá' (5).

Case arranges for Wiltshire to marry Uma. The 'service' is performed by Black Jack, a black associate of Case, in the deteriorated store operated by Captain Billy Randall, a dissolute, seedy, alcoholic man of seventy. Wiltshire thinks the fake marriages are not 'the least fault of us white men' (11) but of missionaries who demand these proprieties instead of letting nature take its course. 'If they had let the natives be, I had never needed this deception, but taken all the wives I wished, and left them when I pleased, with a clear conscience' (11). 'I was one of those most opposed to any nonsense about native women, having seen so many whites eaten up by their wives' relatives' (12). Wiltshire regards the Polynesian Uma as a 'child or a kind dog' (12). When he takes her home, he reacts: 'I was ashamed to be so much moved about a native, ashamed of the marriage too' (13).

This act of racial transgression begins to alter Wiltshire's idea of his manhood. Yet, this alteration does not occur rapidly. A few days after the 'marriage', Wiltshire rebukes Uma in a white-dominant, bullying manner: 'I gave her a bit of the rough side of my tongue, as she deserved. She stood up at once, like a sentry to his officer; for I must say she was always well brought up, and had a great respect for whites' (27). As Katherine Linehan notes, this is a 'military master-servant relationship' (416) at this point.

Two days later, having opened a clean, orderly shop, Wiltshire realises no one will patronise his store. He realises he and Uma have been tabooed. At first, Wiltshire turns to Case to remedy the matter. Wiltshire boasts: 'You tell them who I am. I'm a white man, and a British subject, and no end of a big chief at home' (23). That, of course, is a lie. Wiltshire is nothing at home but a non-descript lower class male. But out in the South Seas, the penis/phallus equation works if one is white. He continues: 'I've come here to do them good, and bring them civilization; and no sooner have I got my trade sorted out than they go and taboo me … I demand the reason of this treatment as a white man and a British subject' (23–4).

Wiltshire persists in his white superior mode as he reflects: 'I know how to deal with Kanakas; give them plain sense and fair dealing, and – I'll do them that much justice – they knuckle under every time. They haven't any real government or any real law, that's what you've got to knock into their heads; and even if they had, it would be a good joke if it was to apply to a white man. It would be a strange thing if we came all this way and couldn't do what we pleased' (24). Wiltshire's assumed racial superiority proves ignorant and damaging. He later admits to Tarleton: 'I'm just a trader; I'm just a common, low, God-damned white man and British subject' (35).

Still, he begins to realise that he loves Uma, 'Kanaka and all' (28). The false economic racial superiority does not parallel his erotic attitude, as he begins to care genuinely for Uma. In a surprising shift in gender expectations, Wiltshire begins to work producing copra with his wife and her mother; furthermore, he begins to be the cook in the household. These are alterations to the masculine template which Stevenson wishes to emphasise in the narrative.

Rosyln Jolly (*Review* 1999) remarks about Wiltshire's decisions: 'The identification of Wiltshire with the feminine is linked to his explicit rejection of the masculine, anti-domestic sphere inhabited by Case and his partners Randall and Black Jack' (475). Furthermore, when Wiltshire takes Uma home the first night, he pours out all the gin in his house. This is an additional rejection of Case's and Randall's brutal masculine world, as Jolly comments: 'The pouring out of the gin marks almost ritualistically Wiltshire's rejection of all that Randall represents and his desire instead to safeguard his domestic life and the interests of his wife' (476).

When he meets Tarleton, the missionary, he says his name is Wiltshire, though on the beach he is 'Welsher' or an imperialist swindler (35). Tarleton, at Wiltshire's request, properly marries the two in Wiltshire's own house. The economic and the erotic intertwine when Tarleton, the man who marries them, tells Wiltshire: 'Case is very clever and seems really wicked' (38). Tarleton informs Wiltshire that Case probably murdered several of his other competitors on the island. Linehan notes: 'Case, who makes whites as well as natives pawns in a game played for power, profit, and pleasure, represents a hard-boiled version of Wiltshire's worst tendencies' (417).

To solve his economic dilemma, Wiltshire decides to 'set off upon a voyage of discovery' into the bush, where he suspects Case has 'some kind of establishment' (51). Case first discovers a Tyrolean harp, which had disturbed the natives into believing in devil-worship. Then he finds the devils' stockade, 'a line of queer figures, idols or scarecrows, or what not, ... as fresh as toys out of a shop' (54). He remembers that Case 'was a good forger of island curiosities' (54). He finally discovers one 'shining face ... big and ugly, like a pantomime mask' (55). This is the idol Case has used to terrify the natives, appearing fearsome because of its 'luminous paint' (55).

Wiltshire realises he has to destroy Tiapolo, the devil-shrine, which he dynamites. In the ensuing fight, both he and Uma are wounded by Case. Wiltshire manages to knife Case: 'I drew my knife and got it in the place ... . With that I gave him the cold steel for all it was worth ... . The blood came over my hands, I remember, hot as tea ... The first thing I attended to was to give him the knife again half-a-dozen times up to the handle. I believe he was dead already, but it did him no harm and did me good' (67–8). The intensity of the violence here echoes that of Ballantyne's *The Coral Island*.

Wiltshire agrees to leave Falesá when his firm transfers him. His main concern is his children: 'I'm stuck here, I fancy. I don't like to leave the kids, you see; and – there's no use talking – they're better here than what they would be in a white man's country, though Ben took the eldest up to Auckland, where he's being schooled with the best' (71). However, for his two daughters Wiltshire has more specifically gendered issues: 'But what bothers me is the girls. They're only half-castes, of course; I know that as well as you do, and there's nobody thinks less of half-castes than I do; but they're mine, and about all I've got' (71). The text is a hybrid genre of adventure and domestic forms; the daughters are also hybrids.

Ending on this racial inflection, Stevenson stresses not only Wiltshire's altered manhood but also its degree of alteration. He has moved beyond the male homosocial world of 'the beach'. He has sought a legitimate 'respectable' marriage in his union with Uma. His son he is raising in a socially progressive manner. Jolly (1999) remarks: 'Wiltshire's thinking remains trapped within a racial ideology from which his emotions have been liberated, and which can provide no answers to the social problems posed by his half-caste children' (481). His mulatto daughters are subject to the same racial attitudes which he brought into Falesá. As Robert Kiely notes, Stevenson does not 'introduce even the faintest irony in the tale' (170), which renders the story realistic as an adventure text. Wiltshire's regenerative transformation, presented in this non-ironic stark manner, is partial but undoubtedly accurate.

Jolly (1999) notices about the tale: 'Defined first in adventure terms, as the ability to fight, masculinity is redefined here in terms of domestic commitment [exhibiting] a tension between opposing notions of masculinity as male aggression and manliness as feminine care and restraint ... . [The story is Stevenson's] exploration of the relation between adventurous masculinity and domestic manliness' (479, 482). This transformation is indicated by the fact that after

Tarleton sets Wiltshire's leg following the fight with Case, Wiltshire limps: 'Mr Tarleton set my leg, and made a regular missionary splice of it, so that I limp to this day' (69).

Wiltshire will go no more a-roving in quite the same way. This limp reflects a transmuted masculinity conflicted beyond the conventions of some adventure narratives. Wiltshire joins other protagonists who endure physical disfigurement in adventure texts, such as Dick Heldar in *The Light That Failed*, Peachey Carnehan in *The Man Who Would Be King* or Jack Durrance in *The Four Feathers*. These men differ from the physical vigour of the protagonists of *Captains Courageous*, *The Riddle of the Sands*, *Prester John* or *King Solomon's Mines*, complex texts where nevertheless physical endurance preserves the protagonists. Kiely writes of Stevenson's later South Sea stories:

> The brittle surface of popular adventure – the picturesque locale as backdrop, the simple hero pitted against the caricature villain, the mysterious evil explained by mechanical trickery – is under serious strain in his later South Sea fiction. The Victorian veneer was bound to buckle and crack when laid over the moral and physical topography of the tropics … The exotic fable discloses moral complications which threaten to shatter its own simple frame. (179)

The maimed protagonists of some adventure fiction reveal in graphic form the complications presented in their narratives.

The maiming can be psychological and inhibiting. Wiltshire must hope to find white men like himself, willing legitimately to marry his daughters. Given his own self as template, Wiltshire realizes this will be the toughest trade of his career, with his daughters as the commodity. The tale ends on a question about his daughters: 'I can't reconcile my mind with their taking up with Kanakas, and I'd like to know where I'm to find the whites?' (71), indicating that Wiltshire is still controlled to some extent by his racist ideas. Stevenson incorporates the domestic scenario into the adventure genre in 'The Beach of Falesá' in a powerful, disturbing analysis of imperialism – erotic and economic. Hence, Stevenson concludes with the interrogative.

Hope: *The Prisoner of Zenda* (1894)

Published in April 1894, Anthony Hope's *The Prisoner of Zenda* was an immense best-seller. Gary Hoppenstand records that the novel had sold 7,000 copies by June and 12,000 copies by November (viii). 'Within two years, it was in its 31st edition' (Wallace 26). Using the plot of a nearly-identical double (as in, for example, Dickens' *A Tale of Two Cities*), the novel is a flawless investigation of masculinity as a script, a role, a construction, a disguise. Rudolf Rassendyll is an ideal English gentleman who decides to attend the coronation of a distant relative, also Rudolf, of Elphberg, in Ruritania.

Because of political intrigue provoked by the king's half-brother Michael, Duke of Strelsau, who also desires the throne, Rassendyll is compelled to impersonate the actual king at the coronation. He does so for three months. The real king is held prisoner at the Castle of Zenda by the henchmen of 'Black Michael' the half-brother. Eventually, the king is freed and Rassendyll, having fallen in love with the king's fiancée Princess Flavia, leaves Ruritania and returns to England. The novel is a brilliant analysis of masculinity and the chivalric code of the gentleman.

Anthony Hope recorded in his autobiography the genesis of *The Prisoner of Zenda*: 'One day – it was the 28th of November 1893 – I was walking back from the Westminster County Court (where I had won my case) to the Temple when the idea of "Ruritania" came into my head … I finished the first draft in just a month – on the 29th of December' (119). Margery Fisher notes that this invention of a mythical Central European country supplied a 'compound of energy and idealism, of courtly formality and personal passion' (86). Ruritania provided a 'detachment' by which Anthony Hope could explore 'the Victorian version of medieval chivalry' (82). The distance also enables fantasies of intrigue and glamour.

It was an immensely clever strategy to analyse masculinity, according to Mark Girouard: 'Anthony Hope's inspired invention of Ruritania allowed him to move his English hero straight from modern clubland into a world of castles, kings, beautiful women, and feudal loyalties' (265). Hope was conscious of this strategy and tradition: 'The root idea of *The Prisoner of Zenda* is, of course, merely a variant on the old and widespread theme of "mistaken identity". … I think that the two variants which struck the popular fancy in my little book were royalty and red hair; the former is always a safe card to play, and its combination with the latter had a touch of novelty' (120–21).

In an address in April 1897 to the Royal Institution, Hope said about the 'romance' genre: 'It has no monopoly of this expression [romance], but it is its privilege to render it in a singularly clear, distinct, and pure form; it can give to love an ideal object, to ambition a boundless field, to courage a high occasion … It shows [men] what they would be if they could … and what their acts would show them to be if an opportunity offered' (cited in Mallet 114). The novel therefore tests an ideal conception of masculinity, the chivalric ideal. The subtitle of the novel is: *Being the History of Three Months in the Life of an English Gentleman*. Hope wants to interrogate this code of the gentleman. Is it applicable at the end of the century?

He does so with an ambiguous protagonist. Rassendyll, at the beginning of the novel he narrates, is immediately confronted with questions about masculine identity. Rudolf's sister-in-law, Rose, sets the theme of masculinity in its first line: 'I wonder when in the world you're going to do anything, Rudolf?' She continues: 'You are nine-and-twenty … and you've done nothing' (5). Rudolf rejects the doctrines of masculinity dictated by Thomas Carlyle: he refuses to 'do' anything and he is not one of Carlyle's heroes who perform deeds. Indeed, Rassendyll at the beginning of the text is a rebel against this idea of masculine action and self-assertion. In other words, he is a danger to the dominant notion of active manliness.

Physically, Rassendyll is also different: he has red hair and the Elphberg straight nose, the result of the indiscretion of an ancestor in 1733, who had an affair with Rudolf the Third of Ruritania. Rassendyll recognises 'the uselessness of the life I had led' (8). In addition to being left money, Rassendyll also has 'a roving disposition' (8), which will propel him to his adventure to attend the coronation in Ruritania of Rudolf the Fifth.

Arriving in Ruritania, Rassendyll decides to stay in Zenda. There he learns that Black Michael desires not only the throne but also his half-brother's betrothed. Two of the king's retainers, the Chancellor Colonel Sapt and his aide-de-camp Fritz von Tarlenheim, note his resemblance to the king. Rassendyll reflects like a born adventurer: 'Had I realised what a very plainly-written pedigree I carried about with me, I should have thought long before I visited Ruritania. However, I was in for it now … . The King of Ruritania might have been Rudolf Rassendyll, and I, Rudolf, the King' (23). When the monarch's wine is drugged by Black Michael, he cannot attend the coronation. Pressed by the two retainers, Rassendyll agrees to impersonate the king to save the throne.

After the coronation, Hope repeatedly refers to Rassendyll's function as playing a role, suggesting that after all masculinity, even royalty, is a question of role-playing, not actuality. Sapt remarks: 'Lad … if you play the man, you may save the king yet' (52). Rassendyll thinks: 'The farce had to be reality for us now … . A real king's life is perhaps a hard one; but a pretended king's is, I warrant, much harder' (57–8). 'I had to keep the princess devoted to me – and yet indifferent to me: I had to show affection for her – and not to feel it' (61). 'Was I right to play the part, or wrong to play the part?' he wonders (66). 'I need only say that the secret of my imposture defied detection' (67). Making love to Princess Flavia, Rassendyll thinks to himself he is 'an impostor' (79).

As the action advances, this role-playing is perceived by others. Rupert of Hentzau, Prince Michael's bodyguard and henchman, calls Rassendyll 'the play-actor' (114). He will label Rassendyll this again just before their duel (146). 'And I did not love to hear Rupert call me a play-actor' (114). Rassendyll decides that the scheming Duke Michael was also a 'play-actor' (115). Hence, not only Rassendyll but also other men in the novel are involved in role-playing. Rassendyll claims 'I have been an imposter for the profit of another' (127–8).

Having made Princess Flavia fall in love with him, Rassendyll must confess to her at the conclusion: 'I am not the king!' (158). The restored king, formerly a playboy, compliments Rassendyll: 'You have shown me how to play the king' (160). In these insistent references, Anthony Hope questions whether there is any masculine paradigm apart from role-playing. Men in the novel perform a script. Masculinity is a question of acting, impersonation.

There are three component elements to Rassendyll's script. First, he refers to his adventure as a 'game' at several places in the text, whether it be 'play' or 'intrigue' intended. 'The game had begun' he asserts (33). He begins to become a new man: 'I saw the strong points in our game. And then I was a young man and I loved action' (53). Sapt remarks: 'Well played!' (53). These attitudes are united in the comment: 'I had a fine game to play in Strelsau' (60). Rassendyll tells Sapt: 'We must play high; we must force the game' (70). 'I have my game to play too' says Antoinette de Mauban, Prince Michael's mistress (71). 'I must be left to play my game with Michael my own way' (110), Rassendyll decides before the rescue attempt to save the king.

Another dimension of this chivalric behaviour is swordsmanship. Early in the novel, Rassendyll kills a sentinel. Later in three pages he kills three men, all henchmen of Black Michael's retinue. First is De Gautet: 'He fell dead in the doorway without a word or a groan' (140). Then the Belgian, Bersonin: 'He was no swordsman, though he fought bravely, and in a moment he lay on the floor before me' (141). Then the Englishman Detchard: 'He slipped; he fell. Like a dart I was upon him. I caught him by the throat, and before he could recover himself I drove my point through his neck' (142). As in many adventure texts such as *Treasure Island*, transgression is the road to male self-realisation.

Rassendyll also exemplifies the chivalric code of pure love and self-denial in his parting from the Princess Flavia. In the chapter entitled 'If Love Were all' (159), Rassendylll acknowledges that Flavia is legitimately disturbed 'by the fear that I had counterfeited the lover as I had acted the king' (162). He tells her: 'I love you with all my heart and soul! … There has been but one woman in the world to me – and there will be no other. But God forgive me the wrong I've done you! (162).

When Rassendyll asks Princess Flavia to leave with him, she refuses: 'Honour binds a woman too, Rudolf … I know that I must stay' (163–4). Rassendyll evokes the dramatic trope once more: 'My part is lighter; for your ring shall be on my finger and your heart in my heart, and no touch save of your lips will ever be on mine' (164). When he calls her 'My queen and my beauty!" she replies: 'My lover and true knight!' (164).

Rassendyll at the conclusion tells Sapt and Fritz that 'We have been men' (165). Indeed, Rassendyll in Ruritania has abandoned the idleness of clubland. Fritz tells him: 'Heaven doesn't always make the right men kings!' (165). Anthony Hope questions the very basis of royalty, as indeed Rassendyll is a finer man than Rudolf the Fifth since he adheres to chivalric purity and honour.

Rassendyll returns to become an English gentleman again, but his role-playing at Zenda has given him a gift: 'It was only I, Rudolf Rassendyll, an English gentleman, a cadet of a good house, but a man of no wealth nor position, nor of much rank … For, be I what I might now, I had been for three months a king; which, if not a thing to be proud of, is at least an experience to have undergone' (165). Hope argues for a democratising of the chivalric ideal, as Margery Fisher notes of Rassendyll: 'His courage and nobility are innate rather than acquired' (85). Hoppenstand claims that 'the events of *The Prisoner of Zenda* serve as a rite-of-passage for an indolent young man' (xviii).

Rassendyll returns to England to live 'a very quiet life' (171). He and Flavia exchange red roses annually through Fritz as emissary. 'I love the noblest lady in the world … There was nothing in my love that made her fall short in her high duty' (173). His love for Flavia ensures that he will adhere to a chaste masculine life: 'I will live as becomes the man whom she loves' (173).

Why does Hope espouse the gentlemanly chivalric code in *The Prisoner of Zenda*? According to Joseph Bristow: 'British culture invested so much energy in glamorizing male heroes because they represented … a tremendous lack: they were not to be found in the empire' (225). Hence, Hope argues for an impossible template in *The Prisoner of Zenda*. Yet as Hoppenstand contends: novels such as this 'idealized and reinforced the cultural ideology of the British Empire' (xvii–xviii).

Anthony Hope is famous also for having written the greatest example of a sub-genre of novels called 'Cardboard Kingdoms' by critic Raymond Wallace:

> I refer to a group of novels which I have dubbed the Cardboard kingdoms, works
> of fiction which employ fictitious countries as significant plot elements, usually
> as the principal setting for the action … . The common theme is generally one of
> struggle for the sovereignty, the maintenance in power of a rightful sovereign,
> the recovery from a usurper, or the displacement of a despot (23)

Wallace regards George Meredith's *Harry Richmond* of 1871 as the first of its kind.

For Wallace, Anthony Hope 'found the formula' (25) for this type of narrative in *The Prisoner of Zenda*. It contains the seven elements Wallace contends identify the sub-genre (29): 1. The Fictitious Country; 2. The Crown (or Government) is Threatened; 3. The Wicked Uncle (or brother, half-brother, cousin, nephew, or other claimant to the throne); 4. The Intervening Stranger (usually the hero) a foreigner (like Rassendyll); 5. The Remarkable Coincidence (here, the resemblance of the King and Rassendyll); 6. The Chase (hero and villain pursue each other); 7. The Duel (here Rassendyll slays at least four men). It is a powerful template for literature. But, given its endurance, it is also a genuine template for masculinity. While extremely idealised, it does not mean it is not functioning to construct dimensions of manly behaviours and attitudes.

According to Patrick Howarth, *The Prisoner of Zenda* stands distinct from the tales of Haggard: 'In this the adventures take place, not against a closely observed African or Asian background, but in a country of the imagination' (124). But in addition, Rassendyll has a unique quality: 'He has neither the philistinism nor the anti-intellectual bias of Newbolt Man' (124–5). Rassendyll is a man of action with a mind.

This model of masculinity was evoked intensely, as Mark Girouard has demonstrated, during the First World War. If it was a role, then many were called to play the game. Charles Mallet records that 300,000 copies had been sold in England by 1934 (79). Roger Lancelyn Green is correct to designate the novel as 'among the lesser masterpieces of the period' (184), but it remains a masterpiece in reinforcing a masculine ideal of love, self-denial, chivalry and bravery which British culture would evoke twenty years later in the Great War.

Stacpoole: *The Blue Lagoon* (1908)

Henry De Vere Stacpoole's *The Blue Lagoon* of 1908 is an unusual adventure text in that it incorporates the pastoralist tradition, shows the male maturation process as one of de-civilising and ends in a suicide of the male protagonist, Richard (Dick) Lestrange and his lover and cousin Emmeline (Lestrange). Their child, a boy with the gender-bending name Hannah (since that is the only child's name the castaways know) in a sequel to *The Blue Lagoon*, *The Garden of God* (1923), survives his parents when his grandfather rescues him.

Stacpoole described the origins of the novel: 'Early in 1907, lying awake and pondering, not for the first time in my life, on the extraordinary world we live in, the idea came to me of what it must have been like to the cave men who had no language and for whom a sunset had no name tacked on to it, a storm no name, Life no name, death no name and birth no name, and the idea came to me of two children, knowing nothing about any of these things, find themselves alone on a desert island facing these nameless wonders' (cited in Hardin 209). Four decades after its publication, *The Blue Lagoon* 'stayed in print and over one million copies of it were sold in English alone' (Woods 131).

Stacpoole recorded in 1946, in the twenty-first edition of his novel, the reception the text received: '*The Blue Lagoon* took the public at once by its newness and remote charm, and almost at once began to travel the world, leaving behind it all sorts of things other than its reader: "Blue Lagoon" swimming pools, canoe lakes, bathing beaches, inns, and crockery ware. Paris scented itself with a perfume Blue Lagoon; Como, during the late [Second World] war and the present peace, founded a Blue Lagoon Rest Club for servicemen' (cited in Woods 131).

This combination of idyllic pastoral (echoing the tradition of Longus' *Daphne and Chloe* and Saint-Pierre's *Paul et Virginie* [1787]) united with the adventure genre renders *The Blue Lagoon* a striking investigation of the evolution of masculinity. 'The book saw twenty-four printings in thirteen years' (Hardin 205). By training a physician, Stacpoole was an expert on the South Pacific islands and their vegetation. The descriptions of floral and animal life on the island and at sea are significant environmentalist records. According to Hunter: 'Edwardian adventures keep returning to Eden. It is there in … Stacpoole's *The Blue Lagoon*' (85). Stacpoole is concerned with a world without language or labels. Just as Saint-Pierre's tale is set on Mauritius (Ile-de-France) and contains descriptions of storms, so too does *The Blue Lagoon* follow Saint-Pierre's model.

The Blue Lagoon is a *Bildungsroman* in that it chronicles the maturation of Dick Lestrange from eight years old to around sixteen or seventeen. In search of a better climate as a consumptive, Dick's father Arthur Lestrange, Dick, and

Arthur's niece Emmeline (an orphan), are travelling from Boston to Los Angeles. Below the line in the Pacific, their ship, the *Northumberland*, suddenly catches fire from the cargo of blasting powder in the hold of the ship. During the abandonment of the ship, the children become separated from Arthur Lestrange, being left in a dinghy with the ship's cook, Paddy Button, 'a garrulous and bibulous old Irish sailor, who is their mentor or retainer-figure' (Hunter 85), who until his death in a drunken stupor acts as a counselor/father to the children.

Human brutality ensues. Stacpoole shows a disturbing scene in Chapter 10 when people in the lifeboats will not share water with each other: 'By chance the worst lot of the *Northumberland*'s crew were in the long-boat veritable – "scowbankers" scum; and how scum clings to life you will never know, until you have been amongst it in an open boat at sea. [Captain] Le Farge had no more command over this lot than you have who are reading this book' (54). People in the quarter-boat are 'begging for water when there was none. It was like the prayers one might expect to hear in hell' (55). Stacpoole is famous in the text for combining such grisly detail with idyllic fantasy.

Dick, Em and Paddy come upon an unmanned timber brig, the *Shenandoah*, in the sea, and having boarded it, obtain supplies. Eventually, they arrive at an island somewhere south of the Marquesas, 'the most lonely and beautiful in the world' (58). It appears a Paradise at first: 'the blue and tranquil lagoon' (61), 'heart-achingly beautiful' (62), replete with a cascade of water and cocoa-nut groves. Jefferson Hunter remarks: 'The force behind the empty landscapes in Edwardian books is the sheer pressure of numbers in Edwardian life. The function of landscapes is to provide a clear field of experience for heroic action, or for sexual action in the case of books like *The Blue Lagoon*' (86).

But in fact Stacpoole is too much the naturalist to regard the island as an untouched Eden. The presence of a shark (62) is noted, an animal destined to play a part in the tale. Early in their residence on the island, Dick finds a skull: 'It was a lichen-covered skull, with a great dent in the back of it where it had been cloven by an axe or some sharp instrument' (70). Paddy remarks: 'There's been black doin's here in days gone by' (70). The narrator remarks: 'Nowhere in the world, perhaps, so well as here, could you appreciate Nature's splendid indifference to the great affairs of Man' (72). This indifference is then symbolised by the presence of poisonous 'crimson arita berries' (72).

As times passes, Dick begins to exhibit the de-civilising process by wandering around naked. 'After a while, if you have no special ties to bind you to civilisation, Nature will begin to do for you what she does for the savage' the narrator notes (79). To amuse Paddy, Dick draws a stick figure of Henry the Eighth in the sand, but just as quickly they leave 'Henry and his hat a figure on the sand to be obliterated by the wind' (83). Civilised history is discarded as the children 'mature' into adolescence. It is irrelevant, in contrast to dealing with what is immediately apparent before the castaways: 'Months of semi-savagery had made also a good deal of difference in Dick's appearance … He was the promise of a fine man' (87). Dick 'would as often as not be running about stark naked' (91). The novel stresses the naked male body as signifier of masculinity, affirming its genitality as strenuously as the clothed male urban figure denies it.

When Paddy disappears, dying in a drunken binge, Dick is not disturbed at the loss of his mentor: 'Dick had no illusions at all upon the matter … He felt the old man's limitations … . He was always being checked by the go-as-you-please methods of his elder. Dick came of the people who make sewing machines and typewriters. Mr Button came of a people notable for ballads, tender hearts, and potheen. That was the main difference' (103).

The discovery of Paddy's corpse is grisly. A little crab darts out of the dead man's gaping mouth. 'The thing, for them, had no precedent, and no vocabulary. They had come across death raw and real, uncooked by religion, undeodorised by the sayings of sages and poets' (111). While Dick's father, Arthur Lestrange, had told them of a 'good God' (112), he had said nothing of retribution or death or funerals. In any event, 'this knowledge of [God] would have been no comfort now. Belief in God is no comfort to a frightened child' (112). Stacpoole defies religious authorities, strongly suggesting there would be no God at all if civilisation did not invent him. 'He stood in the centre of an awful and profound indifference' (162). As Richard Hardin notes, 'childhood *was* lost, and not without pain' (214).

In Book II, years have passed. Em and Dick are now around sixteen. 'Dick had been frightened enough at first; but the feeling wore away in time' (119). Stacpoole again focuses on his now strong adolescent body: 'He was well worth looking at and considering, both from a physical and psychological point of view … . Auburn-haired and tall, looking more like seventeen than sixteen with a restless and daring expression, half a child, half a man, half a civilized being, half a savage, he had both progressed and retrograded during the five years of savage life … . Life was all business for him. He would talk to Emmeline, but always in short sentences' (120). As for Emmeline, 'her own personality had suddenly and strangely become merged in his' (121–2). Apart from civilisation, stereotypical gender roles nevertheless emerge.

On the reef fishing, Dick sheds his clothes: 'The surroundings here seemed to develop all that was savage in him. In a startling way; he would kill, and kill, just for the pleasure of killing' (123). This process parallels that of Nature. Stacpoole describes the 'eternal battle' of coral reefs 'with the waves' (126), evoking similar passages in Ballantyne's *The Coral Island* half a century earlier.

When an octopod ensnares Dick, it is Emmeline who races to give Dick the spear to slay the animal. Yet she is not recognised as the rescuer: 'He was not thinking of her. Wild with rage, and uttering hoarse cries, he plunged the broken spear again and again into the depths of the pool … . One might have thought that he had rescued her from death, not she him … . [He was] taking all the glory of the thing to himself, and seeming quite to ignore the important part she had played in it' (131–2).

Stacpoole stresses Dick's naked body as the spectacle of masculinity its adolescent maturity manifests. It anticipates a similar male spectacularity of Leggatt's naked body at the beginning of Conrad's *The Secret Sharer*. One can conclude, from events soon occurring, that he has experienced masturbation and nocturnal emissions as he reaches sexual maturity. Gregory Woods emphasises that boys 'are expected to endure initiation rites further to those which their developing bodies impose on them. Incipient virility is thus constructed not only biologically, but also, even here in the apparent isolation of island life, socially' (132). In *The Blue Lagoon* Dick Lestrange demonstrates that 'masculinity exists in a state of disequilibrium between nature and society' (Woods 145).

The narrator views this appearance of gendered power calmly: 'It was not for any callousness or want of gratitude, but simply from the fact that for the last five years he had been the be-all and end-all of their tiny community – the Imperial master ... [Em] was his shadow and his slave. He was her sun' (132). Stacpoole links Dick's domination on the island with the white imperial project. He would dominate an island or a colony. Stacpoole wonders if Dick would have been more contented in civilisation: 'Who knows if he would have been happier?' (147).

This domination accompanies their first sexual encounter. Seated beneath a bloodied 'Easter Island' idol, Emmeline bends a cane into a bow, which accidentally strikes Dick on the face: 'Almost on the instant he turned and slapped her on the shoulder. She started at him for a moment in troubled amazement ... As she looked at him like that, he suddenly and fiercely clasped her in his arms. He held her like this for a moment, dazed, stupefied, not knowing what to do with her. Then her lips told him, for they met his in an endless kiss' (149). The adolescents 'become wholly innocent versions of Adam and Eve' (Hunter 85).

The narrator states about their sexual relationship: 'An affair absolutely natural, absolutely blameless, and without sin ... . It was a marriage according to Nature, without feasts or guests, consummated with accidental cynicism under the shadow of a religion a thousand years dead ... one a part of the other' (151). The result is that Dick has new respect for Em: 'He talked to her no longer in short sentences' (153). 'Love-making would come on them in fits, and then everything would be forgotten' (154). Eventually, Em gives birth to a male child, whom they name Hannah, as it is the only baby's name they know from their experience of Boston. Jefferson Hunter is correct that this novel is 'responding to a strait-laced society' (86) in these episodes.

A vicious hurricane appears, which destroys their habitation, a harbinger of their end. 'Mischance had come, and spared them and the baby. The blue had spoken, but had not called them' (180). Gender relations have reverted to a power imbalance. When they come to a site where Dick had a ferocious encounter with an albacore, about which he had not told Em, the narrator remarks: 'It was the first time she had heard of it; a fact which shows into what a state of savagery he had been lapsing ... Contempt for women is the first law of savagery, and perhaps the last law of some old and profound philosophy' (188). A terrifying shark, in fact, had eaten his catch.

Disaster strikes. While Dick is fishing, the dinghy floats out to sea, minus one of the sculls. Dick swims frantically to get over its gunwale, just in time to avoid a shark. The shark is the 'spirit of the lagoon' (192), true Nature in its brutal indifference. Both sculls are gone. Dick, Em and the baby are swept out to sea. 'Dick stood in despair … . He could do nothing' (193). They commit suicide by eating arita berries, a branch of which Em had taken into the boat.

The father, Arthur Lestrange, charters a boat to find them after some evidence of their location is discovered. He locates the dinghy just after the couple and the baby have consumed the poisonous berries. When Lestrange asks 'Are they dead?' the Captain, Stannistreet, remarks: 'No; they are asleep' (218). The conclusion appears ambiguous. One learns in the sequel that Em and Dick in fact are dead, although the son lives.

The Blue Lagoon records the maturation of Dick Lestrange, but it is a maturation away from rather than toward conventional civilised masculinity. Its implicit concept is that genuine maleness, with all its strengths and prejudices, is realised in such isolated environments. Dick is aware through the symbolic actions of the cyclone or the shark that Nature, if not malevolent, is indifferent to his existence. This fact carries particular force since Stacpoole has dropped God out of the equation. Dick's adventure is into himself as surely as is the adventure of a Conrad protagonist. In this novel, however, the 'other' culture is solely the self, with its sexual initiation and the experience of paternity. While these experiences would appear conventional, the fact that Dick matures without other male paradigms of behaviour before him renders these exceptional. Dick's experiences bear out Muscogiuri's declaration that 'shipwreck takes on the value of a break, which brings about the (psychic) death of (social and national) identity … a death coincident with a rebirth and an invaluable sea-change' (213).

This is not to say that this masculine paradigm evolved in nature is good or satisfying. In this post-Darwinian text, while masculinity enables survival, it leads to self-destruction. Even so authoritarian an individual as Dick commits suicide. He does not want to be rescued. The text does not say whether this final act of suicide is one of despair or love. If the latter, one must read the suicide of the lovers as a *Liebestod* in the tradition of Romeo and Juliet or Tristan and Isolde. It is safe to say, however, that the mature Dick Lestrange is nevertheless an existential stranger, as his surname indicates: it incorporates French (*l'étranger* and *Le-*) with the English *strange*. Unlike the protagonists of *The Coral Island*, he has no longing to be liberated from the island or rescued. He does not live to be haunted like Jim Hawkins in *Treasure Island* because Dick has no concern for finding money. Dick Lestrange chooses death before that nightmare.

Conrad: *A Smile of Fortune* (1911)

Written in the summer of 1910, Conrad's *A Smile of Fortune* was composed after a nervous breakdown. The story was published in the *London Magazine* in February 1911. Paul Kirschner has demonstrated that the narrative has a close affinity with a story by Guy de Maupassant. The unnamed narrator is, as in *The Secret Sharer*, a young Captain. He takes his ship to Mauritius, the 'Pearl of the Ocean', where he expects to load the ship with sugar cane. In the course of the tale, the young Captain is torn between the commercialism of his enterprise and his attraction to Alice, the illegitimate daughter of one of two Jacobus brothers.

These two brothers, according to Salley Vickers, 'represent twin strains in the captain' (viii). One is Ernest Jacobus, a wealthy merchant in the port who has the respect of the town although he has a mulatto illegitimate son as an office boy, whom he abuses. The other Jacobus brother, Alfred, is a ship-chandler with a daughter, presumably his, by a lady rider circus performer. As Vickers observes, Alfred is 'a social pariah' (viii).

Conrad leaves us in no doubt about the existential nature of this conflict between economics and eroticism. The young Captain's ambiguous response to his economic mission is detailed early in the tale:

> Ah! These commercial interests – spoiling the finest life under the sun. Why must the sea be used for trade – and for war as well? Why kill and traffic on it, pursuing selfish aims of no great importance after all? It would have been so much nicer just to sail about with here and there a port and a bit of land to stretch one's legs on, buy a few books and get a change of cooking for a while. But, living in a world more or less homicidal and desperately mercantile, it was plainly my duty to make the best of its opportunities. (6)

The tale is one of several by Conrad, e.g., *The Secret Sharer*, deploying this sea-land antithesis. The Captain notes: 'On coming in from sea one has to pick up the conditions of an utterly unrelated existence' (5).

Daphna Erdinast-Vulcan (1999) calls attention to the parallels between Shakespeare's *The Tempest* and Conrad's *A Smile of Fortune*: 'The ingredients are all there: an exotic enchanted island, a man who had been cast out by a society dominated by his brutish brother, a beautiful daughter living with her father in utter seclusion, and a young man who comes ashore after a stormy night at sea' (135). Indeed, at the beginning, the young Captain admits about the island: 'I became entranced by this blue, pinnacled apparition, almost transparent against the light of the sky, a mere emanation, the astral body of an island risen to greet me from afar. It is a rare phenomenon' (3).

Alfred Jacobus visits the ship to do business. He also asks the Captain if he is married, to which the young man responds: 'No, I am not married … Neither married nor even engaged' (10). A bit later, he feels 'convinced that I would never marry' (16). Thus, within a few pages, Conrad underscores this tension between economics and eroticism.

If Shakespeare's *The Tempest* is one parallel for Conrad's story, the adventure narrative is another. Before visiting the garden of Alfred Jacobus, the narrator imagines Jacobus and his daughter as the material of a romantic adventure rescue:

> When my friend left me I had a conception of Jacobus and his daughter existing,
> a lonely pair of castaways, on a desert island; the girl sheltering in the house as
> if it were a cavern in a cliff, and Jacobus going out to pick up a living for both
> on the beach – exactly like two shipwrecked people who always hope for some
> rescuer to bring them back at last into touch with the rest of mankind. (35)

In his fantasies, the narrator is the rescuer of the enchanted princess locked in her garden prison, like Sleeping Beauty. The narrator persists in this view when he does see Alice: 'She was as much of a castaway as any one ever wrecked on a desert island' (53). Such erotic rescue fantasies will ultimately be demolished by the force of economic exchange.

Having seen the wealthy merchant Ernest Jacobus abuse the mulatto young man, the narrator decides that Alfred is the more tolerable of the two brothers, contrary to the town's opinion. In the same chapter, two key events occur: first, the narrator discovers he does not have enough bags of a special type to transport his sugar and, second, he meets Alice, the daughter of the circus performer, in Alfred Jacobus' garden. The economic and erotic scenarios are thus juxtaposed.

When the narrator visits Alfred Jacobus' house, he is 'entranced' (38) by the garden, in a clear echo of Shakespeare's *The Tempest*. The Captain is equally mesmerised by Jacobus' daughter Alice, especially by her hair; 'It was a mass of black, lustrous locks, twisted anyhow high on her head … It gave you a sensation of heavy pressure on the top of your head and an impression of magnificently cynical untidiness' (39). This Alice, like Lewis Carroll's protagonist, appears to be in 'wonderland' so far as the Captain is concerned.

He is also sexually aroused by her thin clothing: 'She leaned forward, hugging herself with crossed legs; a dingy amber-coloured, flounced wrapper of some thin stuff revealed the young supple body … . What she had on under that dingy, loose, amber wrapper must have been of the most flimsy and airy character … light attire' (39–40). Her remark to every address is 'Don't care!' (42, 48). Early on, she questions what brings the Captain to her house, and he replies: 'And suppose it's you? You would not call that business? Would you?' (58). His repeated visits to Alice, however, will indicate not love but voyeurism.

Alice is, however, sexually ambiguous in her demeanour. Her voice is twice described as 'harsh' (42, 58) albeit seductive. She has a 'generous, fine, somewhat masculine hand' (57). 'Her attitude, like certain tones of her voice, had in it something masculine' (58). This gender ambiguity, however, had appeared earlier in the narrative when Alfred Jacobus had greeted the Captain with a bouquet of flowers. The narrator recorded: 'He made me feel as if I were a pretty girl' (20). Between the Captain and Alice there is some blurring of gendered identities. Schwarz contends that Jacobus is 'testing whether the captain is a homosexual' (12). Whether or not this is true, the Captain's masculinity is destabilised.

This blurring, however, has a serious consequence because the enthralled but disturbed Captain becomes both masochistic and sadistic. Several times he records that Alice's 'indifference' (51, 53) is nevertheless seductive. But the attraction is humiliating. 'It was like being the slave of some depraved habit' (53). He realises: 'It was what I was coming for daily; troubled, ashamed, eager; finding in my nearness to her a unique sensation that I indulged with dread, self-contempt, and deep pleasure, as if it were a secret vice bound to end in my undoing, like the habit of some drug or other that ruins and degrades its slave' (56). Schwarz (1982) concludes that 'the narrator is pathologically terrified of women' (12).

One wonders if Conrad derived some of this sadism from W.H. Hudson's *Green Mansions* of 1904. There, the protagonist Abel visits the bird-girl/nature-goddess Rima and frequently comments on her gossamer clothing. He also torments her by absenting himself without notice from Rima's presence. Abel deploys both voyeurism and sadism as a method of exerting power over Rima, which he is happy to perceive.

At the same time, in *A Smile of Fortune,* the Captain intends to intimidate Alice: 'I cannot go so far as to say I had terrified her. But she was troubled by my truculence' (51). In a statement of both fear and defiance, Alice tells the Captain: 'If you were to shut me up in an empty place … I could always strangle myself with my hair' (59). Schwarz (1982) observes about the Captain and Alice's relationship: 'The frustrated and repressed captain *chooses* a bastard, a scapegoat of society, because he *needs* to cast himself in the dominant role' (18). One can only agree with Paul Kirschner (1966) that 'Conrad's Captain seems cerebral and vicious' (76).

Overwhelmed by her 'supreme indifference' (62), the Captain kisses her, but the kiss is a torment: 'The first kiss I planted on her closed lips was vicious enough to have been a bite' (62). He is erotically charged because she is indifferent. 'She did not resist, and of course I did not stop at one. She let me go on, not as if she were inanimate – I felt her there, close against me, young, full of vigour, of life, a strong desirable creature, but as if she did not care in the least, in the absolute assurance of her safety, what I did or left undone' (62).

Realising that her father has witnessed this embrace, the Captain, to avoid a scandal and because he experiences a 'contemptuous disgust' (66), allows Alfred Jacobus to blackmail him. In return for the sugar bags, he is forced to pay for a load of potatoes the ship-chandler wishes to get off his hands. The young Captain must take the potatoes if he will not take the daughter. Alice has become a base commodity, with the Captain choosing the economic option rather than the erotic chance.

Conrad invokes another kind of tale in addition to the adventure narrative or the enchanted drama, that of the fairy tale of Cinderella. After their embrace was discovered by her father, Alice had fled from the Captain and her father, leaving behind her shoe. The two men meet over this slipper:

> I followed the direction of his glance. In the absolute stillness of the house we stared at the high-heeled slipper the girl had lost in her flight. We stared. It lay overturned … . It was not really a slipper, but a low shoe of blue, glazed kid, rubbed and shabby. It had straps to go over the instep, but the girl only thrust

> her feet in, after her slovenly manner. Jacobus raised his eyes from the shoe to
> look at me. (65)

The narrator realises that his Cinderella is less alluring than his fantasy conceived.
When she returns, he puts the shoe on her foot, correcting her slovenliness: 'I put
on the shoe, buttoning the instep-strap. It was an inanimate foot' (69). Having
gone from fantasised 'slipper' to ordinary 'shoe', the shoe fits but the prince is
fleeing.

The Captain's disgust at the economic coercion from Jacobus and at his own
choice also becomes a disgust for Alice. When the Captain sees her again, he treats
her as the commodity she has become. 'I don't know why or whence I received
the impression that she had come too late. She ought to have appeared at my call'
(69). When she exhibits independence, he treats her as a slave. 'I felt more like
wailing over the lost illusion of vague desire, over the sudden conviction that I
would never find again near her the strange, half-evil, half-tender sensation that
had given its acrid flavour to so many days, which had made her appear tragic and
promising, pitiful and provoking. That was all over' (69–70).

When he departs, she tries to kiss him 'but I was no longer moved' (71). He
tells her he is 'now doing business with your father … That's the sort of man
I am' (70). The Captain now chooses economics over eroticism, concealing his
misogyny and perhaps impotence behind this façade. 'I realised clearly with a
sort of terror my complete detachment from that unfortunate creature' (70). As
Jeremy Hawthorn observes: 'The captain deserts Alice at the point at which his
desire dies and she appears before him as an independent individual … At this
point, when he has to deal with her as an equal interested in and attracted to him,
his desire evaporates' (120). Schwarz (1982) summarises: 'We are listening to the
confessions of a disturbed young man who had become obsessed with an even
more disturbed young woman' (16).

The narrator reflects on the experience: 'I felt in my heart that the further one
ventures the better one understands how everything in our life is common, short,
and empty; that it is in seeking the unknown in our sensations that we discover
how mediocre are our attempts and how soon defeated!' (71). 'I was glad enough
to be at sea, but not with the gladness of old days' (73).

This realisation has major consequences. Due to a famine, the Captain manages
to sell the potatoes for a great sum when he reaches Australia. Jerome Zuckerman
regards this transaction, where the Captain sells the potatoes 'at exorbitant prices',
as evidence of his 'complicity in Jacobus' baseness; he is willing to exploit others
as Jacobus had been willing to exploit him. Just as Jacobus used the sexual
attractions of his daughter, so also the Captain uses the hardships of a people …
[Hence] the ironic smile of fortune of the title' (101–2).

Because of his superior performance, the Captain is asked by his employers
to return to the 'Pearl of the Ocean'; he declines. Zuckerman believes he is now
aware of his sordid nature: 'Ensnared in moral corruption and thus in his own eyes
rendered unfit for rule, he resigns his command' to face 'an uncertain future' (102).

Furthermore, the Captain fears becoming involved with either Alfred Jacobus or his daughter Alice. He cannot revisit the nightmare of sex. Earlier, a friend had warned him: 'Of course, if that girl were disposed of it would certainly facilitate –' (51). Recalling that Alfred Jacobus asked at their first meeting if he were married, the Captain realises that the ship-chandler was all along deceiving him, planning to get rid of his daughter.

When he resigns his command, the Captain feels the situation was 'driving me out of the ship I had learned to love … . I sat heavy hearted at that parting, seeing all my plans destroyed, my modest future endangered – for this command was like a foot in the stirrup for a young man' (78–9). Instead of embracing command as do the young captains of *The Secret Sharer* or *The Shadow-Line*, this Captain is alienated from all identity at the tale's conclusion. According to William Lafferty, the Captain 'is uncertain of what kind of man he is' (63). The difference is that the other two stories do not involve heterosexual love. Conrad seems to argue that being uninvolved with a woman is best for a sailor. The Captain in *A Smile of Fortune* is a sado-masochist who in the end is demolished by both eroticism and economics. Yet, according to Zivah Perel, he is similar to other Conrad protagonists: 'The men in Conrad's fiction … share the common trait of bachelorhood. Their resistance to forming permanent male-female relationships becomes critical in their dissent against the Victorian standards of masculinity that value marriage and childbearing' (117).

The tale seems particularly to summarise Conrad's jaded attitude toward the maritime enterprise. John Peck argues that several factors contributed to Conrad's disillusionment: 'There was the impact of Darwin's ideas. There was the increasingly competitive, land-grabbing colonialism of the late nineteenth century. There was a neo-mercantilist mentality, in which protectionism increasingly usurped the concept and practice of free trade. And there was the sense of being at the end of an era, as sail finally gave way to steam' (171). *A Smile of Fortune* with its drop-out protagonist appears to confirm Conrad's sense of malaise. His erotic encounter with Alice has revealed the fragility of his masculine identity, whether in the form of enchanted drama, beloved fairy tale or alluring adventure.

Conrad: 'The Planter of Malata' (1914)

Joseph Conrad's 'The Planter of Malata' was written in November and December 1913. It was published in the *Metropolitan Magazine* in its June and July issues of 1914. In his Note to the collection *Within the Tides* (1920) in which the tale was included, Conrad declared that 'the primary intention of [the tale] was esthetic; an essay in description and narrative around a given psychological situation' and that 'the scene near the rock … from the point of view of psychology [is] crucial' (Wright, ed. 212). He described the story 'as a very nearly successful attempt at doing a very difficult thing' (212). Thomas Moser famously declared that Conrad's 'decline' was due to the fact he could not deal with erotic passion. In 'The Planter of Malata', on the contrary, Conrad exhibits the ability to deal with sexual passion via a strategy of scorched earth/no prisoners.

The tale involves the destabilisation of masculinity on the part of its protagonist, Geoffrey Renouard, a man of action, an experimental scientist and a loner engulfed in a consuming love affair with Felicia Moorsom, who has come to a large colonial city, Sydney in the manuscript, to find her fiancé Arthur, who was unjustly accused of embezzlement and fled England. Felicia has come to locate Arthur as an act of 'reparation' (276), to repair him and restore him to his merited status. The Editor informs Renouard that the Moorsom party has arrived and that 'they are out looking for a man' (252), a line which Renouard repeats to himself. According to Stanley Renner, this statement makes the story 'about a lost sense of masculinity in the culture' (5).

Prior to meeting Felicia Moorsom, Renouard, 'with his fine bronzed face ... was a lean, lounging, active man' (241). He is an 'explorer' (251). He has been involved in a 'five-years' program of scientific adventure' (243) involving plant experimentation at his silk plantation on the island of Malata. But he had prior adventures: he had settled in Malata 'after five years of adventure and exploration' (273).

These adventures and ventures have given him a rough reputation. 'You are a fellow that doesn't count the cost' his Editor acquaintance (not friend) tells him (249). Later, Felicia Moorsom's father states: 'I am told that he has made an enemy of almost every man who had to work with him ... He never counted the cost they say. Not even of lives' (272). Felicia rebukes Renouard later by describing him as 'a man who, I understand, has never counted the cost' (276). Renouard, then, is to all appearances an intelligent adventurer and risk-taker, unafraid of challenges. The Editor reminds him: 'You know what has been said of you? That you couldn't get on with anybody you couldn't kick' (260). However, as Joel Kehler declares, 'everyone but Renouard does "count the cost"' (154).

Furthermore, the idea of adventure takes on a new meaning in this tale. As Juliet McLauchlan stresses, this passionate attraction 'involves exploration into his own personality, and here the discovery is emptiness' (189). Having explored in the physical world, Renouard is here again adventuring, but in the psychological erotic world. This is the intention of his name, deriving from the French verb *renouer*, that is, 'to tie again', 'to knot again', 'to resume', 'to renew', 'to resume relationship.' It is a high risk behaviour which will both enlighten him and destroy him.

Renouard's first vision of Felicia Moorsom is at a dinner party:

> She was tall and supple, carrying nobly on her straight body a head of a character which to him appeared peculiar, something ... pagan, crowned with a great wealth of hair ... Her hair was magnificently red and her eyes very black. It was a troubling effect ... All that mass of arranged hair appeared incandescent, chiseled and fluid, with the daring suggestion of a helmet of burnished copper and the flowing lines of molten metal ... . Her shoulders and her bare arms

gleamed with an extraordinary splendour … Under the red coppery gold of the hair [she seemed] as though she had been a being made of ivory and precious metals changed into living tissue. (246–7)

To Renouard she is 'a condescending and strong-headed goddess' (265).

Conrad evokes the myth of Galatea. Renouard has fashioned her, like Pygmalion, into a fantasised statue which has come alive. This Galatea, however, will not be his. 'In the darkness of his cabin, he did not create a faint mental vision of her person for himself, but, more intimately affected, he scented distinctly the faint perfume she used. [He was] oppressed by the sensation of something that had happened to him and could not be undone … . that consciousness of something that could no longer be helped' (256–7). Then, Renouard sees Felicia as an 'amazon' (271). He becomes a 'mortal envelope, emptied of everything but hopeless passion' (273). As the relationship evolves, 'he was afraid … She was fate itself' (276).

This awareness is reflected subconsciously in a dream Renouard has on his schooner. He dreams of a head of a statue which resembles Felicia Moorsom, which eventually crumbles 'and at last turned into a handful of dust' (263). He is profoundly disassociated from himself: 'On closer examination he perceived that the reflection of himself in the mirror was not really the true Renouard' (263). He knows the dream is 'demonic' (264). He perceives his own self as the other.

Renouard can define this 'demonic' dimension: 'He accepted the immense misfortune of being in love with a woman who was in search of another man … He feared it instinctively as a sick man may fear death. For it seemed that it must be the death of him … It seems that a woman betrays us simply by this that she exists, that she breathes' (265). He fears he is 'going to pieces' (265). To him, she is a 'tragic Venus' (267).

Part of this destabilising of masculinity in Renouard is reflected by references aligning him to Pallas or Minerva. Renouard 'had such a profile as may be seen amongst the bronzes of classical museums, pure under a crested helmet – recalled vaguely a Minerva's head' (269). Later, 'his suddenly lowered eyelids brought out startlingly his resemblance to antique bronze, the profile of Pallas, still, austere, bowed a little in the shadow of the rock' (297). This goddess, albeit a woman, sprang from Zeus' head. Renouard then is both intensely masculine but disturbingly incorporates within him a virginal goddess of wisdom and war.

Part of Renouard's experience in his relationship is to discover the feminine in himself, but as his alignment with Minerva demonstrates, it is the feminine of a female-male goddess. In reality, Felicia Moorsom is the virginal, asexual Minerva or Diana. As the latter, she is a huntress on a mission to dominate or destroy any Arthur, her fiancée or Renouard, who stands in her way. Erdinast-Vulcan observes about Minerva/Felicia that Renouard's identification with her 'is a measure of his metamorphosis which accelerates until he becomes a mere reflection of her will' (158–9). Renouard is willing, she notes, 'to enter Miss Moorsom's false romance, to step into the role of the object of the quest' (159). He is offered 'a choice between his former 'masculine', 'true' self and the exhausted, passive creature of the false romance woven by Felicia' (160). 'Conrad writes about a character who loses his "masculine self" when he is assimilated into the false "feminine discourse" of romance' (Erdinast-Vulcan 164).

This goddess Venus/Felicia is a handful of dust, as Renouard's dream advised. Felicia's false wisdom is given ironic point by her constant assertions that she stands for truth in this venture to find Arthur: 'I think I may say I have an instinct for truth' (272); 'I stand for truth here' (276); 'It's I who stand for truth' (297); 'Here I stand for truth itself' (299). In reality, her vainglorious reclamation of Arthur is to act as a female Pygmalion, to recreate him to repossess him.

Felicia represents the decadence of shore life, including its repudiation of actual sexuality and its emptiness. Her father informs Renouard about Felicia's hollow nature: 'You don't know what it is to have moved, breathed, existed, and even triumphed in the mere smother and froth of life – the brilliant froth. Their thoughts, sentiments, opinions, feelings, actions too, are nothing but agitation in empty space – to amuse life – a sort of superior debauchery, exciting and fatiguing, meaning nothing, leading nowhere. She is a creature of that circle' (270). Felicia is an alluring *femme fatale* but a worthless one.

The Editor discovers that Renouard's assistant, who calls himself Walter, is in reality the sought-for Arthur, on whom Renouard took pity and brought to the island of Malata. Before arriving from Malata, Renouard had buried Arthur after he was injured fatally in an accident. 'To bury him was the last service Renouard had rendered to his assistant before leaving the island on this trip to town' (282). Unable to reveal the truth to the Moorsoms, Renouard invites them to come to Malata to find Walter.

Before they do arrive, Renouard swims from the schooner to the island to tell his attendants to lie about the fate of Walter. Ted Billy labels this episode 'the planter's ontological swim' (153). This swim, the male returning to the womb, prefigures Renouard's end and reveals his existential state:

> Renouard set his direction by a big star that, dipping on the horizon, seemed to look curiously into his face. On this swim back, he felt the mournful fatigue of all that length of the traversed road, which brought him no nearer to his desire... It was as if his love had sapped the invisible supports of his strength. There came a moment when it seemed to him that he must have swum beyond the confines of life. He had a sensation of eternity close at hand, demanding no effort offering its peace. It was easy to swim like this beyond the confines of life looking at a star … He lay in his hammock utterly exhausted and with a confused feeling that he had been beyond the confines of life, somewhere near a star, and that it was very quiet there. (287)

Finally, on the rocky promontory of Malata, Renouard admits to Felicia that he buried Arthur. He informs her that Arthur 'wasn't impressive. He was pitiful. My worst enemy could have told you he wasn't good enough to be one of Renouard's victims. It didn't take me long to judge that he was drugging himself. Not drinking. Drugs' (296). Felicia's fiancé, with the absurdly chivalric name of Arthur, was a self-destructive loser. Even more, when Arthur/Walter died, 'he muttered something about his innocence and something that sounded like a curse on some woman, then turned to the wall – and just grew cold' (297). Both Arthur and Renouard will curse Felicia. Renouard recognises that 'now you will not believe in me – not even in me who must in truth be what I am – even to death' (297). The setting of this revelation reinforces Owen Knowles' contention that 'the keynote of Conrad's story is initially set by the bold contrast between the primitive outcrop of Malata and decadent mainland' (1979, 183).

Nevertheless, as the bearer of truth, Renouard drives home his point: 'Are you grieving for your dignity? [Arthur] was a mediocre soul and could have given you but an unworthy existence' (298). Then he lashes into her falseness: 'You are merely the topmost layer, disdainful and superior, the mere pure froth and bubble on the inscrutable depths which someday will toss you out of existence ... You are the eternal love itself – only, O Divinity, it isn't your body, it is your soul that is made of foam' (298). Renouard alludes to the birth of Aphrodite/Venus from the sea/semen foam, but this Aphrodite has no body, or she has a body but no sexuality.

But this revelation costs Renouard: 'Fire ran through his veins, turned his passion to ashes, burnt him out and left him empty, without force – almost without desire' (299). He acknowledges that Felicia is sexually repressed, which demolishes his own erotic desire. He recognises that she is 'so used to the forms of repression enveloping, softening the crude impulses of old humanity that she no longer believed in their existence as if it were an exploded legend. She did not recognise what had happened to her (299). When he alludes to the legitimate power of sex, she tells him in French that she is 'repelled by all that' (300). According to Hawthorn (2004), Felicia's response in French implies 'revulsion so strong as to render her incapable of expressing her horror of sex in her own language' (132). Within the Moorsom name, the French *moeurs* (customs, habits) inscribes this repression in Felicia. She has no genuine self, just 'manners'. Hovering within her name is also the Latin *mors* or death.

Transmuted in his exported masculinity, Renouard has had an erotic adventure that, unlike his others in the world, has led to self-knowledge and death: 'His resolution had failed him ... This walk up the hill and down again was like the supreme effort of an explorer trying to penetrate the interior of an unknown country ... Decoyed by a mirage, he had gone too far – so far that there was no going back. His strength was at an end. For the first time in his life he had to give up' (300).

After the Moorsoms leave Malata, Renouard dismisses all his servants and releases the schooner. When the Editor returns to the island, he finds the sandals, jacket and sarong Renouard customarily wore when he went bathing. The Editor claims Renouard drowned, but the sailing-master doubts it, as there has been no body discovered. In fact: 'Nothing was ever found – and Renouard's disappearance remained in the main inexplicable. For to whom could it have occurred that a man would set out calmly to swim beyond the confines of life – with a steady stroke – his eyes fixed on a star?' (305). Renouard commits suicide, in a triumphal act of male self-assertion.

McLauchlan states about Renouard: 'Though Renouard's final discovery of selfhood is the discovery of emptiness, yet he is less worthless than Felicia' (190). Is this accurate? Renouard has found his true male self. It is not empty (his previous life may have been) – it is full of passion now. Renner believes that in 'The Planter of Malata' Conrad exposed the pernicious sexlessness attached to women in Edwardian culture, which ultimately destroys both men and women, 'a serious neurosis in culture' (14). Renner suggests that Arthur fled Felicia not because of the embezzlement charge but because of the debilitation of the sexual impulse which results from a sexless cultural ideology. The word 'sentiment', Renner notes, is used repeatedly in the tale 'in reference to the idealization of love as a self-sacrificing spiritual emotion untainted by selfish sexual desire' (17). Conrad, he concludes, records 'a general cultural malaise at the heart of its sexual life' (17).

According to Kehler, Renouard's swim to the star evokes Tennyson's Ulysses, who follows 'knowledge like a sinking star/Beyond the utmost bound of human thought.' Renouard's death is not a suicide but a triumph. Graver comments that Conrad 'treats love with less subtlety than the psychological or moral aspects of masculine self-knowledge' (178). However that may be, Conrad handles the latter subject superbly. One can concur with Said (1966): 'This, to my mind, is Conrad's most pessimistic story, and a masterpiece nonetheless' (162).

Like Ulysses, another explorer, Renouard finds his genuine sexualised manhood sufficient to stand for the truth. As Kehler observes, 'Now it is he that "stands for truth" and she that will have to shore up her sanity with new lies and pretenses' (160). Even if the culture was or is still 'searching for a man', Renouard has found his manhood. Having in his first swim to the island, overwhelmed by *eros*, failed to commit suicide, in his second swim he abandons *eros* and then, triumphantly, embraces *thanatos*.

In a statement about sea fiction which applies to adventure texts in general, John Peck observes: 'The masculine world of the ship might be one where bodies are abused, but it is also a world in which men take pride in their strength and resilience. This exaggerated sense of masculinity … encourages an attitude towards women that is at a far remove from any kind of domestic ideal' (26). The texts in this chapter verify the tension existing between the attitudes of economic adventurers like Conrad's protagonists and the defining of heterosexual relationships. Leo Vincey in *She* is prematurely gray from his sexual encounters. The young Dick Lestrange in *The Blue Lagoon* chooses death. John Wiltshire in 'The Beach of Falesá' marries across racial lines but remains conflicted about his decision. Rassendyll in *The Prisoner of Zenda* escapes his involvement by pleading a higher cause. In each text there remains the tension between the masculine world of adventure and the different context of heterosexuality.

Conclusion

Buchan: *The Thirty-Nine Steps* (1915)

In 1926, John Buchan, author of *Prester John* and by then a novelist of stature with such titles as *The Power-House* (1913), *Greenmantle* (1916), *Mr Standfast* (1919), and *John Macnab* (1925) to his credit and fame, paused to write a short essay 'Adventure Stories, From Defoe to Stevenson' for *John O'London's Weekly*. The essay summarises his attitudes toward adventure fiction even as it records the passage from the adventure novel to the spy novel between the Edwardian and Georgian periods.

Buchan argues that 'in a sense every good novel is a novel of adventure; for there is action in it or it would not be a novel' (274). But Buchan then defines the adventure novel more narrowly: 'We must define the thing quite arbitrarily, I think, as a rapid, close-textured narrative in which the bulk of the incidents involve physical violence and peril, and in which the interest is centred upon these incidents and their immediate human "reactions". Let us add that the incidents should themselves be strange and romantic or, if they are commonplace, they must have a strange and romantic setting' (274). Buchan instances Stevenson's *Kidnapped* as an exemplary adventure text.

Buchan then elaborates that he sees two kinds of adventure texts. One 'skims the cream, is content with a minimum of detail, and trips unashamed within easy distance of unreality' (274). This kind of adventure novel is exemplified, he thinks, by *Treasure Island* and *The Prisoner of Zenda*. The 'other type follows the *Robinson Crusoe* tradition and is at immense pains to give verisimilitude by a multitude of concrete details … The second school are artists in verisimilitude' (274). For Buchan *King Solomon's Mines* and *The Riddle of the Sands* represent this second category. He regards *The Riddle of the Sands* as 'the best story of adventure published in the last quarter of a century … As for the characters, I think they are the most fully realized of any adventure story that I have met, and the atmosphere of grey Northern skies and miles of yeasty water and wet sands is as masterfully reproduced as in any story of Conrad's' (276).

Buchan's essay, albeit brief, is important, for it signals a transition from the adventure text to the spy text during the passing of the Edwardian adventure novel into the powerful Georgian spy novel. Buchan's selection of *The Riddle of the Sands* is particularly noteworthy, for its focus on 'invasion scare' and espionage in an adventure context prefigures this transformation, which will be realised in Buchan's 1915 masterpiece *The Thirty-Nine Steps*. With the urgency of the First World War, international diplomacy and global espionage, the spy story begins to gain prominence in the Georgian period. It does *not* supplant the adventure novel, as the many texts published during and after the Great War attest, but it does reveal the integration of adventure elements into the spy narrative as the German menace and fear of traitors within the gates gain importance.

The protagonist, Richard Hannay, becomes involved in a German threat to destabilise global relations by assassinating Constantine Karolides, a Greek diplomat, provoking a war between England and Germany. Hannay confronts a German spy organisation and the threat of the invasion of Britain by Germany, echoing *The Riddle of the Sands* and its Germanophobia. *The Thirty-Nine Steps* includes such detectival elements as ratiocination and the metropolitan city as a dangerous locale. The latter element is not part of the adventure narrative, which rather stresses foreign and exotic locales. Furthermore, the action is confined to England and Scotland. Adventure has been brought home in this spy novel, for the presence of German spies and domestic traitors has rendered England itself a foreign locale to rival the dangers of any actual foreign land. Buchan's subsequent spy novels, however, often occur in foreign lands.

On the other hand, *The Thirty-Nine Steps* does deploy many of the conventions of adventure fiction: the intrepid hero, the exotic landscapes (the wilds of Scotland), an emphasis on physical strength and the confrontations between hunter and hunted, pursuer and pursued. However, the hunted is a Scotsman returned from South Africa with his wealth, while the hunters are both the British police and German agents. As Tom Ryall states: 'Although *The Thirty-Nine Steps* is not a colonial adventure story it is a story about a colonial adventurer' (156).

Like his adventure cousins, Hannay is a model of masculinity in extremely stressful times. He makes comments such as the following: 'I must keep going myself, ready to act when things got riper' (39); 'Somehow the first success gave me a feeling that I was going to pull the thing through' (57); 'The only thing that kept me going was that I was pretty furious' (65); 'I forced myself to play the game' (105). Richard Usborne asserts in *Clubland Heroes* about this imprinting: 'If not exactly the author set for homework, Buchan was certainly strongly recommended to the schoolboy by parent, uncle, guardian, pastor and master. Buchan backed up their directives and doctrines. Buchan wrote good English. Buchan taught you things. Buchan was good for you' (84).

Buchan's novel also reflects the focus of many adventure texts on the all-male environment. Tom Ryall observes about the novel:

> In the character of Richard Hannay, it constitutes a particular version of masculinity – the heroic adventurer ... untroubled by the presence of the feminine. Buchan's novel sketches a world which is almost exclusively male, producing a conception of masculine identity in which the presence and implications of the feminine is repressed, displaced and possibly repositioned. It may be termed a consciously 'uncomplicated' version of masculinity although, from another perspective, it may be viewed as a version made complex precisely by the repression and displacement of the world of sexuality. (153)

A key difference of Hannay from the protagonists of adventure fiction, however, is his eschewing of personal advantage and reward for an explicit national agenda, service to king and country, as he remarks throughout the text: 'The prospect was pretty dark either way, but anyhow there was a chance, both for myself and for my country ... The odds were horrible, but I had to take them' (66–7); 'I felt the sense of danger and impending calamity, and I had a curious feeling, too, that I alone could avert it, alone could grapple with it' (86). Hannay does not prevent the assassination, but he does foil the conspiracy of war and invasion, in the process alerting the British government to its complacency.

In the course of his escape and pursuit through the Yorkshire and Scottish moors, Hannay comes upon a young innkeeper who wants to write novels. He tells Hannay: 'I want to see life, to travel the world, and write things like Kipling and Conrad' (32). When Hannay gives him a background story fashioned of adventure thrills, the young man comments: 'By God! ... It is all pure Rider Haggard and Conan Doyle' (33). Thus in a few pages, Buchan manages to bring the names of great adventure novelists into his spy tale. By this strategy, he acknowledges the importance of the adventure novel to the spy genre and incorporates it into his text.

Hannay as hero, however, differs in some aspects from the adventure heroes discussed in this book. There are, of course, similarities between the spy hero and the adventure hero: wandering and journeying, being unmarried, colonial associations and experience, action and independence. Common to both adventure and spy texts is the function of imprinting masculinities. On the other hand, Hannay and his associates represent what Richard Usborne famously defined as a 'clubland hero' in the works of Buchan, Sapper and Dornford Yates. These clubland heroes are often clubmen in an inner circle, gentlemen by birth, have an independent income, speak the same language, embrace school ideologies, stress sportsmanship, have friends similar to themselves, are patriotic and stress duty not so much to self as to country.

It is true that some adventure protagonists have university backgrounds, for example, but membership in a club is not necessarily one of their signature traits. Instead, most adventure heroes have associates but are alienated and restless. In the case of Conrad, the men in his sea stories are often existentially isolated, full of skepticism rather than conviction. The contrast between David Crawfurd in *Prester John* and Richard Hannay in *The Thirty-Nine Steps* reveals this difference of adventure heroes from their spy counterparts. While both men get their 'pile' from South Africa, Crawfurd's experiences are in that country, while Hannay faces his challenges in England. Crawfurd's opponents are black; Hannay's are white. The protagonists of Childers' *The Riddle of the Sands* presage the protagonists of spy novels with their university backgrounds and commitment to a national cause. Men in spy novels are not often marooned on islands (Ballantyne), fighting in cardboard kingdoms (Hope), searching for lost treasure (Stevenson) or becalmed on ships (Conrad), although in their exploits they might experience one or two of these.

Thus, Buchan's career from *Prester John* in 1910 to *The Thirty-Nine Steps* in 1915 records not the demise of the adventure text but its incorporation into another genre, the spy thriller, to serve the agenda of the immediate war situation. Flagging Kipling, Haggard and Conrad, *The Thirty-Nine Steps* pays its respects to the legacy of the Victorian and Edwardian adventure novel by assuming its obligation to chronicle and imprint British masculinities. Hundreds of soldiers in the trenches of World War I put the slender volume in their kit.

Select Bibliography

Primary Texts

*indicates the version used as primary cited text in this book

*Ballantyne, R.M. *The Coral Island: A Tale of the Pacific Ocean* (1858), ed. J.S. Bratton. Oxford: Oxford University Press, 1991.

*Buchan, John. *Prester John* (1910), ed. David Daniell. Oxford: Oxford University Press, 1994.

*Buchan, John. *The Thirty–Nine Steps* (1915), ed. Christopher Harvie. Oxford: Oxford University Press, 1993.

*Childers, Erskine. *The Riddle of the Sands* (1903), ed. Norman Donaldson. New York: Dover Publications, 1976.

Childers, Erskine. *The Riddle of the Sands* (1903), Foreword by Geoffrey Household. New York: Penguin Books, 1978.

Childers, Erskine. *The Riddle of the Sands: A Record of Secret Service* (1903), ed. David Trotter. Oxford: Oxford University Press, 1998.

*Conrad, Joseph. 'An Outpost of Progress' (1897), in *Tales of Unrest*. New York: Penguin Books, 1977, 83–110.

*Conrad, Joseph. 'Youth' (1897), in *Heart of Darkness and Other Tales*, ed. Cedric Watts. Oxford: Oxford University Press, 2002, 69–100.

Conrad, Joseph. 'Youth' (1897), in *Youth and The End of the Tether*. New York: Penguin Books, 1975, 7–40.

Conrad, Joseph. 'Youth' (1897), in *Youth, Heart of Darkness, The End of the Tether*, ed. Robert Kimbrough. Oxford: Oxford University Press, 1984, 1–42.

*Conrad, Joseph. 'Geography and Some Explorers', in *Heart of Darkness* (1899), ed. Robert Kimbrough. New York: Norton, 1988, 143–7.

Conrad, Joseph. *Heart of Darkness* (1899), ed. Ross C. Murfin. Boston: St Martin's, 1996.

Conrad, Joseph. *Heart of Darkness* (1899), ed. Ross C. Murfin. New York: St Martin's, 1989.

*Conrad, Joseph. *Heart of Darkness* (1899), ed. Robert Kimbrough. New York: Norton, 1988.

Conrad, Joseph. *Heart of Darkness* (1899), in *Heart of Darkness and Other Tales*, ed. Cedric Watts. Oxford: Oxford University Press, 2002, 101–87.

Conrad, Joseph. *Typhoon* (1902), in *Typhoon and Other Stories*, ed. Paul Kirschner. New York: Penguin Books, 1990, 53–132.

*Conrad, Joseph. *Typhoon* (1902), in *Typhoon and Other Tales*, ed. Cedric Watts. Oxford: Oxford University Press, 1998, 1–74.

Conrad, Joseph. *The Secret Sharer* (1910), in *Conrad's* Secret Sharer *and the Critics*, ed. Bruce Harkness. Belmont CA: Wadsworth, 1962.

Conrad, Joseph. *The Secret Sharer* (1910), ed. Daniel R. Schwartz. Boston: St. Martin's, 1997.

*Conrad, Joseph. *The Secret Sharer: An Episode from the Coast* (1910), in *Typhoon and Other Tales*, ed. Cedric Watts. Oxford: Oxford University Press, 1998, 177–217.

*Conrad, Joseph. *A Smile of Fortune: A Harbour Story* (1911), Foreword by Salley Vickers. London: Hesperus Press, 2007.

*Conrad, Joseph. 'The Planter of Malata' (1914), in *Almayer's Folly and Other Stories*, Afterword by Jocelyn Baines. New York: The New American Library, 1965, 241–305.

Conrad, Joseph. *The Shadow-Line: A Confession* (1917), ed. Jacques Berthoud. New York: Penguin Books, 1986.

*Conrad, Joseph. *The Shadow-Line: A Confession* (1917), ed. Jeremy Hawthorn. Oxford: Oxford University Press, 1985.

*Conrad, Joseph. *Notes on Life and Letters* (1921). London: Dent, 1949.

*Haggard, H. Rider. *King Solomon's Mines* (1885), ed. Dennis Butts. Oxford: Oxford University Press, 1989.

*Haggard, H. Rider. *Allan Quatermain* (1887), ed. Dennis Butts. Oxford: Oxford University Press, 1995.

*Haggard, H. Rider. *She* (1887), ed. Daniel Karlin. Oxford: Oxford University Press, 1991.

Haggard, H. Rider. She: *The Annotated: A Critical Edition of H. Rider Haggard's Victorian Romance*, ed. Norman Etherington. Bloomington: Indiana University Press, 1991.

*Hope, Anthony. *The Prisoner of Zenda* (1894), ed. Tony Watkins. Oxford: Oxford University Press, 2001.

Hope, Anthony. *The Prisoner of Zenda* (1894), in *The Prisoner of Zenda* and *Rupert of Hentzau*, ed. Gary Hoppenstand. New York: Penguin Books, 2000, 3–152.

*Hudson, W.H. *Green Mansions* (1904), ed. Ian Duncan. Oxford: Oxford University Press, 1998.

Hudson, W.H. *Green Mansions* (1904), Introduction by Carlos Baker. New York: Bantam, 1965.

Hudson, W.H. *Green Mansions: A Romance of the Tropical Forest* (1904), Foreword by John Galsworthy. New York: Random House, 1944.

*Kipling, Rudyard. *The Man Who Would Be King* (1888), in *The Man Who Would Be King and Other Stories*, ed. Louis L. Cornell. Oxford: Oxford University Press, 1987, 244–79.

*Kipling, Rudyard. *The Light That Failed* (1891), ed. John M. Lyon. New York: Penguin, 1992.

*Kipling, Rudyard. *Captains Courageous* (1897), ed. Leonee Ormond. Oxford: Oxford University Press, 1995.

*Mason, A.E.W. *The Four Feathers* (1902), ed. Gary Hoppenstand. New York: Penguin, 2001.

*Schreiner, Olive. *Trooper Peter Halket of Mashonaland* (1897). Johannesburg: Donker 2001.

*Stacpoole, Henry De Vere. *The Blue Lagoon* (1908). Gloucester: Dodo Press, 2006.

*Stevenson, Robert Louis. 'A Gossip on Romance' (1882), in *Selected Poetry and Prose*, ed. Bradford A. Booth. Boston: Houghton Mifflin, 1968, 55–66.

*Stevenson, Robert Louis. *Treasure Island* (1883), ed. Emma Letley. Oxford: Oxford University Press, 1985.

*Stevenson, Robert Louis. 'A Humble Remonstrance' (1884), in *Selected Poetry and Prose*, Ed. Bradford A. Booth. Boston: Houghton Mifflin, 1968, 66–75.

Stevenson, Robert Louis. 'The Beach of Falesá' (1892), in *Dr. Jekyll and Mr. Hyde and Other Stories*, ed. Jenni Calder. New York: Penguin, 1979, 99–170.

Stevenson, Robert Louis. 'The Beach of Falesá' (1892), in *Selected Poetry and Prose,* ed. Bradford A. Booth. Boston: Houghton, Mifflin, 1968, 331–91.

*Stevenson, Robert Louis. 'The Beach of Falesá' (1892), in *South Sea Tales*, ed. Roslyn Jolly. Oxford: Oxford University Press, 1999, 3–71.

Stevenson, Robert Louis. *The Ebb-Tide* (1894), in *Dr. Jekyll and Mr. Hyde and Other Stories*, ed. Jenni Calder. New York: Penguin Books, 1979, 171–301.

*Stevenson, Robert Louis. *The Ebb-Tide* (1894), in *South Sea Tales*, ed. Roslyn Jolly. Oxford: Oxford University Press, 1999, 123–252.

Books: Biography, History and Criticism

Ashcroft, Bill, Gareth Griffiths and Helen Tiffin. *Post-Colonial Studies: The Key Concepts*. London: Routledge, 2000.

Ashley, Leonard R.N. *George Alfred Henty and the Victorian Mind*. San Francisco: International Scholars, 1998.

Barash, Carol, ed. *An Olive Schreiner Reader: Writings on Women and South Africa*. London: Pandora Press, 1987.

Batchelor, John. *The Edwardian Novelists*. London: Duckworth, 1982.

Batchelor, John. *The Life of Joseph Conrad*. Oxford and Cambridge: Blackwell Publishers, 1994.

Baxter, Katherine Isobel and Richard J. Hand, eds. *Joseph Conrad and the Performing Arts*. Aldershot, UK: Ashgate, 2009.

Bell, David and Gill Valentine, eds. *Mapping Desire: Geographies of Sexualities*. London: Routledge, 1995.

Berthoud, Jacques. *Joseph Conrad: The Major Phase*. Cambridge: Cambridge University Press, 1978.

Bhabha, Homi K., ed. *Nation and Narration*. London: Routledge, 1990.

Bhabha, Homi K. *The Location of Culture*. London: Routledge, 1994.

Billy, Ted. *A Wilderness of Words: Closure and Disclosure in Conrad's Short Fiction*. Lubbock: Texas Tech University Press, 1997.

Bloom, Clive, ed. *Spy Thrillers From Buchan to Le Carre*. London: Macmillan, 1990.

Boehmer, Ellenke. *Empire Writing: An Anthology of Colonial Literature, 1870–1918*. Oxford: Oxford University Press, 1998.

Bonney, William W. *Thorns and Arabesques*. Baltimore: The Johns Hopkins University Press, 1980.

Boyle, Andrew. *The Riddle of Erskine Childers*. London: Hutchinson, 1977.

Brantlinger, Patrick. *Rule of Darkness: British Literature and Imperialism, 1830–1914*. Ithaca: Cornell University Press, 1988.

Bristow, Joseph. *Empire Boys: Adventures in a Man's World*, ed. Derek Longhurst. London: Harper Collins, 1991.

Brittan, Arthur. *Masculinity and Power*. Oxford, England: Blackwell, 1989.

Brod, Harry, ed. *The Making of Masculinities*. Boston: Allen & Unwin, 1987.

Bruss, Paul. *Conrad's Early Sea Fiction: The Novelist as Navigator*. Lewisburg: Bucknell University Press, 1979.

Buchan, John. *Memory Hold the Door: The Autobiography of John Buchan* (1940), ed. David Daniell. London: J.M. Dent and Sons, 1984.

Buckley, Jerome Hamilton. *William Ernest Henley: A Study in the "Counter-Decadence" of the 'Nineties*. Princeton: Princeton University Press, 1945.

Buckley, Jerome Hamilton. *Season of Youth: The Bildungsroman from Dickens to Golding*. Cambridge: Harvard University Press, 1974.

Calder, Jenni, ed. *Stevenson and Victorian Scotland*. Edinburgh: Edinburgh University Press, 1981.

Campbell, Ian, ed. *Nineteenth-Century Scottish Fiction: A Critical Anthology*. New York: Barnes and Noble, 1979.

Carlyle, Thomas. *On Heroes, Hero-Worship, and the Heroic in History*. London: Dent, 1967.

Carlyle, Thomas. *The Nigger Question*. New York: Appleton-Century-Crofts, 1971.

Cawleti, John G. *Adventure, Mystery, and Romance*. Chicago: University of Chicago Press, 1976.

Cawleti, John G. and Bruce A. Rosenberg. *The Spy Story*. Chicago: University of Chicago Press, 1987.

Cohen, Morton. *Rider Haggard: His Life and Works*. London: Hutchinson, 1960.

Cohen, Morton, ed. *Rudyard Kipling to Rider Haggard*. London: Hutchinson, 1965.

Conrad, Jessie. *Joseph Conrad and His Circle*. New York: E.P. Dutton and Co, Inc., 1935.

Conrad, Joseph. *A Personal Record* and *The Mirror of the Sea* (1912, 1906), ed. Mara Kalnins. New York: Penguin Books, 1998.

Coroneos, Con. *Space, Conrad, and Modernity*. Oxford: Oxford University Press, 2002.

Cox, C.B. *Joseph Conrad: The Modern Imagination*. London: J.M. Dent and Sons, 1974.

Cox, Tom. *Damned Englishman: A Study of Erskine Childers (1870–1922)*. New York: Exposition Press, 1975.

Daleski, H.M. *Joseph Conrad: The Way of Dispossession*. New York: Holmes and Meier, 1976.

Danahay, Martin A. *Gender at Work in Victorian Culture: Literature, Art and Masculinity*. Aldershot, UK: Ashgate, 2005.

Daniell, David. *The Interpreter's House: A Critical Assessment of John Buchan*. London: Nelson, 1985.

Dawson, Graham. *Soldier Heroes: British Adventure, Empire and the Imagining of Masculinities*. London: Routledge, 1994.

Dean, Leonard F. *Joseph Conrad's Heart of Darkness: Backgrounds and Criticisms*. Englewood Cliffs, N.J.: Prentice-Hall, 1960.

Donovan, Stephen. *Joseph Conrad and Popular Culture*. Basingstoke, UK and New York: Palgrave Macmillan, 2005.

Dowling, Andrew. *Manliness and the Male Novelist in Victorian Literature*. Aldershot, UK: Ashgate, 2001.

Dryden, Linda. *Joseph Conrad and the Imperial Romance*. New York: Palgrave Macmillan, Macmillan, 2000.

Eldridge, C.G. *Victorian Imperialism*. Atlantic Highlands, N.J.: Humanities Press, 1978.

Ellis, Peter Berresford. *H. Rider Haggard*. London: Routledge and Kegan Paul, 1978.

Erdinast-Vulcan, Daphna. *The Strange Short Fiction of Joseph Conrad: Writing, Culture, and Subjectivity*. Oxford: Oxford University Press, 1999.

Erdinast-Vulcan, Daphna, Allan H. Simmons, and J.H Stape, eds. *Joseph Conrad: The Short Fiction*. Amsterdam: Editions Rodopi, 2004.

Etherington, Norman. *Rider Haggard*. Boston: Twayne, 1984.

Fisher, Margery. *The Bright Face of Danger*. Boston: The Horn Book, 1986.

Fraser, Robert. *Victorian Quest Romance*. Plymouth: Northcote House, 1998.

Frederick, John T. *William Henry Hudson*. Boston: Twayne, 1972.

Gates, Henry Louis, Jr., ed. *'Race', Writing, and Difference*. Chicago: University of Chicago Press, 1986.

Geddes, Gary. *Conrad's Later Novels*. Montreal: McGill-Queen's University Press, 1980.

Gibson, Andrew and Robert Hampson, eds. *The Conradian: Conrad and Theory*. Amsterdam: Editions Rodopi, 1998.

Giddings, Robert, ed. *Literature and Imperialism*. New York: St. Martin's Press, 1991.

Gilbert, Elliot L., ed. *Kipling and the Critics*. New York: New York University Press, 1965.

Gilbert, Sandra M. and Susan Gubar. *No Man's Land: The Place of the Woman Writer in the Twentieth Century*, Volume 2, Sexchanges. New Haven: Yale University Press, 1989.

Gillon, Adam. *Joseph Conrad*. Boston: Twayne Publishers, 1982.

Gillon, Adam. *Joseph Conrad: Comparative Essays*. Lubbock: Texas Tech University Press, 1994.

Girouard, Mark. *The Return to Camelot: Chivalry and the English Gentleman.* New Haven: Yale University Press, 1981.

Goonetilleke, D.C.R.A. *Developing Countries in British Fiction*. London: Macmillan, 1977.

GoGwilt, Christopher. *The Invention of the West*. Stanford: Stanford University Press, 1995.

Graham, Gerald S. *A Concise History of the British Empire*. London: Thames and Hudson, 1978.

Graver, Lawrence. *Conrad's Short Fiction*. Berkeley: University of California Press, 1969.

Gray, Stephen. *Southern African Literature: An Introduction*. New York: Harper and Row, 1979.

Green, Martin. *Dreams of Adventure, Deeds of Empire*. New York: Basic Books, 1979.

Green, Martin. *The Robinson Crusoe Story*. University Park, PA: Pennsylvania State University Press, 1990.

Green, Martin. *The Adventurous Male: Chapters in the History of the White Male Mind*. University Park, PA: Pennsylvania State University Press, 1993.

Green, Roger Lancelyn. *Tellers of Tales*. London: Edmund Ward Ltd., 1946.

Green, Roger Lancelyn. *A.E.W. Mason*. London: Max Parrish, 1952.

Green, Roger Lancelyn, ed. *Kipling: The Critical Heritage*. New York: Barnes and Noble, 1971.

Gross, John, ed. *The Age of Kipling*. New York: Simon and Schuster, 1972.

Guerard, Albert J. *Conrad the Novelist*. Cambridge: Harvard University Press, 1958.

Gurko, Leo. *Joseph Conrad: Giant in Exile*. New York: The Macmillan Company, 1962.

Haggard, H. Rider. *Diary of an African Journey: The Return of H. Rider Haggard*, ed. Stephen Coan. New York: New York University Press, 2000.

Hall, Donald, ed. *Muscular Christianity: Embodying the Victorian Age.* Cambridge: Cambridge University Press, 1994.

Harkness, Bruce, ed. *Conrad's Heart of Darkness and the Critics*. San Francisco: Wadsworth Publishing Company, 1960.

Harkness, Bruce, ed. *Conrad's Secret Sharer and the Critics*. Belmont, CA: Wadsworth, 1962.

Harlow, Barbara and Mia Carter. *Imperialism and Orientalism: A Documentary Sourcebook*. Oxford: Blackwell Publishers, 1999.

Harman, Claire. *Myself and the Other Fellow: A Life of Robert Louis Stevenson*. New York: Harper, 2005.

Harris, Jose. *Private Lives, Public Spirit: Britain 1870–1914*. London: Penguin, 1993.

Hawthorn, Jeremy. *Joseph Conrad: Language and Fictional Self-Consciousness*. Lincoln, NE: The University of Nebraska Press, 1979.

Hawthorn, Jeremy. *Sexuality and the Erotic in the Fiction of Joseph Conrad*. London: Continuum, 2007.

Hay, Eloise Knapp. *The Political Novels of Joseph Conrad: A Critical Study*. Chicago: Chicago University Press, 1963.

Hewitt, Douglas. *Conrad: A Reassessment*. Totowa, NJ: Rowman and Littlefield, 1975.

Higgins, D.S. *Rider Haggard: A Biography*. New York: Stein and Day, 1983.

Holden, Philip and Richard J. Ruppel, eds. *Imperial Desire: Dissident Sexualities and Colonial Literature*. Minneapolis: University of Minnesota Press, 2003.

Horsley, Lee. *Fictions of Power in English Literature: 1900–1950*. New York: Longman, 1995.

Howarth, Patrick. *Play Up and Play the Game: The Heroes of Popular Fiction*. London: Methuen, 1973.

Howe, Irving. *Politics and the Novel*. New York: Horizon Press, 1957.

Howe, Susanne. *Novels of Empire*. New York: Columbia University Press, 1949.

Hugon, Anne. *The Exploration of Africa: From Cairo to the Cape*. New York: Abrams, 1993.

Hunter, Jefferson. *Edwardian Fiction*. Cambridge: Harvard University Press, 1982.

Hyam, Ronald. *Empire and Sexuality: The British Experience*. Manchester: Manchester University Press, 1990.

Ingram, Allan, ed. *Joseph Conrad: Selected Literary Criticism and* The Shadow-Line. London: Methuen, 1986.

Jean-Aubrey, G. *Joseph Conrad: Life and Letters*, 2 Vols. London: William Heinemann, 1927.

Karl, Frederick R. *A Reader's Guide to Joseph Conrad*. New York: Noonday Press, 1960.

Karl, Frederick R. *Joseph Conrad: The Three Lives*. New York: Farrar, Straus, and Giroux, 1979.

Katz, Wendy R. *Rider Haggard and the Fiction of Empire: A Critical Study of British Imperial Fiction*. Cambridge: Cambridge University Press, 1987.

Kermode, Frank. *Puzzles and Epiphanies*. London: Routledge, 1962.

Kestner, Joseph A. *Mythology and Misogyny*. Madison: University of Wisconsin Press, 1989.

Kestner, Joseph A. *Masculinities in Victorian Painting*. Aldershot, UK: Scolar Press, 1995.

Kestner, Joseph A. *The Edwardian Detective 1901–1915*. Aldershot, UK: Ashgate, 2000.

Kiely, Robert. *Robert Louis Stevenson and the Fiction of Adventure*. Cambridge: Harvard University Press, 1964.

Killam, G.D. *Africa in English Fiction, 1874–1939*. Ibadan: Ibadan University Press, 1968.

Kimmel, Michael S. *Changing Men: New Directions in Research on Men and Masculinity*. Newbury Park, California: Sage, 1987.

Kimmel, Michael S. and Michael A. Messner. *Men's Lives*. New York: Macmillan, 1992.

Klein, Bernhard, ed. *Fictions of the Sea: Critical Perspectives on the Ocean in British Literature and Culture*. Aldershot, UK: Ashgate, 2002.

Knowles, Owen and Gene M. Moore. *Oxford Reader's Companion to Conrad*. Oxford: Oxford University Press, 2000.

Knox-Shaw, Peter. *The Explorer in English Fiction*. New York: St. Martin's Press, 1986.

Lane, Christopher. *The Burdens of Intimacy: Psychoanalysis and Victorian Masculinity*. Chicago: Chicago University Press, 1999.

Lansbury, James. *Korzeniowski*. London: Serpent's Tail, 1992.

Leavis, F.R. *The Great Tradition*. New York: New York University Press, 1964.

Leavis, F.R. *Anna Karenina and Other Essays*. New York: Simon and Schuster, 1969.

Lothe, Jakob. *Conrad's Narrative Method*. Oxford: Clarendon Press, 1989.

Low, Gail Ching-Liang. *White Skin/Black Masks: Representation and Colonialism*. New York: Routledge, 1996.

Lownie, Andrew. *John Buchan: The Presbyterian Cavalier*. Boston: David R. Godine, 1995.

Mack, E.C. *Public Schools and British Opinion since 1860*. Westport: Greenwood Press, 1971.

Mackenzie, John M. *Propaganda and Empire: The Manipulation of British Public Opinion, 1880–1960*. Manchester: Manchester University Press, 1986.

Mackenzie, John M., ed. *Imperialism and Popular Culture*. Manchester: Manchester University Press, 1986.

Mackenzie, John M. *Orientalism: History, Theory, and the Arts*. Manchester: Manchester University Press, 1995.

Mahood, M.M. *The Colonial Encounter*. London: Rex Collings, 1977.

Maixner, Paul, ed. *Robert Louis Stevenson: The Critical Heritage*. London: Routledge, 1981.

Mallet, Charles. *Anthony Hope and His Books*. Port Washington, N.Y.: Kennikat Press, 1968.

Mangan, J.A. and James Walvin, eds. *Manliness and Morality: Middle-Class Masculinity in Britain and America, 1800–1940*. New York: St. Martin's Press, 1987.

Mangan, J.A. *The Games Ethic and Imperialism*. London: Cass, 1998.

McClintock, Anne. *Imperial Leather: Race, Gender and Sexuality in the Colonial Contest*. New York: Routledge, 1995.

McClure, John A. *Kipling and Conrad: The Colonial Fiction*. Cambridge: Harvard University Press, 1981.

McClure, John. *Late Imperial Romance*. London: Verso, 1994.

Meyer, Bernard C. *Joseph Conrad: A Psychoanalytic Biography*. Princeton: Princeton University Press, 1967.

Meyers, Jeffrey. *Fiction and the Colonial Experience*. Ipswich: The Boydell Press, 1972.

Meyers, Jeffrey. *Joseph Conrad: A Biography*. New York: Charles Scribner's Sons, 1991.

Middleton, Peter. *The Inward Gaze: Masculinity and Subjectivity in Modern Culture*. London: Routledge, 1992.

Middleton, Tim. *Joseph Conrad*. London: Routledge, 2006.

Miller, David. *W.H. Hudson and the Elusive Paradise*. New York: St. Martin's Press, 1990.

Millman, Lawrence. *Rider Haggard and the Male Novel*; *What is Pericles?*; *Beckett Gags*. Ph.D. Thesis/Dissertation. New Brunswick, N.J.: Rutgers University, 1974.

Monsman, Gerald. *Olive Schreiner's Fiction: Landscape and Power*. New Brunswick: Rutgers University Press, 1991.

Moore-Gilbert, B.J. *Kipling and "Orientalism"*. New York: St. Martin's Press, 1986.

Moser, Thomas. *Joseph Conrad: Achievement and Decline*. Cambridge: Harvard University Press, 1957.

Moss, Robert F. *Rudyard Kipling and the Fiction of Adolescence*. London: Macmillan, 1982.

Mosse, George L. *The Image of Man*. New York: Oxford UP, 1996.

Mudrick, Marvin, ed. *Conrad: A Collection of Essays*. Englewood Cliffs, N.J.: Prentice-Hall, 1966.

Murfin, Ross C., ed. *Conrad Revisited*. Tuscaloosa: The University of Alabama Press, 1985.

Nadelhaft, Ruth L. *Joseph Conrad*. Atlantic Highlands, NJ: Humanities Press International, 1991.

Najder, Zdzislaw. *Joseph Conrad: A Chronicle*. New York: Quality Book Club, 1983.

Newbolt, Henry. *Selected Poems*, ed. Patrick Dickinson. London: Hodder & Stoughton, 1981.

Orel, Harold. *The Victorian Short Story*. Cambridge: Cambridge University Press, 1986.

Orel, Harold. *Critical Essays on Rudyard Kipling*. Boston: G.K. Hall, 1989.

Parry, Benita. *Conrad and Imperialism: Ideological Boundaries and Visionary Frontiers*. London: The Macmillan Press, 1983.

Peck, John. *Maritime Fiction: Sailors and the Sea in British and American Novels, 1719–1917*. New York: Palgrave, 2001.

Phillips, Richard. *Mapping Men and Empire: A Geography of Adventure*. New York: Routledge, 1996.

Piper, Leonard. *Dangerous Waters: The Life and Death of Erskine Childers*. London: Hambledon and London, 2003.

Pocock, Tom. *Rider Haggard and the Lost Empire*. London: Weidenfeld and Nicolson, 1993.

Porch, Douglas. *Wars of Empire*. London: Cassell and Company, 2000.

Quayle, Eric, ed. *The Collector's Book of Boys' Stories*. London: Studio Vista, 1973.

Ray, Martin, ed. *Joseph Conrad: Interviews and Recollections*. Iowa City: University of Iowa Press, 1990.

Richards, Jeffrey, ed. *Imperialism and Juvenile Literature*. Manchester: Manchester University Press, 1989.

Ridley, Hugh. *Images of Imperial Rule*. New York: St. Martin's Press, 1983.

Rising, Catherine. *Darkness at Heart: Fathers and Sons in Conrad*. Westport: Greenwood Press, 1990.

Rivière, Jacques. *The Ideal Reader*, ed. and trans. Blanche A. Price. New York: Meridian, 1960.

Roberts, Andrew Michael, ed. *The Conradian: Conrad and Gender*. Amsterdam: Editions Rodopi, 1993.

Roberts, Andrew Michael. *Conrad and Masculinity*. New York: Palgrave Macmillan, 2000.

Roper, Michael and John Tosh, eds. *Manful Assertions: Masculinities in Britain since 1800*. London: Routledge, 1991.

Ruppel, Richard J. *Homosexuality in the Life and Work of Joseph Conrad*. New York: Routledge, 2008.

Rutherford, Andrew, ed. *Kipling's Mind and Art*. Stanford: Stanford University Press, 1964.

Said, Edward W. *Orientalism*. New York: Vintage Books, 1979.

Said, Edward W. *Culture and Imperialism*. New York: Alfred A. Knopf, 1993.

Said, Edward W. *Joseph Conrad and the Fiction of Autobiography* (1966), Foreword by Andrew N. Rubin. New York: Columbia University Press, 2008.

Sandison, Alan. *The Wheel of Empire*. New York: St. Martin's Press, 1967.

Schwarz, Daniel R. *Conrad:* Almayer's Folly *to* Under Western Eyes. London: Macmillan, 1980.

Schwarz, Daniel R. *Conrad: The Later Fiction*. London: Macmillan, 1982.

Schwarz, Daniel R., ed. *The Secret Sharer* by Joseph Conrad. New York: St. Martin's, 1997.

Sedgwick, Eve. *Between Men: English Literature and Male Homosocial Desire*. New York: Columbia University Press, 1985.

Seymour-Smith, Martin. *Rudyard Kipling*. London: Macdonald-Queen Anne Press, 1989.

Sherry, Norman. *Conrad and His World*. London: Thames and Hudson, 1972.

Sherry, Norman, ed. *Conrad: The Critical Heritage*. London: Routledge and Kegan Paul, 1973.

Sherry, Norman, ed. *Joseph Conrad: A Commemoration*. London: Macmillan, 1976.

Showalter, Elaine. *Sexual Anarchy: Gender and Culture at the Fin de Siècle*. New York: Penguin Books, 1990.

Silverberg, Robert. *The Realm of Prester John*. Athens: Ohio University Press, 1996.

Silverman, Kaja. *Male Subjectivity at the Margins*. London: Routledge, 1992.

Simmel, Georg. *On Individuality and Social Forms*, ed. Donald N. Levine. Chicago: University of Chicago Press, 1971.

Simmons, Alan H. *Joseph Conrad*. New York: Palgrave Macmillan, 2006.

Smith, Janet Adam. *John Buchan and His World*. New York: Charles Scribner's Sons, 1979.

Snyder, Katherine W. *Bachelors, Manhood, and the Novel, 1850–1925*. Cambridge: Cambridge University Press, 1999.

Stallman, R.W., ed. *The Art of Joseph Conrad*. Athens: Ohio University Press, 1982.

Stape, John. *The Cambridge Companion to Joseph Conrad*. Cambridge: Cambridge University Press, 1996.

Stape, John. *The Several Lives of Joseph Conrad*. New York: Pantheon Books, 2007.

Stearns, Peter N. *Be a Man! Males in Modern Society*. London: Holmes and Meier, 1990.

Stewart, J.I.M. *Rudyard Kipling*. New York: Dodd, Mead, and Company, 1966.

Stiebel, Lindy. *Imagining Africa: Landscape in H. Rider Haggard's African Romances*. Westport: Greenwood Press, 2001.

Street, Brian V. *The Savage in Literature*. London: Routledge and Kegan Paul, 1975.

Sullivan, Zohreh T. *Narratives of Empire: The Fictions of Rudyard Kipling*. Cambridge: Cambridge University Press, 1993.

Sussman, Herbert. *Victorian Masculinities*. Cambridge: Cambridge University Press, 1995.

Tiger, Lionel. *Men in Groups*. New York: Random House, 1969.

Tomalin, Ruth. *W.H. Hudson*. New York: Philosophical Library, 1954.

Tompkins, J.M.S. *The Art of Rudyard Kipling*. Lincoln: University of Nebraska Press, 1959.

Usborne, Richard. *Clubland Heroes*. London: Barrie and Jenkins, 1953.

Van Ghent, Dorothy. *The English Novel: Form and Function*. New York: Rinehart, 1961.

Vance, Norman. *The Sinews of the Spirit*. Cambridge: Cambridge University Press, 1985.

Walker, Cherryl, ed. *Women and Gender in Southern Africa to 1945*. Cape Town: David Philip, 1990.

Wark, Wesley K., ed. *Spy Fiction, Spy Films, and Real Intelligence*. London: Cass, 1991.

Watt, Ian. *Conrad in the Nineteenth Century*. Berkeley: University of California Press, 1979.

Watt, Ian. *Essays on Conrad*. Cambridge: Cambridge University Press, 2000.

Watts, Cedric. *Conrad's Heart of Darkness: A Critical and Contextual Discussion*. Milan: Mursia International, 1977.

Weeks, Jeffrey. *Coming Out*. London: Quartet, 1977.

Weeks, Jeffrey. *Sex, Politics and Society*. London: Longman, 1981.

Weeks, Jeffrey. *Against Nature*. London: Rivers Oram Press, 1991.

White, Andrea. *Joseph Conrad and the Adventure Tradition*. Cambridge: Cambridge University Press, 1993.

Wiley, Paul L. *Conrad's Measure of Man*. Madison: The University of Wisconsin Press, 1954.

Wollaeger, Mark A. *Joseph Conrad and the Fictions of Skepticism*. Stanford: Stanford University Press, 1990.

Wright, Walter F., ed. *Joseph Conrad on Fiction*, Lincoln: University of Nebraska Press, 1964.

Wynne, Catherine. *The Colonial Conan Doyle: British Imperialism, Irish Nationalism, and the Gothic*. Westport: Greenwood Press, 2002.

Zweig, Paul. *The Adventurer: The Fate of Adventure in the Western World*. Princeton: Princeton University Press, 1974.

Articles, Essays and Reviews

Achebe, Chinua. 'An Image of Africa: Racism in Conrad's *Heart of Darkness*', in *Hopes and Impediments: Selected Essays*, Chinua Achebe. London: Heinemann, 1989.

Acheraiou, Amar. 'Floating Words: Sea as Metaphor of Style in "Typhoon"', *The Conradian* 29, no. 1 (Spring 2004), 27–38.

Adams, James Eli. 'The Banality of Transgression?: Recent Works on Masculinity', *Victorian Studies* 26 (Winter 1993), 207–13.

Anderson, Robert S. 'Lord of the Flies on Coral Island', *Canadian Review of Sociology and Anthropology* 4, no. 1 (February 1967), 54–68.

Anonymous. 'Review of *She*', *Pall Mall Gazette* no. 6802 (4 January 1887), p. 5.

Baines, Jocelyn. 'Afterword', in *Almayer's Folly and Other Stories*, Joseph Conrad. New York: The New American Library, 1965, 306–18.

Baines, Jocelyn. 'Conrad's Biography and *The Secret Sharer*', in *The Secret Sharer*, ed. Harkness, 116–21.

Baker, Carlos. 'Introduction', in *Green Mansions* (1904), W.H. Hudson. New York: Bantam Books, 1965, v–xxi.

Baker, Carlos. 'The Source-Book for Hudson's *Green Mansions*', *PMLA* 61, no. 1 (March 1946), 252–7.

Bassnett, Susan. 'Cabin'd Yet Unconfined: Heroic Masculinity in English Seafaring Novels', in *Fictions of the Sea*, ed. Klein, Aldershot UK: Ashgate, 2002, 176–87.

Benson, Carl. 'Conrad's Two Stories of Initiation', *PMLA* 69, no. 1 (March 1954), 46–56.

Berthoud, Jacques. 'Introduction: Autobiography and War', in *The Shadow-Line: A Confession* (1917), Joseph Conrad. New York: Penguin Books, 1986, 7–24.

Bidwell, Paul. 'Legatt and the Promised Land: A New Reading of *The Secret Sharer*', *Conradiana* 3, no. 2 (1969), 26–35.

Bock, Martin. 'Conrad's Voyages of Disorientation: Crossing "The Shadow-Line"', *Conradiana* 17, no. 2 (1985), 83–92.

Booth, Bradford A. 'Introduction', in *Selected Poetry and Prose of Robert Louis Stevenson*, Robert Louis Stevenson. Boston: Houghton Mifflin Company, 1968, vii–xxi.

Bratton, J.S. 'Introduction', in *The Coral Island: A Tale of the Pacific Ocean* (1858), R.M. Ballantyne. Oxford: Oxford University Press, 1991, vii–xxi.

Bratton, J.S. 'Of England, Home and Duty: The Image of England in Victorian and Edwardian Juvenile Fiction', in *Imperialism and Popular Culture*, ed. MacKenzie, 74–93.

Bristow, Joseph. 'Introduction', in *The Oxford Book of Adventure Stories*. Oxford: Oxford University Press, 1996, xi–xxv.

Brown, P.L. '"The Secret Sharer" and the Existential Hero', *Conradiana* 3, no. 3 (1971–72), 22–31.

Bruss, Paul S. '"Typhoon": The Initiation of Jukes', *Conradiana* 5, no. 2 (1973), 46–56.

Buchan, John. 'Introduction', in *Tales of Mystery and Imagination*, Edgar Allan Poe. London: Nelson and Sons, 1911.

Buchan, John. 'Adventure Stories', *John O'London's Weekly* 41, no. 398 (4 December 1926), 274–6.

Bunn, David. 'Embodying Africa: Woman and Romance in Colonial Fiction', *English in Africa* 15, no. 1 (1988), 1–28.

Butts, Dennis. 'Introduction', in *King Solomon's Mines* (1885), H. Rider Haggard. Oxford: Oxford University Press, 1989, vii–xx.

Butts, Dennis. 'Introduction', in *Allan Quatermain* (1885), H. Rider Haggard. Oxford: Oxford University Press, 1995, vii–xx.

Calder, Jenni. 'Introduction', in *Dr. Jekyll and Mr. Hyde and Other Stories*, Robert Louis Stevenson. New York: Penguin Books, 1979, 7–21.

Carabine, Keith. '"The Secret Sharer": A Note on the Dates of Its Composition', *Conradiana* 19, no. 3 (1987), 209–13.

Carrigan, Tim, Bob Connell and John Lee. 'Toward a New Sociology of Masculinity', in *The Making of Masculinities*, ed. Harry Brod. Boston: Allen and Unwin, 1987, 63–100.

Casarino, Cesare. 'The Sublime of the Closet: Or, Joseph Conrad's Secret Sharing', *Boundary 2* 24, no. 2 (Summer 1997), 199–243.

Chon, Sooyoung. '"Typhoon": Silver Dollars and Stars', *Conradiana* 22, no. 1 (1990), 25–43.

Clarke, G.S. 'Can England Be Invaded?', *National Review* 27 (May 1896), 338–56.

Coan, Stephen. 'Introduction', in *Diary of an African Journey: The Return of H. Rider Haggard*, H. Rider Haggard. New York: New York University Press, 2000, 1–43.

Cornell, Louis L. 'Introduction', in *The Man Who Would Be King and Other Stories*, Rudyard Kipling. Oxford: Oxford University Press, 1987, xviii–xxxvii.

Couzens, T.J. 'The Old Africa of a Boy's Dream: Towards Interpreting *Prester John*', *Africa Perspective* 13 (Spring 1979), 34–57.

Curley, Daniel. 'Legate of the Ideal', in *The Secret Sharer*, ed. Harkness, 75–82.

Daleski, H.M. '"The Secret Sharer": Questions of Command', *Critical Quarterly* 17, no. 3 (Autumn 1975), 268–79.

Daniell, David. 'Introduction', in *Prester John* (1910), John Buchan. Oxford: Oxford University Press, 1994, vii–xxvi.

Daniell, David. 'At the Foot of the Thirty-Ninth Step', *John Buchan Journal* 10 (Spring 1991), 15–26.

Davidis, Maria. '"Unarm, Eros!": Adventure, Homoeroticism, and Divine Order in *Prester John*', in *Imperial Desire*, eds. Philip Holden and Richard J. Ruppel. Minneapolis: University of Minnesota Press, 2003, 223–40.

Dawson, Anthony B. 'In the Pink: Self and Empire in "The Secret Sharer"', *Conradiana* 22, no. 3 (1990), 185–96.

Dawson, Graham. 'The Blond Bedouin', in *Manful Assertions*, eds. Michael Roper and John Tosh. London: Routledge, 1991, 113–44.

Dazey, Mary Ann. 'Shared Secret or Secret Sharing in Joseph Conrad's "The Secret Sharer"', *Conradiana* 18, no. 3 (1986), 201–3.

Devers, James. 'More on Symbols in Conrad's "The Secret Sharer"', *Conradiana* 28, no. 1 (1996), 66–76.

Dickinson, Patric. 'Introduction [Henry Newbolt, 1862–1938]', in *Selected Poems of Henry Newbolt*. London: Hodder and Stoughton, 1981.

Dilworth, Thomas R. 'Conrad's Secret Sharer at the Gates of Hell', *Conradiana* 9, no. 3 (1977), 203–17.

Dobrinsky. Joseph. 'The Two Lives of Joseph Conrad in *The Secret Sharer*, *Cahiers victoriens & édouardiens* 21 (April 1985), 33–49.

Donaldson, Norman. 'Introduction', in *The Riddle of the Sands* (1903), Erskine Childers. New York: Dover Publications, 1976, 1–11.

Doyle, Arthur Conan. 'Mr Stevenson's Methods in Fiction', *The National Review* 14 (1890), 646–57.

Doyle, Arthur Conan. 'My First Book', in *Sir Arthur Conan Doyle: Interviews and Recollections*, ed. Harold Orel. New York: St Martin's, 1991, 91–96.

Draudt, Manfred. 'Reality or Delusion?: Narrative Technique and Meaning in Kipling's *The Man Who Would Be King*', *English Studies* 65 (August 1984), 316–26.

Dryden, Linda. '*Heart of Darkness* and *Allan Quatermain*: Apocalypse and Utopia', *Conradiana* 31, no. 3 (Fall 1999), 173–97.

Dunae, Patrick A. 'Boy's Literature and the Idea of Empire, 1870–1914', *Victorian Studies* 24, Number 1 (Autumn 1980), 105–21.

Duncan, Ian. 'Introduction', in *Green Mansions* (1904), W.H. Hudson. Oxford: Oxford University Press, 1998, vii–xxiii.

Dussinger, Gloria R. '"The Secret Sharer": Conrad's Psychological Study', *Texas Studies in Language and Literature* 10, no. 4 (Winter 1969), 599–608.

Dutheil, Martine Hennard, 'The Representation of the Cannibal in Ballantyne's "The Coral Island": Colonial Anxieties in Victorian Popular Fiction', *College Literature* 28, no. 1 (Winter 2001), 105–22.

Eggenschwiler, David. 'Narcissus in "The Secret Sharer": A Secondary Point of View', *Conradiana* 11, no. 1 (1979), 23–40.

Epstein, Hugh. 'The Duality of "Youth": Some Literary Contexts", *The Conradian* 21, no. 2 (1996), 1–14.

Etherington, Norman. 'Rider Haggard's Imperial Romances', *Meanjin* 36 (July 1977), 189–99.

Etherington, Norman. 'South African Origins of Rider Haggard's Early African Romances', *Notes and Queries* 24, no. 5 (October 1977), 436–8.

Etherington, Norman. 'Rider Haggard, Imperialism, and the Layered Personality', *Victorian Studies* 22, no. 1 (1978), 71–88.

Etherington, Norman. 'Critical Introduction', in *The Annotated* She: *A Critical Edition of H. Rider Haggard's Victorian Romance*, H. Rider Haggard. Bloomington: Indiana University Press, 1991, xv–xliii.

Evans, Frank B. 'The Nautical Metaphor in *The Secret Sharer*, *Conradiana* 7, no. 1 (1975), 3– 16.

Evans, Robert O. 'Conrad: A Nautical Image', *Modern Language Notes* 72, no. 2 (February 1957), 98–9.

Fairchild, Hoxie N. 'Rima's Mother', *PMLA* 68, no. 3 (June 1953), 357–70.

Feder, Lillian. 'Marlow's Descent into Hell', *Nineteenth-Century Fiction* 9 (March 1955), 280– 92.

Fiedler, Leslie. 'The Male Novel', *Partisan Review* 37, no. 1 (1970), 74–89.

Fletcher, James V. 'The Creator of Rima: W.H. Hudson, A Belated Romantic', *The Sewanee Review Quarterly* 41 (1933), 24–40.

Fraser, Gail. '"An Outpost of Progress" and *The Secret Agent*', *The Conradian* 11 (1986), 155–69.

Friedmann, Marion. 'Introduction', in *Trooper Peter Halket of Mashonaland* (1897), Olive Schreiner. Johannesburg: AD. Donker/Publisher, 2001, 9–25.

Fussell, Paul, Jr. 'Irony, Freemasonry, and Humane Ethics in Kipling's "The Man Who Would Be King"', *ELH* 25, no. 3 (September 1958), 216–33.

Galsworthy, John. 'Foreword', in *Green Mansions* (1904). New York: Random House, 1944.

Gettmann, Royal A. and Bruce Harkness. 'Morality and Psychology in *The Secret Sharer*', in *The Secret Sharer*, ed. Harkness, 125–32.

Giddings, Robert. 'Cry God for Harry, England and Lord Kitchener: A Tale of Tel-el-Kebir, Suakin, Wadi Haifa and Omduran', in *Literature and Imperialism*, ed. Robert Giddings. New York: St. Martin's Press, 1991, 182–219.

Gilbert, Sandra M. 'Rider Haggard's *Heart of Darkness*', *Partisan Review* 50, no. 3 (1983), 444– 53.

Glover, David. 'The Stuff that Dreams are Made of: Masculinity, Femininity, and the Thriller', in *Gender, Genre, and Narrative Pleasure*, ed. Derek Longhurst. London: Unwin Hyman, 1989, 67–83.

Graver, Lawrence. '"Typhoon": A Profusion of Similes', *College English* 24, no. 1 (October 1962), 62–4.

Gray, Stephen. 'King Solomon's Adventure Hero', *Communique* 4, no. 2 (June 1978), 23–30.

Green, Martin. 'The Robinson Crusoe Story', in *Imperialism and Juvenile Literature*, ed. Jeffrey Richards. Manchester: Manchester University Press, 1989, 34–52.

Greene, Graham. 'The Last Buchan', in *Collected Essays*, Graham Greene. London: The Bodley Head, 1969, 223–5.

Griem, Eberhard. 'Rhetoric and Reality in Conrad's "Typhoon"', *Conradiana* 24, no. 1 (1992), 21–32.

Griffiths, Trevor R. '"This Island's Mine": Caliban and Colonialism', in *The Yearbook of English Studies* 13, eds. G.K. Hunter and C.J. Rawson. London: The Modern Humanities Research Association, 1983, 159–80.

Guerard, Albert J. 'Introduction', in *Heart of Darkness, Almayer's Folly, The Lagoon*, Joseph Conrad. New York: Dell, 1960, 7–23.

H.B. [William E. Henley] 'London Letter' [review of *She*], *Critic* 7 (12 February 1887), 78.

Haggard, H. Rider. 'A Zulu War–Dance', *The Gentleman's Magazine* CCXLL, no. 1759, (July 1877), 94–107.

Haggard, H. Rider. 'Fact and Fiction', *The Athenaem* no. 3063 (10 July 1886), 50, and no. 3066 (July 31 1886), 144.

Haggard, H. Rider. 'About Fiction', *Contemporary Review* 51, no. CCCII (February 1887), 172– 80.

Haggard, H. Rider. 'The Real King Solomon's Mines', *Cassell's Magazine* (July 1907), 144–51.

Haggard, H. Rider. 'The Zulus: The Finest Savage Race in the World', *Pall Mall Magazine* (1908), 764–70.

Hamner, Robert. 'The Enigma of Arrival in "An Outpost of Progress"', *Conradiana* 33, no. 3 (Fall 2001), 171–87.

Hannabuss, Stuart. 'Ballantyne's Message of Empire', in *Imperialism and Juvenile Literature*, ed. Jeffrey Richards. Manchester: Manchester University Press, 1989, 53–71.

Hannabuss, Stuart. 'Islands as Metaphors', *Universities Quarterly: Culture, Education, and Society* 38, no. 1 (Winter 1983/4), 70–82.

Hansford, James. 'Reflection and Self-Consumption in "Youth"', *The Conradian* 12, no. 2 (1987), 150–65.

Hansford, James. 'Money, Language, and the Body in "Typhoon"', *Conradiana* 26, no. 2 and 3 (1994), 135–55.

Hardesty, Patricia W. et al. 'Doctoring the Doctor: How Stevenson Altered the Second Narrator Of *Treasure Island*', *Studies in Scottish Literature* 21 (1986), 1–22.

Hardin, Richard F. 'The Man Who Wrote *The Blue Lagoon*: Stacpoole's Pastoral Center', *English Literature in Transition, 1880–1920* 39, no. 2 (1996), 205–20.

Harkness, Bruce. 'The Secret of *The Secret Sharer* Bared', *College English* 27, no. 1 (October 1965), 55–61.

Harris, Wilson. 'The Frontier on Which *Heart of Darkness* Stands', *Research in African Literatures* 12, no. 1 (Spring 1981), 86–93.

Harvie, Christopher. 'The Politics of Stevenson', in *Stevenson and Victorian Scotland*, ed. Jenni Calder. Edinburgh: Edinburgh University Press, 1981, 107–25.

Hatt, Michael. '"Making a Man of Him": Masculinity and the Black Body in Mid-Nineteenth- Century American Sculpture', *Oxford Art Journal* 15, no. 1 (1992), 21–35.

Hatt, Michael. 'The Male Body in Another Frame: Thomas Eakins' *The Swimming Hole* as a Homoerotic Image', in *The Body*, ed. Andrew Benjamin. London: Academy, 1993a, 8–21.

Hatt, Michael. 'Muscles, Morals, Mind: The Male Body in Thomas Eakins' *Salautat*', in *The Body Imaged*, ed. Kathleen Adler and Marcia Pointon. Cambridge: Cambridge University Press, 1993b, 57–69.

Hawkins, Hunt. 'Conrad's Critique of Imperialism in *Heart of Darkness*', *PMLA* 94, no. 2 (1979), 286–99.

Hawkins, Hunt. 'The Issue of Racism in *Heart of Darkness*', *Conradiana* 14, no. 3 (1982), 163–71.

Hawthorn, Jeremy. 'Introduction' in *The Shadow-Line: A Confession* (1917), Joseph Conrad. Oxford: Oxford University Press, 1985, vii–xxv.

Hawthorn, Jeremy. 'Conrad and the Erotic: "A Smile of Fortune" and "The Planter of Malata"', in *Joseph Conrad: The Short Fiction*, ed. Daphna Erdinast-Vulcan et al., Amsterdam: Rodopi, 2004, 111–41.

Hayes, Timothy S. 'Colonialism in R.L. Stevenson's South Seas Fiction: "Child's Play" in the Pacific', *English Literature in Transition 1880–1920*, 52.2 (Spring 2009), 160–81.

Hiley, Nicholas. 'The Failure of British Counter-Espionage against Germany, 1907–1914', *Historical Journal* 28, no. 4 (1985), 835–62.

Hiley, Nicholas. 'Decoding German Spies: British Spy Fiction, 1908–18', in *Spy Fiction, Spy Films, and Real Intelligence*, ed. Wesley K. Wark. London: Cass, 1991, 55–79.

Himmelfarb, Gertrude. 'John Buchan: An Untimely Appreciation', *Encounter* 84 (September 1960), 46–53.

Hinz, Evelyn J. 'Rider Haggard's *She*: An Archetypal "History of Adventure"', *Studies in the Novel* 4 (Fall 1972), 416–31.

Hodges, Robert R., 'Deep Fellowship: Homosexuality and Male Bonding in the Life and Fiction of Joseph Conrad', *Journal of Homosexuality* 4, no. 4 (Summer 1979), 379–93.

Hoffmann, Charles G. 'Point of View in "The Secret Sharer"', *College English* 23, no 8 (May 1962), 651–4.

Hoppenstand, Gary. 'Introduction', in *The Four Feathers* (1902), A.E.W. Mason. New York: Penguin Books, 2001, vii–xxv.

Hoppenstand, Gary. 'Introduction', in *The Prisoner of Zenda* and *Rupert of Hentzau*, Anthony Hope. New York: Penguin Books, 2000, vii–xxiv.

Household, Geoffrey. 'Foreword', in *The Riddle of the Sands* (1903), Erskine Childers. New York: Penguin Books, 1978, 7–15.

Jackson, David H. '*Treasure Island* as a Late-Victorian Adults' Novel', *The Victorian Newsletter* 72 (Fall 1987), 28–32.

Jeffrey, Keith and Eunan O'Halpin. 'Ireland in Spy Fiction', in *Spy Fiction, Spy Films, and Real Intelligence*, ed. Wesley K. Wark. London: Cass, 1991, 92–116.

Johnson, Barbara, and Marjorie Garber. 'Reading Conrad Psychoanalytically', *College English* 49, no. 6 (October 1987), 628–40.

Jolly, Roslyn. '*The Ebb Tide* and *The Coral Island*', *Scottish Studies Review* 7, no. 2 (Autumn 2006), 79–91.

Jolly, Roslyn. 'Introduction', in *South Sea Tales* (1893), Robert Louis Stevenson. Oxford: Oxford University Press, 1999, ix–xxxiii.

Jolly, Roslyn. 'Stevenson's "Sterling Domestic Fiction": "The Beach of Falsea"', *The Review of English Studies*, New Series, 50, no. 200 (November 1999), 463–82.

Kaarsholm, Preben. 'Kipling and Masculinity', in *Patriotism: The Making and Unmaking of British National Identity* vol. III, ed. Ralph Samuel. London: Routledge, 1989, 215–26.

Kalnins, Mara. 'Introduction', in *A Personal Record* and *The Mirror of the Sea*, Joseph Conrad. New York: Penguin Books, 1998, xvi–xxxiii.

Karlin, Danny. '*Captains Courageous* and American Empire', *Kipling Journal* 63 (September 1989), 11–21.

Karlin, Daniel. 'Introduction', in *She* (1887), H. Rider Haggard. Oxford: Oxford University Press, 1991, vii–xxxi.

Kehler, Joel R. '"The Planter of Malata": Renouard's Sinking Star of Knowledge', *Conradiana* 8, no. 2 (1976), 148–62.

Kennedy, Paul. 'The Riddle of the Sands', *The Times* (3 January 1981), 7.

Kimbrough, Robert. 'Introduction', in *Youth, Heart of Darkness, The End of the Tether*, Joseph Conrad. Oxford: Oxford University Press, 1984, ix–xxvi.

Kimbrough, Robert. 'Introduction', in *Heart of Darkness* (1899), Joseph Conrad. New York: Norton, 1988, ix–xvii.

Kincead-Weekes, Mark. 'Vision in Kipling's Novels', in *Kipling's Mind and Art*, ed. Andrew Rutherford. Stanford CA: Stanford University Press, 1964, 197–234.

Kirschner, Paul. 'Introduction', in *Typhoon and Other Stories* (1903), Joseph Conrad. New York: Penguin, 1990, 3–31.

Kirschner, Paul. 'Conrad and Maupassant: Moral Solitude and "A Smile of Fortune"', *Review of English Studies* 7, no. 3 (July 1966), 62–77.

Knowles, Owen. 'Conrad and Mérimée: The Legend of Venus in "The Planter of Malata"', *Conradiana* 11, no. 2 (1979), 177–84.

Kolupke, Joseph. 'Elephants, Empires, and Blind Men: A Reading of the Figurative Language in Conrad's "Typhoon"', *Conradiana* 20, no. 1 (1988), 71–85.

Kramer, Jürgen. 'Conrad's Crews Revisited', in *Fictions of the Sea*, ed. Klein, 157–75.

Krieger, Murray. 'Conrad's *Youth*: A Naïve Opening to Art and Life', *College English* 20, no. 6 (March 1959), 275–80.

Lafferty, William. 'Conrad's "A Smile of Fortune": The Moral Threat of Commerce', *Conradiana* 7 (1975), 63–74.

Landry, Rudolph J. 'The Source of the Name Rima in *Green Mansions*', *Notes and Queries* 3, no. 12 (1956), 545–6.

Lang, Andrew. 'Review of Rider Haggard's *King Solomon's Mines*', *Saturday Review* 60 (10 October 1885), 485–6.

Lang, Andrew. 'Review of Rider Haggard's *She*', *Academy* 31 (15 January 1887), 35–6.

Le Gallienne, Richard. 'Review of Robert Louis Stevenson's *The Ebb-Tide*', *The Star* (27 September 1894), reprinted in *Retrospective Reviews* (1896), i, 146–9.

Leiter, Louis. 'Echo Structures: Conrad's *The Secret Sharer*, in *The Secret Sharer*, ed. Harkness, 133–50.

Letley, Emma. 'Introduction', in *Treasure Island* (1883), Robert Louis Stevenson. Oxford: Oxford University Press, 1985, vii–xxiii.

Levenson, Michael. 'Secret History in *The Secret Sharer*', in *The Secret Sharer*, ed. Schwarz 163–74.

Linehan, Katherine Bailey. 'Taking Up with Kanakas; Stevenson's Complex Social Criticism in "The Beach of Falesá"', *English Literature in Transition, 1880–1920* 33, no. 4 (1990), 407–22.

London, Bette. 'Mary Shelley, *Frankenstein*, and the Spectacle of Masculinity', *PMLA* 108 (March 1993), 253–66.

Lorch, Thomas M. 'The Barrier Between Youth and Maturity in the Works of Joseph Conrad', *Modern Fiction Studies* 10 (Spring 1964), 73–80.

Lord Meath. 'Have We the "Grit" of Our Forefathers?', *The Nineteenth Century* 64 (September 1908), 421–9.

Lyall, Alfred. 'The English Novel', *Quarterly Review* 179 (October 1894), 530–52.

Lyon, John M. 'Introduction', in *The Light That Failed* (1891), Rudyard Kipling. New York: Penguin Books, 1992, vii–xxvi.

Madison, R.D. 'The Secret Maneuver in "The Secret Sharer"', *Conradiana* 14, no. 3 (1982), 233– 6.

Maisonnat, Claude. 'Alterity and Suicide in "An Outpost of Progress"', *Conradiana* 28, no. 2 (1996), 101–14.

Mangan, J.A. 'Manly Chaps in Control: Blues and Blacks in the Sudan', in *The Games Ethic and Imperialism*. London: Frank Cass Publishers, 1998, 71–100.

Mangan, J.A. 'Noble Specimens of Manhood: Schoolboy Literature and the Creation of a Colonial Chivalric Code', in *Imperialism and Juvenile Literature*, ed. Jeffrey Richards. Manchester: Manchester University Press, 1989, 173–94.

Mann, David D., and William Hardesty, III. 'Stevenson's Revisions of *Treasure Island*: "Writing Down the Whole Particulars"', *Transactions for the Society of Textual Scholarship* 3 (1987), 377–92.

Mathews, James W. 'Ironic Symbolism in Conrad's "Youth"', *Studies in Short Fiction* 11 (Spring 1974), 117–23.

Mazlish, Bruce. 'A Triptych: Freud's *The Interpretation of Dreams*, Rider Haggard's *She*, and Bulwer-Lytton's *The Coming Race*', *Comparative Studies in Society and History* 35, no. 4 (October 1993), 726–45.

McClintock, Anne. 'Maidens, Maps, and Mines: The Reinvention of Patriarchy in Colonial South Africa', *The South Atlantic Quarterly* 87, no. 1 (Winter 1988), 147–92.

McLauchlan, Juliet. 'Conrad's Heart of Emptiness: "The Planter of Malata"', *Conradiana* 18, no. 3 (1986), 180–92.

Meisel, Joseph S. 'The Germans Are Coming!: British Fiction of a German Invasion, 1871–1913', *War, Literature, and the Arts* 2, no. 2 (1990), 41–79.

Meyers, Jeffrey. 'The Idea of Moral Authority in "The Man Who Would Be King"', *Studies in English Literature, 1500–1900* 8, no. 4, Nineteenth Century (Autumn 1968), 711–23.

Miller, Betty. 'Kipling's First Novel', in *The Age of Kipling*, ed. Gross, 1972, 2–6.

Miller, J. Hillis. 'Sharing Secrets', in *The Secret Sharer*, ed. Schwarz, 232–52.

Miller, Norma. 'All Is Vanity Under the Sun: Conrad's Floppy Hat as Biblical Allusion', *Conradiana* 30, no. 1 (Spring 1998), 64–7.

Muscogiuri, Patrizia. 'Cinematographic Seas', in *Fictions of the Sea*, ed. Klein, 203–220.

Morf, Gustav. 'Conrad Versus Apollo', *Conradiana* 11, no. 3 (1979), 281–7.

Morzinski, Mary. '*Heart of Darkness* and Plato's Myth of the Cave', *Conradiana* 34, no. 3 (2002, 227–33.

Moss, John G. 'Three Motifs in Haggard's *She*', *English Literature in Transition* 16, no. 1 (1973), 27–36.

Mudrick, Marvin. 'Conrad and the Terms of Modern Criticism', in *The Secret Sharer*, ed. Harkness, 110–15.

Mulhern, Francis. 'English Reading', in *Nation and Narration*, ed. Homi K. Bhabha. London: Routledge, 1990, 250–64.

Mulvey, Laura. 'Afterthoughts', *Framework* 15–17 (1981), 12–15.

Mulvey, Laura. 'Visual Pleasure and Narrative Cinema', in *Film Theory and Criticism*, ed. Gerald Mast. New York: Oxford University Press, 1985, 803–16.

Murfin, Ross C. 'Introduction', in *Heart of Darkness* (1899), *A Case Study in Contemporary Criticism*, Joseph Conrad. New York: St. Martin's Press, 1989, 3–16.

Murphy, Michael. '"The Secret Sharer": Conrad's Turn of the Winch', *Conradiana* 18, no. 3 (1986), 193–200.

Neale, Steve. 'Masculinity as Spectacle', in *Screening the Male*, eds. Steven Cohan and Ina Rae Hark. London: Routledge, 1993, 9–20.

Newman, Paul B. 'Joseph Conrad and the Ancient Mariner', *Kansas Magazine* (1960), 79–83.

Niemeyer, Carl. '*The Coral Island* Revisited', *College English* 22, no. 4 (January 1961), 241–5.

Niland, Richard. 'Ageing and Individual Experience in "Youth" and "Heart of Darkness"', *The Conradian* 29, no. 1 (Spring 2004), 99–118.

'Ogilvy, Gavin' [J.M. Barrie]. 'Mr H. Rider Haggard', *The British Weekly: A Journal of Science and Christian Progress* (5 August 1887), 218.

O'Hara, J.D. 'Unlearned Lessons in "The Secret Sharer"', *College English* 26, no. 6 (March 1965), 444–50.

Ormond, Leonee. 'Introduction', in *Captains Courageous* (1897), Rudyard Kipling. Oxford: Oxford University Press, 1995, xviii–xxxiv.

Orwell, George. 'Rudyard Kipling', in *A Collection of Essays*. New York: Doubleday and Company, 1954, 123–39.

Paccaud, Josiane. 'The Alienating Imaginary and the Symbolic Law in Conrad's *The Secret Sharer*, *L'Epoque conradienne* (1987), 89–96. [1987#1]

Paccaud, Josiane. 'Under the Other's Eyes: Conrad's *The Secret Sharer*', *The Conradian* 12, no. 1 (1987), 59–73. [1987#2]

Paccaud-Huguet, Josiane. 'Reading Shadows into Lines: Conrad with Lacan', in *Conrad and Theory*, eds. Andrew Gibson and Robert Hampson. Amsterdam: Rodopi, 1998, 146–77.

Page, Norman. 'Kipling's World of Men', *Ariel* 10, no. 2 (1979), 81–93.

Parker, Christopher. 'Race and Empire in the Stories of R.M. Ballantyne', in *Literature and Imperialism*, ed. Robert Giddings. New York: St. Martin's Press, 1991, 44–63.

Paterson, J.A. and W.M. Russell Paterson. '*The Thirty Nine Steps*: Thoughts and Suggestions on Richard Hannay's Travels through Southern Scotland', *John Buchan Journal* 7 (Winter 1987), 14–19.

Patteson, Richard F. '*King Solomon's Mines*: Imperialism and Narrative Structure', *Journal of Narrative Technique* 8 (Spring 1978), 112–23.

Pearson, Nels C. '"Whirr" is King: International Capital and the Paradox of Consciousness in *Typhoon*', *Conradiana* 39, no. 1 (2007), 29–37.

Perel, Zivah. 'Transforming the Hero: Joseph Conrad's Reconfiguring of Masculine Identity in "The Secret Sharer"', *Conradiana* 36, no. 1–2 (Spring/Summer 2004), 111–29.

Phelan, James. 'Reading Secrets', in *The Secret Sharer*, ed. Schwarz, pp. 128–44.

Pittock, Murray. 'Rider Haggard and *Heart of Darkness*', *Conradiana* 19, no. 3 (Autumn 1987), 206–8.

Porter, Barrett G. 'Sherlock Holmes and the German Threat', *The Baker Street Journal: An Irregular Quarterly of Sherlockiana* 34, no. 1 (March 1984), 27–31.

'Reality and Romance', unsigned, *Spectator* 61 (28 April 1888), 569–71.

Renner, Stanley. '"The Planter of Malata", the Love Song of Geoffrey Renouard, and the Question of Conrad's Artistic Integrity', *Conradiana* 30, no. 1 (Spring 1998), 3–23.

Ressler, Steve. 'Conrad's "The Secret Sharer": Affirmation of Action', *Conradiana* 16, no. 3 (1984), 195–214.

'Review of H. Rider Haggard's *King Solomon's Mines*', unsigned, *Academy* 28 (7 November 1885), 304.

'Review of H. Rider Haggard's *King Solomon's Mines*', unsigned, *Independent* 37 (3 December 1885), 13.

'Review of H. Rider Haggard's *King Solomon's Mines*', unsigned, *Public Opinion* 48 (10 October 1885), 551.

'Review of H. Rider Haggard's *King Solomon's Mines*', unsigned, *Queen* 78 (7 November 1885), 512.

'Review of H. Rider Haggard's *King Solomon's Mines*', unsigned, *Spectator* 58 (7 November 1885), 1473.

'Review of H. Rider Haggard's *She*', unsigned, *Athenaeum* 89 (15 January 1887), 93–94.

'Review of H. Rider Haggard's *She*', unsigned, *Blackwood's Magazine* 141 (February 1887), 301–5.

'Review of H. Rider Haggard's *She*', unsigned, *Pall Mall Gazette* #6802 (4 January 1887), 5.

'Review of H. Rider Haggard's *She*', unsigned, *Public Opinion* 51 (4 January 1887), 38.

'Review of H. Rider Haggard's *She*', unsigned, *Spectator* 60 (15 January 1887), 78–9.

'Review of Robert Louis Stevenson's *The Ebb-Tide*', unsigned, *Saturday Review* 78 (22 September 1894), 330.

'Review of Robert Louis Stevenson's *The Ebb-Tide*', unsigned, *Speaker* 10 (29 September 1894), 362–3.

Richards, Jeffrey. 'With Henty to Africa', in *Imperialism and Juvenile Literature*, ed. Jeffrey

Richards. Manchester: Manchester University Press, 1989, 72–106.

Roper, Michael. 'Introduction: Recent Books on Masculinity', *History Workshop* 29 (Spring 1990), 184–7.

Rosenman, John B. 'The L-Shaped Room in "The Secret Sharer"', *The Claflin College Review* 1, no. 1 (1975), 4–8.

Ruskin, John. 'Inaugural Lecture' (1870), in *Empire Writing*, ed. Elleke Boehmer. Oxford: Oxford University Press, 1998, 16–20.

Ryall, Tom. 'One Hundred and Seventeen Steps Towards Masculinity', in *You Tarzan: Masculinity, Movies, and Men*, ed. Pat Kirkham and Janet Thumin. New York: St. Martin's Press, 1993, 153–66.

Salmon, George. 'What Boys Read', *Fortnightly Review* 39, no. 230 (February 1886), 248–59.

Sandison, Alan. 'A Matter of Vision: Rudyard Kipling and Rider Haggard', in *The Age of Kipling*, ed. John Gross. New York: Simon and Schuster, 1972, 127–34.

Schwarz, Daniel R. 'Introduction', in *The Secret Sharer* (1910), A Case Study in Contemporary Criticism, Joseph Conrad. Boston: Bedford/St. Martin's, 1997, 3–23.

Scott, Bonnie Kime. 'Intimacies Engendered in Conrad's *The Secret Sharer*', in *The Secret Sharer*, ed. Schwarz, 197–210.

Seed, David. 'The Adventure of Spying: Erskine Childers's *The Riddle of the Sands*', in *Spy Thrillers From Buchan to Le Carre*, ed. Clive Bloom. London: Macmillan, 1990, 28–43.

Seed, David. 'Erskine Childers and the German Peril', *German Life and Letters* 45, no. 1 (1992), 66–73.

Shaffer, Brian W. '"Rebarbarizing Civilization": Conrad's African Fiction and Spencerian Sociology', *PMLA* 108 (January 1993), 45–58.

Shippey, Thomas A., and Michael Short. 'Framing and Distancing in Kipling's "The Man Who Would Be King"', *Journal of Narrative Technique* 2, no. 2 (May 1972), 75–87.

Simon, John. 'Between the Conception and the Re-Creation Falls "The Shadow-Line"', *The Hudson Review* 32, no. 2 (Summer 1979), 239–44.

Singh, Francis B. 'The Colonialistic Bias of *Heart of Darkness*', *Conradiana* 10, no. 1 (1978), 41–54.

Smith, Craig. 'Every Man Must Kill the Thing He Loves: Empire, Homoerotics, and Nationalism in John Buchan's *Prester John*', *Novel* 28, no. 2 (Winter 1995), 173–200.

Stafford, David. 'John Buchan's Tales of Espionage: A Popular Archive of British History', *Canadian Journal of History* 18, no. 1 (April 1983), 1–21.

Stallman, R.W. 'Conrad and *The Secret Sharer*', in *The Secret Sharer*, ed. Harkness, 94–109.

Steiner, Joan E. 'Conrad's "The Secret Sharer": Complexities of the Doubling Relationship', *Conradiana* 12, no. 3 (1980), 173–86.

Stott, Rebecca. 'The Dark Continent: Africa as Female Body in Haggard's Adventure Fiction', *Feminist Review* no. 32 (Summer 1989), 69–89.

Swinton, Ernest. 'An Eddy of War', *Blackwood's Magazine* CLXXXL, no. MXCVIII (April 1907), 454–72.

Thale, Jerome. 'Marlow's Quest', in *Joseph Conrad's* Heart of Darkness, ed. Leonard F. Dean. New York: Prentice–Hall, 1960, 159–66.

Thomas, Mark Ellis. 'Doubling and Difference in Conrad: "The Secret Sharer," *Lord Jim*, and *The Shadow Line*', *Conradiana* 27, no. 3 (1995), 222–34.

Tolley, A.T. 'Conrad's "Favorite" Story', *Studies in Short Fiction* 3 (1966), 314–20.

Trilling, Lionel. 'Kipling', in *The Liberal Imagination: Essays on Literature and Society*. New York: Anchor Books, 1953, 114–24.

Trotter, David. 'Introduction', in *The Riddle of the Sands: A Record of Secret Service* (1903), Erskine Childers. Oxford: Oxford University Press, 1998, vii–xviii.

Trotter, David. 'The Politics of Adventure in the Early British Spy Novel', in *Spy Fiction, Spy Films, and Real Intelligence*, ed. Wesley K. Wark. London: Cass, 1991, 30–54.

Troy, Mark. '…of no particular significance except to myself": Narrative Posture in Conrad's "The Secret Sharer"', *Studia Neophilologica* 56 (1984), 35–50.

Turner, Jennifer. '"Petticoats" and "Sea Business": Women Characters in Conrad's Edwardian Short Stories', in *Joseph Conrad: The Short Fiction,* ed. Daphna Erdinast-Vulcan et al. Amsterdam: Rodopi, 2004, 142–56.

Vance, Norman. 'Kipling's World of Men', *Ariel* 10, no. 2 (1979), 81–93.

Vickers, Salley. 'Foreword', in *A Smile of Fortune: A Harbour Story* (1911), Joseph Conrad. London: Hesperus Press, 2007, vii–x.

Wallace, Raymond P. 'Cardboard Kingdoms', *San Jose Studies* 13, no. 2 (Spring 1987), 23–34.

Walsh, Dennis M. 'Conrad's "Typhoon" and the Book of *Genesis*', *Studies in Short Fiction* 11 (Winter 1974), 99–101.

Watkins, Tony. 'Introduction', in *The Prisoner of Zenda* (1894), Anthony Hope. Oxford: Oxford University Press, 2001, vii–xxii.

Watson, Fiona. '*Captains Courageous* and the Hispanic World', *Kipling Journal* 57 (September 1983), 11–20.

Watt, Ian. 'Story and Idea in Conrad's *The Shadow-Line*', in *Modern British Fiction: Essays in Criticism*, ed. Mark Shorer. Oxford: Oxford University Press, 1961.

Watts, Cedric. 'Introduction', in *Lord Jim* (1900), Joseph Conrad. New York: Penguin Books, 11–30.

Watts, Cedric. 'The Mirror-tale: an ethico-structural analysis of Conrad's 'The Secret Sharer''', *Critical Quarterly* 19, no. 3 (1976), 25–37.

Watts, Cedric. 'Conrad's Absurdist Techniques: A Terminology', *Conradiana* 9, no. 2 (1977), 141–8.

Watts, Cedric. '"A Bloody Racist': About Achebe's View of Conrad', in *The Yearbook of English Studies* 13, Colonial and Imperial Themes Special Number, ed. G.K. Hunter and C.J. Rawson. London: The Modern Humanities Research Association, 1983, 196–209.

Watts, Cedric. 'The Narrative Enigma of Conrad's "A Smile of Fortune"', *Conradiana* 17, no. 2 (1985), 131–6.

Watts, Cedric. '*The Ebb-Tide* and *Victory*', *Conradiana* 28, no. 2 (1996), 133–7.

Watts, Cedric. 'Introduction', in *Typhoon and Other Tales*, Joseph Conrad. Oxford: Oxford University Press, 1998, xi–xxxiii.

Watts, Cedric. 'Introduction', in *Heart of Darkness and Other Tales*, Joseph Conrad. Oxford: Oxford University Press, 2002, xi–xxviii.

Wegelin, Christof. 'MacWhirr and the Testimony of the Human Voice', *Conradiana* 7, no. 1 (1975), 45–50.

West, Russell. 'Travel and Failure(s) of Masculinity in *Almayer's Folly* and *An Outcast of the Islands*', *L'Epoque conradienne* 23 (1997), 11–28.

Weston, John Howard. '"Youth": Conrad's Irony and Time's Darkness', *Studies in Short Fiction* 11 (Fall 1974), 399–407.

Wheeler, Paul Mobray. 'H. Rider Haggard', *Georgia Review* 20, no. 2 (Summer 1966), 213–19.

White, James F. 'The Third Theme in "The Secret Sharer"', *Conradiana* 21, no. 1 (1989), 37–46.

Wilhelm, Cherry. 'H. Rider Haggard: *Allan Quatermain*', *Crux* 9, no. 2 (May 1975), 48–52.

Williams, Porter, Jr. 'The Brand of Cain in "The Secret Sharer"', *Modern Fiction Studies* 10 (Spring 1964), 27–30.

Williams, Porter, Jr. 'The Matter of Conscience in Conrad's *The Secret Sharer*' *PMLA* 79, no. 5 (December 1964), 626–30.

Wills, John Howard. 'A Neglected Masterpiece: Conrad's *Youth*', *Texas Studies in Language and Literature* 4 (Spring 1963), 591–601.

Willy, Todd G. 'The Call to Imperialism in Conrad's "Youth": An Historical Reconstruction', *Journal of Modern Literature* 8 (1980), 39–50.

Willy, Todd G. 'Measures of the Heart and of the Darkness: Conrad and the Suicides of "New Imperialism"', *Conradiana* 14, no. 3 (1982), 189–98.

Wilson, Edmund. 'The Kipling That Nobody Read', in *Kipling's Mind and Art*, ed. Andrew Rutherford. London: Oliver and Boyd, 1964, 17–69.

Woods, Gregory. 'Fantasy Islands: Popular Topographies of Marooned Masculinities', in *Mapping Desire: Geographies of Sexuality*, ed. David Bell. New York: Routledge, 1995, 126–48.

Wright, Walter F. '*The Secret Sharer* and Human Pity', in *The Secret Sharer*, ed. Harkness, 122–4.

Wyatt, Robert D. 'Joseph Conrad's "The Secret Sharer": Point of View and Mistaken Identities', *Conradiana* 5, no. 1 (1973), 12–27.

Zangwill, Israel. 'In Defence of *Ebb-Tide*', *Critic* [New York] (24 November 1894), xxii n.s., 342–3, in Maixner, ed. *Critical Heritage*, 459–63.

Zuckerman, Jerome. '"A Smile of Fortune": Conrad's Interesting Failure', *Studies in Short Fiction* 1 (Winter 1964), 99–102.

Index